Preface

This book is mainly targeted for MCA (New Course), M.Sc.(CS), MIT etc. exam of Discrete Mathematics for all Open Universities including Indira Gandhi, MJPR University(U.P.). It has been introduced in market after seeing the huge demand of ready to grasp material for exams with high level of quality, and its un-availability in market. We the GullyBaba Publishing House took a step ahead to publish the quality material focusing on exams at the same time giving you indepth knowledge about the subject.

GPH Book is the pioneer effort that provides a unique methodology so as to perform better in exams. If your goal is to attain higher grade use this powerful study tool independently or along with your text.

On the Web : **www.gullybaba.com** *is the vital resource for your exams acting as catalyst to boost up your preparation.*

Acknowledgments :

We appreciate the staff and facility support provided by GullyBaba Publishing House. In particular, we appreciate the encouragement and professional advises received from Mr. Ajay Saini, Mr. Tarun Sharma, H. Faheem Ahmed and many more.

Also we would like to thank typesetting and designing team Mrs. Bhawna Verma, Mr. Shravan Vats, Mr. Mukesh.

We gratefully acknowledges the significant contributions of Mr. Mahesh Chand, Mrs. Bimla Devi, Mrs. Bhawna Verma and our experts in bringing out this publication.

New Delhi

Contents

Chapter-1	Propositional Calculus	1-25
Chapter-2	Techniques Of Proof	26-34
Chapter-3	Boolean Algebra And Circuit Fundamentals	35-76
Chapter-4	Sets, Relations and Functions	77-107
Chapter-5	Counting Principles	108-127
Chapter-6	Partitions And Distribution	128-134
Chapter-7	Basic Symbols	135-137

Question Papers

(1) June: 2005 (Solved)..................140-147
(2) Dec: 2005 (Solved)..................148-154
(3) June: 2006 (Solved)..................155-163
(4) Dec: 2006 (Solved)..................164-170
(5) June: 2007 (Solved)..................171-177
(6) Dec: 2007 (Solved)..................178-184
(7) June: 2008 (Solved)..................185-190
(8) Dec: 2008 (Solved)..................191-196
(9) June: 2009 (Solved)..................197-200
(10) Dec: 2009 (Solved)..................201-204
(11) June: 2010 (Solved)..................205-212
(12) Dec: 2010 (Solved)..................213-219
(13) June: 2011 (Solved)..................220-223
(14) Dec: 2011 (Solved)..................224-227
(15) June: 2012 (Solved)..................228-232
(16) Dec: 2012 (Solved)..................233-239
(17) June: 2013..................240-241
(18) Dec: 2013..................242-243
(19) June: 2014..................244-245
(20) Dec: 2014..................246-247
(21) June: 2015..................248-248
(22) Dec: 2015..................249-250
(23) June: 2016 (Solved)..................251-256
(24) Dec: 2016..................257-259
(25) June: 2017 (Solved)..................260-266
(26) Dec: 2017..................267-268
(27) June: 2018 (Solved)..................269-277
(28) Dec: 2018..................278-279
(29) June: 2019 (Solved)..................280-284
(30) Dec: 2019 (Solved)..................285-292
(31) June: 2020..................293-294
(32) Dec: 2020..................295-296
(33) June: 2021 (Solved)..................297-300
(34) Dec: 2021 (Solved)..................301-306

DISCRETE MATHEMATICS

MCS–013

For
Master In Computer Applications [MCA]

Dr. A.K. Saini
Ph.D, M.PHIL., MCA, M.Sc., MBA

Vimal Kumar Sharma
M.A. (MATHS), B.SC.(MATHS), PGDCCA, PGDCA, CIC

Useful For

IGNOU, KSOU (Karnataka), Bihar University (Muzaffarpur), Nalanda University, Jamia Millia Islamia, Vardhman Mahaveer Open University (Kota), Uttarakhand Open University, Kurukshetra University, Seva Sadan's College of Education (Maharashtra), Lalit Narayan Mithila University, Andhra University, Pt. Sunderlal Sharma (Open) University (Bilaspur), Annamalai University, Bangalore University, Bharathiar University, Bharathidasan University, HP University, Centre for distance and open learning, Kakatiya University (Andhra Pradesh), KOU (Rajasthan), MPBOU (MP), MDU (Haryana), Punjab University, Tamilnadu Open University, Sri Padmavati Mahila Visvavidyalayam (Andhra Pradesh), Sri Venkateswara University (Andhra Pradesh), UCSDE (Kerala), University of Jammu, YCMOU, Rajasthan University, UPRTOU, Kalyani University, Banaras Hindu University (BHU) and all other Indian Universities.

Closer to Nature We use Recycled Paper

GULLYBABA PUBLISHING HOUSE PVT. LTD.
ISO 9001 & ISO 14001 CERTIFIED CO.

Published by:
GullyBaba Publishing House Pvt. Ltd.

Regd. Office:
2525/193, 1st Floor, Onkar Nagar-A,
Tri Nagar, Delhi-110035
(From Kanhaiya Nagar Metro Station Towards Old Bus Stand)
Call: 9991112299, 9312235086
WhatsApp: 9350849407

Branch Office:
1A/2A, 20, Hari Sadan,
Ansari Road, Daryaganj,
New Delhi-110002
Ph.011-45794768
Call & WhatsApp:
8130521616, 8130511234

E-mail: hello@gullybaba.com, **Website:** GullyBaba.com

New Edition

ISBN: 978-18-90864-48-4

Copyright© with Publisher

All rights are reserved. No part of this publication may be reproduced or stored in a retrieval system or transmitted in any form or by any means; electronic, mechanical, photocopying, recording or otherwise, without the written permission of the copyright holder.

Disclaimer: Although the author and publisher have made every effort to ensure that the information in this book is correct, the author and publisher do not assume and hereby disclaim any liability to any party for any loss, damage, or disruption caused by errors or omissions, whether such errors or omissions result from negligence, accident, or any other cause.

If you find any kind of error, please let us know and get reward and or the new book free of cost.

The book is based on IGNOU syllabus. This is only a sample. The book/author/publisher does not impose any guarantee or claim for full marks or to be passed in exam. You are advised only to understand the contents with the help of this book and answer in your words.

All disputes with respect to this publication shall be subject to the jurisdiction of the Courts, Tribunals and Forums of New Delhi, India only.

Home Delivery of GPH Books

You can get GPH books by VPP/COD/Speed Post/Courier.
You can order books by Email/SMS/WhatsApp/Call.
For more details, visit gullybaba.com/faq-books.html
Our packaging department usually dispatches the books within 2 days after receiving your order and it takes nearly 5-6 days in postal/courier services to reach your destination.

Note: Selling this book on any online platform like Amazon, Flipkart, Shopclues, Rediff, etc. without prior written permission of the publisher is prohibited and hence any sales by the SELLER will be termed as ILLEGAL SALE of GPH Books which will attract strict legal action against the offender.

CHAPTER -1
PROPOSITIONAL CALCULUS

CONNECTIVES

Truth Table : Table made by values T and F on the basis of connectives.

Logic : Logic is the study of general patterns of reasoning, without reference to particular meaning or contents.

A ***Statement*** is a sentence which has one and only one of two possible values, called truth values (True or False) are also called propositions e.g. 'Shahjahanpur is a city in UP.' is a Statement.

Truth Value If a statement is true, then its truth value is T and if it is false, then its truth value is F.

Simple statement A statement is said to be simple, if it cannot be broken down into two or more sentences. For e.g. Neeraj is a student of IGNOU.

Compound statement A statement which is combination of two or more simple statements is called a compound statement e.g. Ramesh is a doctor and Rahul is not a doctor.

Connectives : The words which combine simple statements to form a compound statement are called connectives e.g. AND, OR.

Types of Connects	*Symbol used*
And	$\wedge$ (Called conjunction)
Or	$\vee$ (Called disjunction)
Not	$\sim$ (Called negation or denial)
Implies	$\Rightarrow$ (Called implication)
If and only if	$\leftrightarrow$ (Called double implication)

Conjunction : If two simple statements P and q are connected by word 'and', then the resulting compound statement " p and q" is called a conjunction of P and q and is written as "$P \wedge q$"

P	Q	P ∧ Q
T	T	T
T	F	F
F	T	F
F	F	F

Disjunction or Alternation : If two simple statements p and q are connected by the word 'or', the resulting compound statement "p or q" is called disjunction of p and q and is written in symbolic from as "p ∨ q".

P	Q	P ∨ Q
T	T	T
T	F	T
F	T	T
F	F	F

Negation : An assertion that statement fails or denial of a statement is called the negation of the statement. The negation of a statement p in symbolic form is written as "~p".
Regarding the truth value of the negation ~p of statement p, we have
~ p has truth value T, whenever p has truth value F.
~p has truth value F, whenever p has truth value T.

Negation of compound Statements
(1) Negation of Conjunction The negation of a conjunction p ∧ q is the disjunction of the negation of P and the negation of q. Thus, it is written as: -
~(p ∧ q) = (~ p) ∨ (~ q)

(2) Negation of disjunction The negation of a disjunction P ∨ q is the conjunction of the negation of p and the negation of q. Thus it is written as :
~(p ∨ q) = (~ P) ∧(~ q)

(3) Negation of a Negation : Negation of negation of a statement is the statement itself. It is written as :
~(~p) = P.

P	⌐P
T	F
F	T

Conditional statement **(If ----- Then)** : In mathematics many Statement, are of the type "If p then q". Such statements are called conditional statements and are denoted by
P $\Rightarrow$ q or p $\to$ q read as 'p implies q'.

P	Q	P→Q	P	Q	P⇔Q
T	T	T	T	T	T
T	F	F	T	F	F
F	T	T	F	T	F
F	F	T	F	F	T

Biconditional statement : In mathematics some statements are of the form "p if and only if q". Such statements are called bi conditional statements and are denoted by
p $\Leftrightarrow$ q or p $\leftrightarrow$ q.

Regarding the truth values of p $\to$ q and p $\leftrightarrow$ q, we have
(i) The conditional p $\to$ q is false only if p is true and q is false. Accordingly, if p is false then P $\to$ q is true regardless of the truth value of q.

(ii) The biconditional p $\leftrightarrow$ q is true whenever p and q have the same truth values otherwise it is false.

<u>Connective</u>	<u>Statement</u>	<u>Symbol</u>	<u>Symbolicform</u>	<u>Negation</u>
And	conjunction	$\wedge$	p $\wedge$ q	(~p) $\vee$ (~q)
or	disjunction	$\vee$	p $\vee$ q	(~p) $\wedge$ (~q)
not	Negation	~	~p	~(~p) = p
if then	implication	$\to$	p $\to$ q	p $\wedge$ (~q)
if and only if	biconditional	$\leftrightarrow$	p $\leftrightarrow$ q	p $\wedge$ (~ q)] $\vee$ [q $\wedge$ (~q)]

Tautologies : A statement is said to be a tautology if it is true for all logical possibilities. In other words. A statement whose truth values is always True is called a tautology.

P	⌐P	P$\vee$⌐P
T	F	T
F	T	T

Contradiction : A statement is said to be a contradiction if it is false for all logical possibilities. In other words, a statement whose truth value is always place is called contradiction.

P	⌐P	P∧⌐P
T	F	F
F	T	F

Logical Equivalence : Two statements S_1 (p, q, r....) and S_2 (p, q, r ------) are said to be logically equivalent, or simply equivalent if they have the same truth values for all logical possibilities and is denoted by e.g.
$P \Leftrightarrow Q$ is logic equivalent is $(P \Rightarrow Q) \wedge (Q \Rightarrow P)$
S_1 (p, q, r....) $\cong S_2$ (p, q, r ------)
In other words, S_1 and S_2 are logically equivalent if they have identical truth tables.
E.g. $P \Leftrightarrow Q$ is logical equivalent to $(P \Rightarrow Q) \wedge (Q \Rightarrow P)$.

Duality : Two compound statements S_1 and S_2 are said to be duals of each other if one can be obtained from the other by replacing $\wedge$ by $\vee$ and $\vee$ by $\wedge$. The connectives $\wedge$ and $\vee$ are also called duals of each other.
for eg (a) The dual of $(P \vee Q) \wedge R$ is $(P \wedge Q) \vee R$
(b) The dual of $\rceil(P \vee Q) \vee (P \vee \rceil)(Q \wedge \rceil s))$ is
$\rceil(P \wedge Q) \vee (P \wedge \rceil)(Q \vee \rceil s)$

Algebra of Statements
Statements satisfying many laws, some of which are as follows: -
(1) Idempotent laws : If p is any statement, then
(a) $p \vee q = p$ \qquad\qquad (b) $P \wedge P = p$

(2) Associative laws : If p, q, r, are any three statements, then
(a) $p \vee (q \vee r) = (p \vee q) \vee r$ \qquad (b) $P \wedge (q \wedge r) = (q \wedge p) \wedge r$.

(3) commutative laws : If p and q are two statements, then
(a) $P \vee q = q \vee p$ \qquad\qquad (b) $P \wedge q = q \wedge p$.

(4) Distributive laws : If p, q, r are three statements, then
(a) $P \wedge (q \vee r) = (p \wedge q) \vee (p \wedge r)$

(5) Identity laws : If P is any statement, t is tautology and c is contradiction, then
(a) $P \vee t = t$ \qquad\qquad (b) $P \wedge t = p$
(c) $P \vee c = p$ \qquad\qquad (d) $P \wedge c = c$

(6) Complement laws : If t is a tautology, C is contradiction and p is any statement, then.
(a) $p \vee (\sim p) \cong t$ (b) $p \wedge (\sim p) \cong c$
(c) $\sim t \cong c$ (d) $\sim c \cong t$

(7) Involution law : If p is any statement, then
$\sim (\sim p) \cong p$

(8) Demorgan's law : If P and q are two statements, then
(a) $\sim (p \vee q) \cong (\sim p) \wedge (\sim q)$
(b) $\sim (p \wedge q) \cong (\sim P) \vee (\sim q)$

(9) Double Negation law : $\sim(\sim p) \equiv p$
Logical Quantifiers :

Quantifiers

The universal quantification of a predicate p(x) is the statement" For all values of x, P(x) is true we assume here that only values of x that make sense in P(x) are considered. If we wish to restrict the values of x, we can, for e.g., write $\forall x \geq 0$ or $\forall n \in z$. The symbol $\forall$ is called the universal quantification of P(x) is denoted $\forall x\ P(x)$.

In some situation we only require that there be at least one value for which the predicate is true. The existential quantification of a predicate P(x) is the statement. "There exists a value of x for which P(x) is true". The existential quantification of P(x) is denoted by $\exists x\ P(x)$. The symbol $\exists$ is called the existential quantifier.

Mathematically the quantifier "for all", which is ' $\forall$ ' (for every) and given by '$(\forall x \in U)\ p(x)$ or 'p(x), $\forall x \in U$' and where U is universal quantifier. Quantifiers are of two kinds (i) universal (U) and (ii) existential ($\exists$).

Examples of Universal Quantifiers :

* Any integer is either positive or negative which is rewritten as -
*' For all x, if x is an integer, then x is either positive or negative.

Example of Existential Quantifier :

* Some real numbers are integers which is rewritten as
*' $\exists$ atleast one x such that x is a real number and x is an integer.

Precedence Rule : According to this rule the order of preference in which the connectives are applied in a formula of propositions that has no brackets is :

(a) $\sim$
(b) $\wedge$
(c) $\vee$ and $\oplus$
(d) $\rightarrow$ and $\leftrightarrow$

Always note that the 'inclusive or' and 'exclusive or' are both third in the order of preference. However, if both these appear in a statement, we first apply the left most one. So, for instance, in $p \vee q \oplus \sim p$, we first apply $\vee$ and then $\oplus$. The same applies to the 'implication' and the 'biconditional', which are both fourth in the order of preference.

Some Important Questions :

Q1. Establish the equivalence $(P \vee Q) \Rightarrow R \equiv (P \Rightarrow R) \wedge (Q \Rightarrow R)$

Truth table for LHS

P	Q	R	PVQ	(PVQ) $\Rightarrow$ R
F	F	F	F	T
F	F	T	F	T
F	T	F	T	F
F	T	T	T	T
T	F	F	T	F
T	F	T	T	T
T	T	F	T	F
T	T	T	T	T

Truth table for RHS

P	Q	R	P$\Rightarrow$R	Q$\Rightarrow$R	(P$\Rightarrow$ R) $\wedge$ (Q $\Rightarrow$ R)
F	F	F	T	T	T
F	F	T	T	T	T
F	T	F	T	F	F
F	T	T	T	T	T
T	F	F	F	T	F
T	F	T	T	T	T
T	T	F	F	F	F
T	T	T	T	T	T

LHS = RHS
$\Rightarrow$ Given Expression is proved.

Q2. Express P $\Rightarrow$ Q terms of $\{\neg, \vee\}$ only

$\{\neg, \rightarrow\}$
Truth table for $\neg$ is

P	$\neg$P
F	T
T	F

Truth table for $\rightarrow$ is

P	Q	P$\rightarrow$Q
F	F	T
F	T	T
T	F	F
T	T	T

Q3. Construct truth table for the following formula :
(A$\Rightarrow$B) $\wedge$ (A$\vee$ $\neg$ B) where $\neg$, $\Rightarrow$, $\wedge$ and $\vee$ respectively denote negation, conditional, conjunction and disjunction.

A	B	$\neg$B	A$\rightarrow$B	$\neg$(A$\rightarrow$B)	(A$\vee$$\neg$B)	$\neg$(A$\rightarrow$B)$\wedge$(A$\vee$$\neg$B)
F	F	T	T	F	T	F
F	T	F	T	F	F	F
T	F	T	F	T	T	T
T	T	F	T	F	T	T

Q4. Construct truth table for the following formula :
($\neg$P $\wedge$ $\neg$Q) $\Leftrightarrow$ (P$\Rightarrow$Q)

P	Q	$\neg$P	$\neg$Q	$\neg$Q$\wedge$$\neg$Q	P$\Rightarrow$Q	($\neg$P$\wedge$$\neg$Q)
F	F	T	T	T	T	T
F	T	T	F	F	T	T
T	F	F	T	F	F	T
T	**T**	**F**	**F**	**F**	**T**	**T**

Q5. Construct truth table for the following formula : (G $\vee$ $\neg$ H) $\Rightarrow$ (G $\wedge$H) where '$\vee$', '$\neg$', '$\Rightarrow$' and '$\wedge$' denote respectively disjunctions, negation, conditional and conjunction.

(G $\vee$7H) $\Rightarrow$ (G $\wedge$ H)

G	H	7H	G$\vee$7H	G $\wedge$ H	(G$\vee$7H) $\Rightarrow$ G$\wedge$ H
F	F	T	T	F	F
F	T	F	F	F	T
T	F	T	T	F	F
T	T	F	T	T	T

Q6. Express $P \Leftrightarrow Q$ in terms of [¬, ∨] only.

$P \Leftrightarrow Q$ in terms of {¬, V}
¬ = NOT logic
∨ = OR logic
⇔ = Equivalence if and only if biconditional.
$P \Leftrightarrow Q = (P \wedge Q) \wedge (¬P \wedge ¬Q) (P \wedge Q) \vee (¬P \wedge ¬Q)$
We know that $= m \wedge n = (¬m \vee ¬n)$
$\Rightarrow P \Leftrightarrow Q = (¬P \vee ¬Q) \vee (¬¬P \vee ¬¬Q)$
$P \Leftrightarrow Q = (¬P \vee ¬Q) \vee (P \vee Q)$

Q7. Construct truth table for the following formula : ¬[(P∧¬Q) ∨ (¬P ∧ Q)]

$\Leftrightarrow [(P \vee R) \wedge (Q \vee R)] \wedge (¬P \vee R)$
$\Leftrightarrow [(P \vee R) \wedge (Q \vee R)] \wedge (¬P \wedge R)$
Taking Negation
$\Leftrightarrow ¬[(P \vee R) \wedge (Q \wedge R) \wedge (¬P \vee R)$
$\Leftrightarrow ¬[(P \vee R) \vee ¬(Q \vee R) \vee (¬P \vee R)$
$\Leftrightarrow (¬P \wedge ¬R) \vee (¬Q \wedge ¬R) \wedge (¬¬P \vee ¬R)$
$\Leftrightarrow (¬P \wedge ¬R) \vee (¬Q \wedge ¬R) \vee (P \wedge ¬R)$
which is the required disjunctive normal form.

Q8. Obtain the equivalent normal form for the formula : ¬G ∧ (H ⇔ G).

Disjunctive normal form of
  $7G \wedge (H \Leftrightarrow G)$
[∴ 'A⇔B' ⇔ (A∧B) ∨ (7A ∧ 7B)
  ∴ $7G \wedge (H \Leftrightarrow G)$
= $7G \wedge (H \wedge G) \vee (7H \wedge 7G)$
= $7G \wedge (H \wedge G) \vee 7G \wedge (7H \wedge 7G)$
= $(7G \wedge H) \wedge (7G \wedge G) \vee (7G \wedge 7H) \wedge (7G \wedge 7G)$
TG ∧ G will always be 0.
and anything adding with 0.
0 or anything = anything
= $(7G \wedge 7H) \wedge (7G \wedge 7G)$
Now, A ∧ A = A
  $(7G \wedge 7H) \wedge 7G$

Q9. Construct truth table for the following formula : ¬(P ∨ ¬Q) ⇔ (P ⇔ Q)

¬(P ∨ ¬Q) ⇔ (P (P ⇔ Q)

P	Q	¬Q	P ∨ ¬Q	¬(P∨Q)	P⇒Q	¬(P∨¬Q) ⇔ ((P≡Q)
0	0	1	1	0	1	0

MCS-13 GPH Solution Book   9

0	1	0	0	1	1	1
1	0	1	1	0	0	1
1	1	0	1	0	1	0

Q10. The binary logical operator ↓ is defined as $P \downarrow Q = \neg(P \vee Q)$. Show that the operation ↓ is functionally complete.

$$P \downarrow Q = \neg(P \vee Q) \quad [\text{NOR}]$$

I $\quad P \downarrow P = \neg(P \wedge P)$
$\quad\quad = \neg P \; [\text{NOT}]$

II $\quad \neg P \downarrow \neg Q = \neg(\neg P \vee \neg)Q$
$\quad\quad = (\neg\neg P \wedge \neg\neg Q)$
$\quad\quad = P \wedge Q \; [\text{AND}]$

III $\quad (P \downarrow Q) \downarrow (P \downarrow Q) = \neg(P \downarrow Q)$
$\quad\quad = \neg\neg(P \vee Q)$
$\quad\quad = (P \vee Q) \; [\text{OR}]$

Q11. Show that the set $(\neg, \rightarrow)$ of operators is a complete set of operators.

All the five connectivities $\wedge, \vee, \neg, \Rightarrow$ and $\Leftrightarrow$ we can replace all these connectivities by either $\wedge$ or $\vee$.

as $Q \Rightarrow R$
$= (\neg Q \vee R)$
and $Q \Leftrightarrow R$
$= (\neg Q \vee R) \wedge (\neg R \vee Q)$
Further $\wedge$ can be represented as $\vee$.
$Q \wedge R$
$= \neg(\neg Q \vee \neg R)$
So, $(\neg, \vee)$ is complete set,
Now,
$P \Rightarrow Q = \neg P \vee Q$, we have
$P \vee Q = \neg P \vee Q$

As $(\neg, \vee)$ is functionally complete so the above proof shows that $\{\neg, \Rightarrow\}$ is also functionally complete set.

Q12. Find the dual of the propositional formula: $((P \vee Q) \wedge (Q \wedge \neg S)) \vee (P \vee F)$, where F stands for FALSE.

To find dual of on expression change:

$\quad\quad\quad$ AND to OR
$\quad\quad\quad\quad$ 1 to 0
$\quad\quad\quad\quad$ 0 to 1

$((\neg P \vee Q) \wedge (Q \wedge \neg S)) \vee (P \vee F)$ has dual
$((\neg P \wedge Q) \vee (Q \vee \neg S)) \wedge (P \wedge T)$

Note :
(1) F (False) is changed with T (True)
(2) ⌐(NOT) are not changed
(3) ∧ changed to ∨
(4) ∨ changed to ∧

Q13. Establish the equivalence
(i) $P \Leftrightarrow Q \equiv \neg(P \vee Q) \vee (P \wedge Q)$
(ii) $\neg(P \Leftrightarrow Q) \equiv (P \wedge \neg Q) \vee (\neg P \wedge Q)$
(iii) $P \Rightarrow Q (Q \Rightarrow R) \equiv (P \wedge Q) \Rightarrow R$
(iv) $P \Rightarrow (Q \vee R) \equiv (P \Rightarrow Q) \vee (P \Rightarrow R)$
(v) $(P \Rightarrow Q) \Rightarrow (P \wedge Q) \equiv (\neg P \Rightarrow Q) \wedge (Q \Rightarrow P)$
(vi) $(P \vee Q) \Rightarrow R \equiv (P \Rightarrow R) \wedge (Q \Rightarrow R)$

(i) Taking R.H.S.
$\neg(P \vee Q) \vee (P \wedge Q)$
$\equiv (\neg P \wedge \neg Q) \vee (P \wedge Q)$
$\equiv [(\neg P \wedge \neg Q) \vee P)] \wedge [(\neg P \wedge \neg Q) \vee Q]$
$\equiv [\neg P \vee P) \wedge (\neg Q \vee P)] \wedge [(\neg P \vee Q) \wedge (\neg Q \vee Q)]$
$\equiv (\neg Q \vee P) \wedge (\neg P \vee Q)$
$\equiv (Q \Rightarrow P) \wedge (P \Rightarrow Q)$
$\equiv P \Leftrightarrow Q$

(ii) Taking L.H.S.
$\neg(P \Leftrightarrow Q)$
$\equiv \neg[(P \Rightarrow Q) \wedge (Q \Rightarrow P)]$
$\equiv \neg[(\neg P \vee Q) \wedge (\neg Q \vee P)]$
$\equiv (P \wedge \neg Q) \vee (\neg P \wedge Q)$

(iii) Taking R.H.S.
$(P \wedge Q) \Rightarrow R$
$\equiv \neg(P \wedge Q) \vee R \equiv P \Rightarrow Q (Q \Rightarrow R)$

(iv) Taking L.H.S.
$P \Rightarrow (Q \vee R)$
$\equiv \neg P \vee (Q \vee R)$
$\equiv (\neg P \vee Q) \vee (\neg P \vee R)$
$\equiv (P \Rightarrow Q) \vee (P \Rightarrow R)$

(v) Taking L.H.S.
$(P \Rightarrow Q) \Rightarrow (P \wedge Q)$
$\equiv \neg(P \Rightarrow Q) \vee (P \wedge Q)$

$\equiv [\neg P \vee (P \wedge Q)] \Rightarrow [\neg Q \vee (P \wedge Q)]$
$\equiv (\neg P \Rightarrow Q) \wedge (Q \Rightarrow P)$

(vi) Taking L.H.S.
$(P \vee Q) R$
$\equiv \neg (P \vee Q) \vee R$
$\equiv (\neg P \wedge \neg Q) \vee R$
$\equiv (\neg P \vee R) \wedge (\neg Q \vee R)$
$\equiv (P \to R) \wedge (Q \to R)$

Q14. Establish the equivalence and write its dual equivalence
a) $(P \wedge Q) \vee [\neg P \vee (\neg P \vee Q)] \equiv \neg P \vee Q$
b) $\neg P \wedge (\neg Q \wedge R) \vee (Q \wedge R) \vee (P \wedge R) \equiv R$

(a) L.H.S $\equiv (P \wedge Q) \vee [\neg P \vee (\neg P \vee Q)] \equiv (P \wedge Q) \vee [(\neg P \vee \neg P) \vee Q)]$
$\equiv (P \wedge Q) \vee (\neg P \vee Q)$
Now, $(P \wedge Q) \wedge (\neg P \vee Q) \equiv [(P \wedge Q) \wedge \neg P] \vee [(P \wedge Q) \wedge Q]$
$\equiv [(P \wedge Q) \wedge \neg P] \vee (P \wedge Q) (P \wedge Q)$ by absorption
$(P \wedge Q) \vee (\neg P \vee Q) \equiv [(P \wedge Q) \wedge (\neg P \vee Q)] \vee (\neg P \vee Q)$
$\equiv \neg P \vee Q$ by absorption
$\equiv$ RHS

The dual equivalence is $(P \vee Q) \wedge [\neg P \wedge (\neg P \wedge Q)] \equiv \neg P \wedge Q$

(b) $\neg P \wedge (\neg Q \wedge R) \vee (Q \wedge R) \vee (P \wedge R) \equiv R$
Taking LHS
$\neg P \wedge (\neg Q \wedge R) \vee (Q \wedge R) \vee (P \wedge R)$
$\equiv \neg P \wedge [\neg Q \vee R) \wedge R] \vee (P \wedge R)$
$\equiv \neg P \wedge (Q \wedge R) \vee (P \wedge R)$
$\equiv (\neg P \wedge Q \wedge R) \vee (P \wedge R)$
$\equiv (P \wedge Q \wedge R) \vee (P \wedge R)$
$\equiv (Q \wedge R) \vee R$
$\equiv R$ .... by absorption
The Dual equivalence is $\neg P \vee (\neg Q \vee R) \wedge (Q \vee R) \wedge (P \vee R) \equiv R$

Q15. Show that the following formulas are tautologies :
a) $[(A \vee B) \vee (B \wedge C) \vee (C \wedge A)] \Leftrightarrow (A \vee B) \vee (B \vee C) \vee (C \vee A)$
b) $P \Rightarrow (Q \Rightarrow P)$
c) $(P \Rightarrow Q) \Rightarrow [P \vee (Q \wedge R) \wedge Q \wedge (P \vee R)]$
We can solve these kind of problem either using truth table method or by equivalence method

(a) $[(A \vee B) \vee (B \wedge C) \vee (C \wedge A)] \Leftrightarrow (A \vee B) \vee (B \vee C) \vee (C \vee A)$

We prove the formula by using truth tables.
For LHS.

A	B	C	A∨B	B∧C	C∧A	(A∨B) ∨ (B∧C)	(A∨B) ∨ (B∧C) ∨ (C∧A)
T	T	T	T	T	T	T	T
T	T	F	T	F	F	T	T
T	F	T	T	F	T	T	T
T	F	F	T	F	F	T	T
F	T	T	T	T	F	T	T
F	T	F	T	F	F	T	T
F	F	T	F	F	F	F	F
F	F	F	F	F	F	F	F

For RHS. The truth table is as follows:

A	B	C	A∨B	B∨C	C∨A	(A∨B) ∨ (B∨C)	(A∨B) ∨ (B∨C) ∨ (C∨A)
T	T	T	T	T	T	T	T
T	T	F	T	T	T	T	T
T	F	T	T	T	T	T	T
T	F	F	T	F	T	T	T
F	T	T	T	T	T	T	T
F	T	F	T	T	F	T	T
F	F	T	F	T	T	T	T
F	F	F	F	F	F	F	F

Since the truth tables of LHS and RHS are not same therefore the given formulae is not a tautology.

(b) $P \Rightarrow (Q \Rightarrow P) = \neg P \vee (Q \Rightarrow P)$
$$= \neg P \vee (\neg Q \vee P)$$
$$= (\neg P \vee \neg Q) \vee P$$
$$= \neg (P \wedge Q) \vee P$$
$$= (P \wedge Q) \rightarrow P$$

which is true : Hence the given formule is tautology.

(c)(i) $P \Rightarrow (Q \Rightarrow R) \equiv \neg P \vee (Q \Rightarrow R) \equiv \neg P \vee (\neg Q \vee R)]$
$\equiv (\neg P \vee \neg Q) \vee R) \equiv \neg(P \vee Q) \vee R$
$\equiv (P \vee Q) \Rightarrow R$

(ii) $(P \Rightarrow Q) \Rightarrow (P \wedge Q) \equiv \neg(P \Rightarrow Q) \vee (P \wedge Q)$
$\equiv (P \wedge \neg Q) \vee (P \wedge Q) \equiv P \wedge (Q \vee \neg Q)$

$(\neg P \Rightarrow Q) \wedge (Q \Rightarrow P) \equiv (P \vee Q) \wedge (\neg Q \vee P) \equiv (P \vee Q) \wedge (P \vee \neg Q)$
$\equiv P \vee (Q \wedge \neg Q)$

Now if $P \wedge (Q \vee \neg Q)$ is true, then so is P. Hence $P \vee (Q \wedge \neg Q)$ is true. On the other hand if $P \vee (Q \wedge \neg Q)$ is true. Then at least one of them is true. But $Q \wedge \neg Q$ false always. Therefore P is true. Thus $P \wedge (Q \vee \neg Q)$ is also true because $Q \vee \neg Q$ is true always. Thus these are true in identical cases and thus these are equivalent. Actually we have seen that the two sides are equivalent to P.

Q16. Write an equivalent formula for $P \wedge (Q \Leftrightarrow R) \vee (R \Leftrightarrow P)$ which does not involve biconditional.

Given $P \wedge (Q \Leftrightarrow R) \vee (R \Leftrightarrow P)$
$\Leftrightarrow [P \wedge ((Q \Rightarrow R) \wedge (R \Rightarrow Q)) \vee ((R \Rightarrow P) \wedge (P \Rightarrow R))]$

Q17. Write an equivalent formula for $P \wedge (Q \Leftrightarrow R)$ which is free biconditional as well as conditional.

Given $P \wedge (Q \Leftrightarrow R) \Leftrightarrow P \wedge ((Q \Rightarrow R) \wedge (R \Rightarrow Q))$
$\Leftrightarrow [P \wedge ((\neg Q \vee R) \wedge (\neg R \vee Q))]$

Q18. Check whether the following equivalence is valid or not :
$((P \wedge Q) \Rightarrow R) \equiv (P \Rightarrow R) \wedge (Q \Rightarrow R)$
Explain why or why not.

The given equivalence is: -
$((P \wedge Q) \Rightarrow R) \equiv (P \Rightarrow R) \wedge (Q \Rightarrow R)$
It can be check by using the truth table.
The above relation is valid if the given equivalence is a tautology.
Now truth table for $(P \wedge Q) \Rightarrow R$ is: -

P	Q	R	P∧Q	(P∧Q)⇒R
F	F	F	F	T
F	F	T	F	T
F	T	F	F	T
F	T	T	F	T
T	F	F	F	T
T	F	T	F	T
T	T	F	T	F
T	T	T	T	T

And truth table for (P ⇒ R) ∧ (Q ⇒ R) is :-

P	Q	R	P⇒R	Q⇒R	(P⇒R)∧(Q⇒R)
F	F	F	T	T	T
F	F	T	T	T	T
F	T	F	T	F	F
F	T	T	T	T	T
T	F	F	F	T	F
T	F	T	T	T	T
T	T	F	F	F	F
T	T	T	T	T	T

Clearly from both truth table, the corresponding values are not same. Therefore the given equivalence is not valid.

Q19. There are two restaurants next to each other. One has a sign that says 'Good food is not cheap' and the other has a sign that says ' Cheap food is not good'. Are both the signs saying the same thing?

Let G denote the statement that the food is good and C the statement that the food is cheap. Hence the first sign says 'G ⇒ ⌐C' and the second says 'C ⇒ ⌐G'. It will now be clear from the following truth table that one is the contra positive of other and hence they mean the same thing.

G	C	$\neg$G	$\neg$C	G$\Rightarrow\neg$C	C$\Rightarrow\neg$G
F	F	T	T	T	T
F	T	T	F	T	T
T	F	F	T	T	T
T	T	F	F	F	F

Q20. Write the negation of the following :
(a) If the determinant of a system of linear equations is zero then either the system has no solution or has an infinite number of solutions.
(b) If two plus two is five then moon is made of green cheese.
                                                            [DEC02, Q2(b, ii)]
(c) If either housing is scarce or people like to live with their in-laws, and if people do not like to live with their in-laws, then housing is scarce.
(d) Either an employee follows the service rules or has to suffer.
                                                            [JUNE03, Q2(c, ii)]
(e) Either today is not a Sunday or today is not a Wednesday.

(a) The negation of the above statement is as follows :
It is not true that if determinant of a system of linear equation is zero then either the system has no solution of has an infinite number of solution.
It can also be written as :
If the determinant of a system of linear equations is not zero then the system has finite number of solution.
(b) The negation of the above statement is " it is not true" that if two plus two is five then moon is made of green cheese.
(c) The negation of above statement is " It is not true" that if either housing is scarce or people like to live with their in laws, and if people do not like to live with their in laws then housing is scarce.
(d) The negation of above statement is either an employee not follows the service rules or he has not to suffer.
(e) The negation of above statement is :
It is not the case that either today is not a Sunday or today is not a Wednesday.
In other words it is written as :
either today is Sunday or today is a Wednesday.

Q21. Express P$\Rightarrow$ Q, P$\Leftrightarrow$ Q using $\uparrow$ and $\downarrow$ only.
i) $P \Rightarrow Q \equiv \neg PQS \vee Q \equiv \neg P \wedge \neg(\neg Q)$
    $\equiv \neg(P \wedge \neg Q)$
    $\equiv P \uparrow \neg Q \equiv P \uparrow (Q \uparrow Q)$
ii) $P \Leftrightarrow Q \equiv (P \Rightarrow Q) \wedge (Q \Rightarrow P)$
    $\equiv \neg[(P \Rightarrow Q) \uparrow (Q \Rightarrow P)]$
    $\equiv [(P \Rightarrow Q) \uparrow (Q \Rightarrow P)] \uparrow [(P \Rightarrow Q) \uparrow (Q \Rightarrow P)]$

$$\equiv [(P \uparrow (Q \uparrow Q)) \uparrow (Q \uparrow (P \uparrow P)] \uparrow [(P \uparrow (Q \uparrow Q)) \uparrow (Q \uparrow (P \uparrow P))]$$

Of course these expressions are not unique, Another such expression would be

$$P \Leftrightarrow Q \equiv (\neg P \vee Q) \wedge (P \vee \neg Q)$$
$$\equiv [(\neg P \vee Q) \wedge P] \vee [(\neg P \vee Q) \wedge \neg Q]$$
$$\equiv (\neg P \wedge P) \vee (Q \wedge P) \vee (\neg P \wedge \neg Q) \vee (Q \wedge \neg Q)$$
$$\equiv (P \wedge Q) \vee (\neg P \wedge \neg Q)$$
$$\equiv (P \wedge Q) \vee \neg(P \vee Q) \equiv \neg\neg((P \wedge Q) \vee \neg(P \vee Q))$$
$$\equiv \neg(\neg(P \wedge Q) \wedge (P \vee Q)]$$
$$\equiv \neg(P \wedge Q) \uparrow (P \vee Q)$$
$$\equiv (P \uparrow Q) \uparrow [(P \uparrow P) \uparrow (Q \uparrow Q)]$$

Q22. Express P ↓ Q using ↑ only.

$$P \downarrow Q \equiv \neg(P \vee Q) \equiv (P \vee Q) \uparrow (P \vee Q)$$
$$\equiv [(P \uparrow P) \uparrow (Q \uparrow Q)] \uparrow [\{P \uparrow P) \uparrow (Q \uparrow Q)]$$

Q23. Establish the analogues of De Morgan's Laws involving ↑ and ↓ :
(i) $\neg (P \uparrow Q) \equiv \neg P \downarrow \neg Q$
(ii) $\neg (P \downarrow Q) \equiv \neg P \uparrow \neg Q$

(i) The R.H.S.
$$\equiv \neg P \downarrow \neg Q$$
$$\equiv \neg(\neg P \vee \neg Q)$$
$$\equiv P \wedge Q$$
$$\equiv \neg(\neg(P \wedge Q))$$
$$\equiv \neg (P \uparrow Q)$$
$$\equiv \text{L.H.S.}$$

(ii) The R.H.S.
$$\equiv \neg P \uparrow \neg Q$$
$$\equiv \neg(\neg P \wedge \neg Q)$$
$$\equiv \neg(\neg(P \vee Q))$$
$$\equiv \neg (P \downarrow Q)$$
$$\equiv \text{L.H.S.}$$

Q24. Find truth table for
(i) $\sim(p \vee q)$
(ii) $(p \wedge q) \vee [\sim(p \wedge q)]$

(i)

p	q	(p∨q)	~(p∨q)
T	T	T	F
T	F	T	F
F	T	T	F
F	F	F	T

(ii)

p	q	(p∧q)	~(p∧q)	(p∧q)∨~(p∧q)
T	T	T	F	T
T	F	F	T	T
F	T	F	T	T
F	F	F	T	T

Q25. Find which sentences are statements and which are not :
(i) Asia is a continent.
(ii) How are you ?
(iii) Moon revolves around the sun.
(iv) Smoking is injurious to health.
(v) 2^n+n is an even number for infinitely many n
(vi) Mathematics is fun
(vii) $2^n = n^2$

(i), (iii), (iv), (v) are statements because each of them is universally true or universally false. (ii) is not a statement, it is a question. (vi) is a subjective sentence. (viii) can be a statement when value(s) which n takes is /are given.

Q26. Deduce whether the following pairs are equivalent
(i) $(P \vee Q) \wedge \neg(P \wedge Q)$, $(P \wedge \neg Q) \vee (\neg P \wedge Q)$
(ii) $(P \Rightarrow Q) \vee \neg(P \vee Q)$, $(P \Rightarrow Q) \wedge (P \Leftrightarrow Q)$

(i) $(P \vee Q) \wedge \neg(P \wedge Q) \equiv (P \vee Q) \wedge (\neg P \vee \neg Q)$
$\equiv [(P \vee Q) \wedge \neg P] \vee [(P \vee Q) \wedge \neg Q]$
$\equiv (P \wedge \neg P) \vee (Q \wedge \neg P) \vee (P \wedge \neg Q) \vee (Q \wedge \neg Q)$
$\equiv (\neg P \wedge Q) \vee (P \wedge \neg Q)$

which is in p.d.n.f. in which he second formula already appears. Thus the two formulae are equivalent.

(ii) To check whether the given pairs are equivalent or not, we construct truth tables for the given formulae: Now truth table for the formula $(P \Rightarrow Q) \vee \neg(P \vee Q)$ is as follows:

P	Q	P⇒Q	P∨Q	⌐(P∨Q)	(P⇒Q)∨⌐(P∨Q)
T	T	T	T	F	T
T	F	F	T	F	F
F	T	T	T	F	T
F	F	T	F	T	T

Now, truth table for the formula
$(P \Rightarrow Q) \wedge (P \Leftrightarrow Q)$ is as follows:

P	Q	P⇒Q	P⇔Q	(P⇒Q)∧(P⇔Q)
T	T	T	T	T
T	F	F	F	F
F	T	T	F	F
F	F	T	T	T

Since the truth values of both formulae are not same therefore these are not equivalent.
Hence given pair is not equivalent.

Q27. Show that the following are equivalent formulas :
(i) $P \vee (P \wedge Q) \Leftrightarrow P$
(ii) $P \vee (\neg P \wedge Q) \Leftrightarrow P \vee Q$
(i) $P \Leftrightarrow P \wedge (Q \vee \neg Q) \Leftrightarrow (P \wedge Q) \vee (P \wedge \neg Q)$
$P \vee (P \wedge Q) \Leftrightarrow (P \wedge (Q \vee \neg Q)) \vee (P \wedge Q)$
$\Leftrightarrow (P \wedge Q) \vee (P \wedge \neg Q)$

(ii) L.H.S. $\equiv P \vee (\neg P \wedge Q)$
$\equiv (P \wedge \neg P) \wedge (P \vee Q)$
$\equiv P \vee Q$
$\equiv$ R.H.S.

Q28. Determine whether the following formulae are tautology, contradiction or satisfiable.
(i) $[P \wedge (P \Rightarrow Q)] \Rightarrow \neg Q$
(ii) $[(P \Rightarrow Q) \wedge (Q \Rightarrow R)] (P \wedge \neg R)$
(i) $[P \wedge (P \Rightarrow Q] \Rightarrow \neg Q \equiv \neg [P \wedge (P \Rightarrow Q)] \vee \neg Q$
$\equiv \neg P \vee (\neg P \Rightarrow \neg Q) \vee Q$ $\neg P \vee (P (P \wedge \neg Q) \vee \neg Q$. (d.n.f.)
$\equiv [(\neg P \vee \neg Q) \vee P] \wedge (\neg P \vee \neg Q. \vee \neg Q)$
$\equiv (\neg P \vee \neg Q) \equiv \neg P \vee \neg Q,$
This formula is not a tautology (it is false for P true, Q true), nor at contradiction (it is true for P false, Q false). It is of course satisfiable.

(ii) The given formula is
$[(P \Rightarrow Q) \wedge (Q \Rightarrow R)] \wedge (P \wedge \neg R)$
First we make truth table for
$(P \Rightarrow Q) \wedge (Q \Rightarrow R)$ as follows:

P	Q	P⇒Q	R	Q⇒R	(P⇒Q)∧(Q⇒R)
T	T	T	T	T	T
T	F	F	T	T	F
F	T	T	F	F	F
F	F	T	F	T	T

Now truth table for the formula
$[(P \Rightarrow Q) \wedge (Q \Rightarrow R)] \wedge (P \wedge \neg R)$ as follows:

P	R	¬R	P∧¬R	(P⇒Q)∧(Q⇒R)	[(P⇒Q)∧(Q⇒R)]∧(P∧¬R)
T	T	F	F	T	F
T	F	T	T	F	F
F	T	F	F	F	F
F	F	T	F	T	F

Since from the above table it follows that all truth values are false. Hence the given formula is a contradiction.

Q29. Find the dual to the propositional formula :
$((\neg P \vee Q) \wedge (Q \vee \neg S)) \vee (P \vee F)$, where F stands for FALSE.
The given propositional formula is
$((\neg P \vee Q) \wedge (Q \vee \neg S)) \vee (P \vee F)$
Since the dual of formula is obtained by replacing '∨' by '∧' & '∧' by '∨'.
Therefore dual of given formula is as follow:
$((\neg P \wedge Q) \wedge (Q \wedge \neg S)) \wedge (P \wedge F) \wedge$ where F stands for FALSE.

Q30. Determine the validity of the conclusion (represented by 'C: ')
form the given set of
premises
(i) {A → (B ∧ O), (B ∨ D) → E, D ∨ A}   C : E
(ii) {P → Q ∧ R, Q ∨ S → ¬, S ∨ P}   C : L
(iii) {[P → Q] → → S, ¬S, P}   C : Q
(iv) {P → Q ∧ R, Q ∨ S → L, S ∨ P}   C : L
(v) P→~ Q, P ∨ R, ~R ∨ ~ S, S with conclusion   C : ~ Q
(vi) {P ⇔ Q, R ∨ ¬S, Q ⇒ S, ¬P ⇒ R}   C : R
#: {P ↔ Q, R ∨ ¬S, Q → S, ¬P → R}   C : R

(vii) If the earth is flat and it has only due moon then the sun comes about the earth.

(i) To determine the validity we are using the truth table for the conclusion one by one.

Truth table for (B ∧O) is:

B	O	B∧O
T	T	T
T	F	F
F	T	F
F	F	F

Truth table for (A → (B ∧ O)) is:

A	B∧O	A→ B∧O
T	T	T
T	F	F
F	T	T
F	F	T

Now truth table for (B ∨ D) is:

B	D	B ∨ D
T	T	T
T	F	T
F	T	T
F	F	F

and Truth table for (B ∨ D) → E is:

B ∨ D	E	(B ∨ D) → E
T	T	T
T	T	T
T	F	F
F	F	T

Now truth table for (D ∨ A) is :

D	A	D ∨ A
T	T	T
T	F	T
T	T	T
F	F	F

Now from the table (ii), (iv) & (v), e observe that the truth value for A, B, O, D, & E gives the true values for A → (B ∧ O), (B ∨ D) → E & D ∨ A. Hence C: E is valid for these values and invalid for other values of A, B, O, D & E.

(ii) To determine the validity we are using the truth tables for the conclusion, one by one.
So, we have.

Truth table for P → Q   **Now truth table for (P→ Q) ∧ R**

P	Q	P → Q
T	T	T
T	F	F
F	T	T
F	F	T

P→Q	Q	(P→Q)∧R
T	T	T
F	T	F
T	F	F
T	F	F

Now truth table for Q ∨ S

Q	S	Q ∨ S
T	T	T
T	F	T
F	T	T
F	F	F

Now truth table for ⌐S ∨ P is as follows:

S	P	⌐S	⌐S ∨ P
T	T	F	T
T	F	F	F
F	T	T	T
F	F	T	T

Now truth table for Q∨ S → ⌐S∨ P is as follows:

Q ∨ S	⌐S ∨ P	Q ∨ S → ⌐S ∨ P
T	T	T
T	F	F
T	T	T
F	T	T

Now from tables (ii), (v), we observe that the truth value for P, Q, R, S gives the true values for
P → Q ∧ R and Q ∨ S →⌐S ∨ P
Hence, C: E is valid for these values and invalid for other values of P, Q, R and S.

(iii) [P ⇒ Q) ⇒ R] ⇒ S,⌐S, P.
Conclusion : Q.
Let the premises be all true. Then in particular S is false. Then (P ⇒ Q) ⇒ must be false, otherwise would be false. Hence (P ⇒ Q) must be true and R must be false. Now as P and
P ⇒ Q. both are true, Q must be true. Therefore the conclusion is valid.

(iv) Premise : P ⇒ (Q ∧ R), Q ∨ S ⇒ L , S ∨ P}
Conclusion : L
If P is true, then truth of P ⇒ (Q ∧ R) gives that Q ∧ R is true. Then Q and hence Q ∨ S must be true. Now the truth of (Q ∨ S) ⇒ L gives that L must

be true. On the other hand if P is false then S cannot be true as S ∨ P is true. Then Q ∨ S is also true giving the truth of L because of truth of (Q ∨ S) ⇒ L.

(v) To Check the validity with conclusions firstly we have to make the truth tables for the premises:-

Now truth table for P → ~ Q is as follows:

P	Q	~Q	P→~Q
T	T	F	F
T	F	T	T
F	T	F	T
F	F	T	T

Now truth table for P ∨ R is as follows:

P	R	P ∨ R
T	T	T
T	F	T
F	T	T
F	F	F

Also truth table for ~R ∨ ~S

R	S	~R	~S	~R∨~S
T	T	F	F	F
T	F	F	T	T
F	T	T	F	T
F	F	T	T	T

Since all the premises are true for the row 2 and for that C : NQ is also true hence conclusion is valid.

(vi) Premises : P ⇔ Q, R ∨ ⌐S, Q ⇒ S, ⌐P ⇒ R.
Suppose that the premises are all true. If the conclusion R is not rue, then R is false, As ⌐P ⇒ R be true, ⌐P may not be false in. P must be true. Now truth of P ⇒ Q gives that P and Q must have the same truth value. Therefore Q must also be true. As Q⇒ S is also true, S must be true. As R and ù S are both false now, We get that R ∨ ⌐S is false. But the premises are all supposed to be true. Thus the conclusion R can not be false and so the conclusion is valid as it is true whenever the premises are true.

(vii) If the premise 'Earth' is round' is true, then the statement 'earth is flat' is false. Then 'The earth is flat and it has only one moon' is also false. Therefore the conclusion is true irrespective of the truth of the second part as the antecedent is false. Therefore the conclusion is valid.

Q31. Construct a program for generating truth tables – mainline and function logic.

Solution :

```
C       Mainline
C       This program evaluates a statement formula
C       And generate its truth table.
C
C       Variables
C       Title   :       Title for the statement formula
C       Name    :       Variable Names
C       Value   :       Logical value of statement formula
C       Number:         Number of Rows in the truth table
C
C       Declarations and Titles
                Integer*2 Name (3)/'P', 'Q', 'R'/
                Real * B Title (4)/'.Not. (P.',' And . Q).O',
'R.(R.OR.',' P)
                Logical Case (10), Logic. Value
                Integer Base (10), Length (10)

C       Initialize Base, Length, Case, N, and Number.

                N = 3
                Number = 2 ** N
                Dn 1K = 1, N
                Base (K) = 2 ** (N – K)
                Length (K) = Base (K)
                Case (K) = .False.
        1       Continue

C.      Output Headings

                Write (6, 10) Title
        10      Format ('1'. 13X, 'Variables', 13X, 4AB)
                Write (6, 20) Name
        20      Format (' ', 8X, 'Case 1 2 3',/, ' ', 13X, 3(A2,2X),
                21X, 'Value',/)

C       Find value of the statement formula, output truth values,
C       And Generate New Truth values for the Logical Variables.
                Do 2 1 = 1 Number
```

```
                    Value = Logic (Case, N)
                    Write (6, 30), (Case(K), K = 1, N), Value
          30        Format (' ', 13X, 3 (L 1, 3X), 23X, L1)
                    Call Next (Case, N, Base, Length)
          2         Continue
                    Stop
                    End

                    Logical Function Logic (Case, N)

    C               This Function defines the statement formula to be evaluated.
                    Logical Case (N)
                    Logic = .Not. (Case(1). And. (Case 2)). or. (Case(3).
                    Or. Case (1))
                    Return
                    End
          Case
```

Variables			.Not. (P. and. Q).Or.(R. OR. P)
1	2	3	
P	Q	R	**Value**
F	F	F	T
F	F	T	T
F	T	F	T
F	T	T	T
T	F	F	T
T	F	T	T
T	T	F	T
T	T	T	T

Q.32 Let us consider that the statement "If it is raining and if rain implies that no one can go to see a film, then no one can go to see a film". As a compound proposition. Show that this proposition is a tautology, by using the properties of logical equivalence.

($\forall\, t \in [0, \infty\,]$) ($\forall\, x \in H$)p(x,t) is the given statement where p(x,t) is the predicate 'The politician can fool x at time t second.', and H is the set of human beings. Its negation is ($\exists\, t \in [0, \infty\, [$) ($\exists\, x \in H$) (~[(x,t), i.e., there is somebody who is not fooled by the politician at least for one moment.
(ii) The given statement is

($\forall x \in R$) ($\exists y \in R$) ($x = y^2$). Its negation is
($\exists x \in R$) ($\forall y \in R$) (x is not equal to y^2), i.e.,
there is a real number which is not the square of any real number.
(iii) The given statement is
($\exists x \in L$) ($\forall t \in [0, \infty[$) p(x,t), where L is the set of lawyers and p(x,t):x does not lie at time t. The negation is
($\forall x \in L$) ($\exists t \in [0. \infty]$) (~p), i.e., every lawyer tells a lie at some time.

Q33. Check whether the following argument is valid, using a truth table. "If Shalini leaves home before 9.00 AM or it she takes a taxi, she will reach office in time. She did leave after 10.00 AM and she did reach office in time. Therefore, Shalini must have taken a taxi."

[DEC05, Q5(b)]

For checking the given argument, we will find is there any tautology or not. So,
p = Shalini leaves home before 9:00 A.M.
q = Shalini takes a taxi
r = Shalini reaches office in time

p	q	r	~p	~p∧q	(~p∧r→q)
T	T	T	F	F	T
T	T	F	F	F	T
T	F	T	F	F	T
T	F	F	F	F	T
F	T	T	T	T	T
F	T	F	T	F	T
F	F	T	T	F	T
F	F	F	T	F	T

From the truth table we see that in the last column, there is T in every row, therefore, there is Tautology and our given argument is valid i.e. Shalini must have taken a taxi.

Chapter-2
Techniques Of Proof

Proof and disproof :
A proof of a proposition p is mathematical argument consisting of a sequence of statements $p_1, p_2, ..., p_n$ from which p logically follows. So, p is the conclusion of this argument.

Sometimes, instead of showing that a statement p is true, we try to prove that it is false, i.e. that ~p is true. Such a proof is called a **disproof** of p.

Theorem and Conjectures : Sometimes it happens that we feel a certain statement is true, but we don't succeed in proving it. It may also happen that we can't disprove it. Such statements are called conjectures. If and when a conjecture is proved, it would be called a theorem. If it is disproved, then its negative will be theorem. In other words the statement that is proved to be true is called a theorem.

Premise and its kind : Each statement in the sequence $p_1, p_2....p_n$, is called the premise (hypothesis/assumption). Premises may be of 4 kinds.
(i) a proposition that has been proved earlier (e.g. to prove that the complex roots of a polynomial in R[x] occur in pairs; or
(ii) a proposition that follows logically from the earlier propositions given in the proof; or
(iii) a mathematical fact that has never been proved, but is universally accepted as true (e.g. two points determine a line). Such a fact is called an axiom (or a postulate);
(iv) the definition of a mathematical term (e.g. assuming the definition of '$\subseteq$' in the proof of $A \cap B \subseteq A$).

Methods of Proof : Methods of proof are of two types :
(i) direct proof
(ii) indirect proof
(i) A direct proof of $p \Rightarrow q$ is a logically valid argument that begins with the assumptions that p is true and, in one or more applications of the law of detachment, concludes that q must be true.

So, to construct a direct proof of $p \Rightarrow q$, we start by assuming that p is true. Then, in one or more steps of the form $p \Rightarrow q_1, q_1 \Rightarrow q_2, ..., q_n \Rightarrow q$, we conclude that q is true.

Indirect proof : This may be subdivided by two ways (i) proof by contrapositive (ii) proof by contradiction

(i) Proof by contrapositive : This way, we use the fact that the preposition $p \Rightarrow q$ is logically equivalent to its contrapositive $(\sim q \Rightarrow \sim p)$,

$$(p \Rightarrow q) = (\sim q \Rightarrow \sim p)$$

Because of this equivalence, to prove $p \Rightarrow q$, we can, instead, prove $\sim q \Rightarrow \sim p$. This means that we can assume that $\sim q$ is true, and then try to prove that $\sim p$ is true.

(ii) Proof by contradiction : In this method, to prove q is true, we begins by supposing that q is false (i.e., $\sim q$ is true). Then, by a logical argument we reach a contradiction $r \wedge \sim r$ for some statement that is always false. This can only happen when $\sim q$ is false also. Therefore q must be true.

This method is also called reduction ad absurdum because it relies on reducing a given assumption to an absurdity.

Counter example : An example (problem) which reflects that a statement is false is called counter example to such a statement.

The natural condition offers the disprove statement of the form $p \rightarrow q$ required an example, where $p \wedge \sim q$ is true. i.e. premise p holds but the conclusion q does not hold.

Natural Numbers : The set of numbers used for counting, called natural numbers and denoted by N. these numbers starts from 1 not from 0.
$N = \{1, 2, 3, 4, 5.........\}$

Peano's Postulates : Peano, given the postulates in respect of defining the characteristics of natural numbers. These are as follows :

P_1 1 is natural number $1 \in n$

P_2 for each natural number n, $\exists$ one natural number n+ called its successor
e.g. $10^+ = 10 + 1 = 11$
$x^+ = x+1, \forall x \in N$

P_3 1 is not the successor of any number, i.e. for every $n \in N$, $n+1 \neq 1$

P_4 If m and $n \in N$, $m^+ = n^+$ then $m = n$
i.e. if two natural numbers m and n have same successor, then they are identical.

P_5 Any subset A of N, which has the property.

(i) $1 \in A$, (ii) $x+ \in A$
whenever $1 \in A$, is equal to N

Trichotomy Law : If $x, y \in N$, then only one possibility is true from the following
(i) $x = y$ (ii) $x > y$ (iii) $x < y$

Mathematical Induction : If $p(n)$ be any statement for all $n \in N$ and is true, where N be the set of natural numbers, then provided that
(i) $P(1)$ is true.
(ii) $P(k)$ is true that is $P(k^+)$ is true where $k \in N$

Vacuous Proof and trivial proof :
A vacuous proof make use of the fact that if p is false, the $p \to q$ is true, regardless of the truth value of q. So, to vacuously prove $p \to q$, all we need to do is to show that p is false.
A trivial proof of $p \to q$ is one based on the fact that if q is true then $p \to q$ is true, regardless of the truth value of p.

Some Important Solved Questions :
Q1. Prove by mathematical induction, that $10^{2n-1}+1$ is divisible by 11
Let $p(n)$; $10^{2n-1}+1$ is divisible by 11
for $n = 1$, $f(1)$ is true because, $p(1) = 10^{2 \times 1 - 1}+1$
$\qquad = 11$, which is divisible by 11
Let us suppose that the statement is true
for $n = k$ i.e.
$p(k) : 10^{2k-1}+1$ is divisible by 11

$$\begin{aligned}P(k^+) = 10^{2(k+1)-1}+1 &= 10^{2k+2-1}+1 \\ &= 10^{2k-1+2}+1 \\ &= 10^{2k-1} 10^2 +1 \\ &= 10^{2k-1}\ 100 + 1 \\ &= 10^{2k-1}\ (99+1)+1 \\ &= 99(10^{2k-1})+10^{2k-1}+1 \\ &= 11(9)\ (10^{2k-1}) + p(k) \text{ where } p(k) = 10^{2k-1}+1 \\ &= \text{a number which is divisible by 11}\end{aligned}$$

Because $11(9)10^{2k-1}$ and $p(k)$ both are divisible by 11
therefore we conclude that, if $p(k)$ is true then $p(k^+)$ is also true.
Hence $p(n) : 10^{2n-1}+1$ is divisible by 11 is true.

Q2. Prove by the principle of mathematical induction that $x^n - y^n$ is divisible by $x+y$ when $n \in N$ and n is even.

$x^n - y^n$ is divisible by $(x+y)$ for n is even
∵ n is even we start from n = 2
∴ $P(2) : x^2 - y^2 = (x+y)(x-y)$, which is divisible by $(x+y)$
∴ P(2) is true.
Let us suppose that for even value of n i.e.. n=2k, the statement is true.
i.e. $P(2k) : x^{2k} - y^{2k}$ is divisible by $(x+y)$

then we have to check $P(2k^+)$ is true.
i.e. $P(2k+2) : x^{2k+2} - y^{2k+2}$ is divisible by $(x+y)$
$P(2k+2) : x^{2k+2} - y^{2k+2}$

$= x^{2k} \cdot x^2 - y^{2k} \cdot y^2$
$= (x^{2k}x^2 - x^{2k}y^2) + (x^{2k} \cdot y^2 - y^{2k}y^2)$
(adding & subtracting by $x^{2k}y^2$)
$= x^{2k}(x^2-y^2) + y^2(x^{2k}-y^{2k})$
$= x^{2k}(x+y)(x-y) + y^2(x^{2k}-y^{2k})$
which is divisible by $(x+y)$ becaue the first number is clearly divisible by $(x+y)$ and second number by $p(2k)$
∴ $p(2k^+)$ is true
∴ $p(n)$ is true $\forall n \in N$.

Q3. Prove by mathematical induction. that $\sum_{i=1}^{n} \frac{1}{\sqrt{n}} \leq 2\sqrt{n}-1 \quad \forall \mathbf{n} \in \mathbf{N}$.

Let $p(n) : \sum_{i=1}^{n} \frac{1}{\sqrt{n}} \leq 2\sqrt{n}-1$

Let n =1, p(n) is true because

$\frac{1}{\sqrt{1}} \leq 2\sqrt{1} - 1$

$1 \leq 2-1$
$1 \leq 1$ which is ture.
let n = 2, p(2) : is true since

$\frac{1}{\sqrt{2}} \leq 2\sqrt{2} - 1$

then given statement is true for n = k

$p(k) \sum_{i=1}^{k} \frac{1}{\sqrt{k}} \leq 2\sqrt{k}-1$

Now we have to show $p(k^+)$ is true

Let, $\dfrac{1}{\sqrt{1}} + \dfrac{1}{\sqrt{2}} + \dfrac{1}{\sqrt{3}} + ... + \dfrac{1}{\sqrt{k}} \leq 2\sqrt{k}-1$

we add $\dfrac{1}{\sqrt{k+1}}$ to both sides

therefore $\dfrac{1}{\sqrt{1}} + \dfrac{1}{\sqrt{2}} + \dfrac{1}{\sqrt{3}} + ... + \dfrac{1}{\sqrt{k}} + \dfrac{1}{\sqrt{k+1}} \leq 2\sqrt{k}-1 + \dfrac{1}{\sqrt{k+1}}$

$\leq \dfrac{(2\sqrt{k}-1)(\sqrt{k+1})+1}{\sqrt{k+1}}$

$\leq \dfrac{(2\sqrt{k}(\sqrt{k+1})-\sqrt{k+1}+1}{\sqrt{k+1}}$

$\leq \dfrac{2\sqrt{k(k+1)}+1-\sqrt{k+1}}{\sqrt{k+1}}$

(which is greater than or equal to 1)

i.e. $2\sqrt{k(k+1)}-\sqrt{k+1}+1 \geq 1$

whatever be the value of k.

∴ p(k+1) is true

∴ $\forall n \in N$, P(n) is true.

Q4. Prove by principle of mathematical induction, $7^{2n}+2^{3n-3}3^{n-1}$ is divisible by 25 $\forall n \in N$

Let p(n) : $7^{2n}+2^{3n-3}.3^{n-1}$ be divisible by 25
for n = 1,
p(1) = $7^2 + 2^0.3^0$ = 50 which is divisible by 25
Let statement is true for n=k
i.e. p(k) is true.
p(k) : $7^{2k}+2^{3k-3}.3^{k-1}$ is divisible by 25
Now we have to test p(k⁺) is true.

p(k⁺) = $7^{2(k+1)} + 2^{3(k+1)-3}.3^{(k+1)-1}$
= $7^{2k+2}+2^{3k+3-3}.3^{k-1}.3$
= $49(7^{2k}) + 2^{3k-3}.8.3.3^{k-1}$
= $49 (7^{2k}) + (24) 2^{3k-3}.3^{k-1}$
= $(50-1) 7^{2k} + (25-1) 2^{3k-3}.3^{k-1}$
= $(50) 7^{2k}-7^{2k}+(25) 2^{3k-3}.3^{k-1}-2^{3k-3}.3^{k-1}$
= $25 (7^{2k}(2) + 2^{3k-3}.3^{k-1})-(7^{2k}+2^{3k-3}3^{k-1})$
= $25 [2(7^{2k}) + 2^{3k-3}.3^{k-1}] - p(k)$

= which is divisible by 25 as p(k) is divisible by 25.
Hence p(k⁺) is true
P(n) is true $\forall n \in N$.

Q5. Consider suitable counter example and discuss the following statement :
i) $\forall x \in Z, x \in Q \setminus N$.
ii) $(x+y)^n = x^n + y^n$ $\forall n \in N, z, y \in Z$.

i) **Theorem :** The area of every equilateral triangle of side a and perimeter 2a is divisible by 3.
Proof : Since there is no equilateral triangle that satisfies the hypothesis, the proposition is vacuously true.

ii) **Theorem :** If a natural number c is divisible by 5, then the perimeter of the equilateral triangle of side c is 3c.
Proof : Since the conclusion is always true, the proposition is trivially true.

Q6. Show that $\sqrt{2}$ is irrational.
We prove the given statement by contradiction.
Let $\sqrt{2}$ is rational and equal to p/q where $q \neq 0$ and, p and q have no factor common to it.
$\sqrt{2} = p/q$
$p = \sqrt{2}q \Rightarrow p^2 = 2q^2 \Rightarrow 2p^2 \Rightarrow 2/p$
Therefore, by definition, p=2q for some $r \in Z$.
Therefore $p^2 = 4r^2$
$p^2 = 2q^2$ also.
So $4r^2 = 2q^2 \Rightarrow 2r^2 = q^2 \Rightarrow 2/q^2 \Rightarrow 2/q$
But now we find that 2 divides both p and q which contradicts our earlier assumption that p and q have no common factor.
Therefore, we conclude that our assumption that $\sqrt{2}$ is rational is false, ie. $\sqrt{2}$ is irrational.

Q7. Give a direct proof of the theorem. The square of an even integer is an even integer.
Sol. Mathematically, Let the statement may be written as
$(\forall x \in Z)(p(x) \Rightarrow q(x))$
where p(x) : x is even, and
q(x) : x^2 is even, i.e. q(x) is the same as $p(x^2)$
The direct proof, then goes as follows

Let x be an even number (i.e. we assume p(x) is true).
Then x = 2n, for some integer n (we apply the definition of an even number).
Then $x^2 = (2n)^2 = 4n^2 = 2(2n^2)$
x^2 is even (i.e. q(x) is true).

Q8. Give a direct proof of the statement 'the product of two odd integers is odd'

Let two odd integers are x & y and our hypothesis is p:x and y are odd. And we want to show that
q : xy is odd as conclusion.
Let us first prove that $p \Rightarrow q$.
Since x is odd, x =2m +1 for some integer m.
Similarly, y=2n+1 for some integer n.
Then xy - (2m+1) (2n+1) = 2(2mn+m+n+)+1
Therefore, xy is odd
So we have shown that $p \Rightarrow q$.
Now we can apply modus ponens to $p \wedge (p \Rightarrow q)$ to get the required conclusion.
Note that the essence of this direct proof lies in showing $p \Rightarrow q$.

Q9. Check whether the following argument is valid?
$(p \to q \vee \sim r) \wedge (q \to p) \Rightarrow (p \to r)$

premises → $p \to q \wedge \sim r$, $q \to p$
Conclusion → $p \to r$

p	q	r	~r	q∧~r	p→q∧~r	q→p	p→r
T	T	T	F	T	T	T	T
T	T	F	T	T	T	T	F
T	F	T	F	F	F	T	T
T	F	F	T	T	T	T	F
F	T	T	F	T	T	F	T
F	T	F	T	T	T	F	T
F	F	T	F	F	T	T	T
F	F	F	T	T	T	T	T

The premises are true in Rows 1, 2, 4, 7, 8. So, the argument will be valid if the conclusion is also true in these rows. But this does not happen in Row 2, for instance. Therefore, the argument is invalid.

Q10. Give an argument to show that the mathematical statement.
'For any two sets A and B, $A \cap B \subseteq A$' is true.

Let x be an arbitrary element and $x \in A \cap B$
$\Rightarrow x \in A$ and $x \in B$.
therefore $x \in A$.
This is true for every x in $A \cap B$.
Therefore, $A \cap B \subseteq A$, by definition of '$\subseteq$'.

Q11. By principle of mathematical induction show that any integer n≥2 is either a prime or a product of primes.

p(n) : n is a prime or n is a product of prime.
Since prime numbers begin from n=2
∴ P(2) : 2 is a prime
∴ P(2) is true.
let n =k and let P(n) is true for n=k
P(k) : k is a prime or product of prime
Now we have to check $P(k^+)$ is true
Let k+1 is not a prime, then it is a composite number and
k+1 = lm (Let) ---------(i)
where l $2 \leq l \leq k$ and $2 \leq m \leq k$
and by induction method we can say P(l) and P(m) are true and therefore l and m are either primes or product of primes.
∴ (i) we conclude that
k+1 = product of primes
∴ P(k+1) is true i.e. $P(k^+)$ is true.
Hence P(n) is true for every value of n, $n \in N$.

Q12. Prove by induction that $n^3 - n$ is divisible by 3 for all positive integers.
[DEC05, Q1(d)]

$P(n) : n^3-n$ is divisible by 3
Let n = 2   ($\because n \geq 2$)
$(2)^3-2 = 8-2 = 6$ divided by 3
∴ P(2) is true.
∴ The given statement is true for n=k
∴ $P(K) : K^3-K$ is divisible by 3.
It will be true for n = k+1, let us check
∴ P(K) is true
∴ $P(K) : K^3 - K = 3m$ (let m, being any integer)
$P(K^+) = (K+1)^3-(K+1)$
$= (K+1)\{(K+1)^2-1\}$
$= (K+1)\{K^2+1+2K-1\}$
$= (K+1)(K^2+2K)$

$= K^3+2K^2+K^2+2K$
$= K^3+3K^2+2K$
$= \mathbf{K^3-K+3K^2+3K}$
$= (K^3-K)+3(K^2+K)$
$= P(K)+3(K^2+K)$ **is true**

Since I part of given statement is divisible by 3 because P(K) is true, and part II is multiple of 3 which is always divisible by 3 confirmly.
∴ P(K⁺) is true i.e. P(K+1) is true.

∴ We conclude that the given statement is true for every value of n
∴ P(n) is true $\forall$ n $\in$ N, hence proved.

CHAPTER-3

BOOLEAN ALGEBRA AND CIRCUIT FUNDAMENTALS

A Boolean algebra **B** is an algebraic structure which consists of a set X ($\neq \emptyset$) having two binary operations (denoted by $\vee$ and $\wedge$), one unary operation (denoted by ') and two specially defined elements **O** and **I** (say), which satisfy the following rules for all $x, y, z, \in \mathbf{X}$.

General Laws of Boolean Algebra : Let $x, y, z \in x$, then we have
1. **Associative Laws :** $x \vee (y \vee z) = (x \vee y) \vee z$,
   $x \wedge (y \wedge z) = (x \wedge y) \wedge z$
2. **Commutative Laws:** $x \vee y = y \vee x$,
   $x \wedge y = y \wedge x$
3. **Distributive Laws:** $x \vee (y \wedge z) = (x \vee y) \wedge (x \vee z)$
   $x \wedge (y \vee z) = (x \wedge y) \vee (x \wedge z)$
4. **Identity Laws :** $x \vee O = x$,
   $x \wedge I = x$
5. **Complementation laws :** $x \wedge x' = O$
   $x \vee x' = I$

Switch : It is a device which is attached to a point in an electric circuit and which controls the flow of electric current in an electronic circuit. Switch can be in two states which are as follows :

(i) OPEN (when a switch is OFF) : No current flows in the circuit. A switch in the off state is called an OPEN switch. An open switch is represented as : -

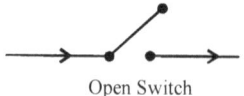
Open Switch

(ii) CLOSE (When a switch is ON) : Current flows in the circuit A switch in on state is a CLOSED switch and is represented as :

Closed Switch

State Values : If x be any switch then 1 is used for close and 0 is used for open switch. These values 1 and 0 are called the states of switch.

Invert of Switch x' is called invert of switch x i.e. if x is open then x' is closed and vice-versa.

Truth Table

x	x'
0	1
1	0

Boolean Variables : The variable which accepts only two values 0 and 1 are called Boolean variables.

Combination of Switches : Two switches may be connected into two ways (i) series combination (ii) parallel combination

Series combination : In this combination two switches are connected in series. In this connection the current will flow and bulb light up only when both switches are closed. If any of the switch is not close, bulb will not glow.

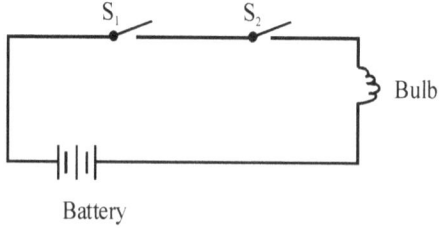
Battery

Truth Table is :

S_1	S_2	S_1 ser S_2
0	0	0
0	1	0
1	0	0
1	1	1

where S_1 ser. S_2 means S_1 serial S_2

Parallel combination : In this combination two (more than two) are connected in parallel. In this connection the current in circuit will flow and bulb glow up when any of switch is close.

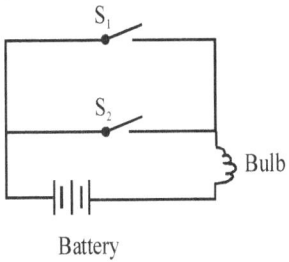

Battery

Truth Table is

S_1	S_2	S_1 parallel S_2
0	0	0
0	1	1
1	0	1
1	1	1

Boolean Algebra : Boolean algebra provides an economical and straight forward approach to the design types of switching circuits, just as an ordinary algebraic expression may be simplified by means of the basic theorems, the expression describing a given switching circuit network may also be reduced or simplified using Boolean algebra. Boolean algebra is now being used extensively in designing the circuitry used in computers.

Fundamental concepts of Boolean Algebra
1. Use of binary digits : In a normal algebraic expression, a variable can take any numerical value. Since Boolean algebra deals with the binary number system, the variables used in the boolean equation may assume only two possible

values 0 or 1.

2. Logical Addition : The symbol '+' is used for logical addition operation. It is also used as 'OR' operator. We may define the '+' symbol (OR) by listing all possible combinations of A and B and the resulting value of C in the equation A+B=C. It may be noted that since the variables A and B can have only two possible values (0 or 1) so only four (2^2) combinations of inputs are possible. The resulting output values for each of the four points are given in the truth table below for "OR" operator.

TABLE 1
Truth table for Logical OR (+) operator :

INPUTS		OUTPUT
A	B	A+B=C
0	0	0
0	1	1
1	0	1
1	1	1

3. Logical Multiplication : The symbol '.' is used for logical multiplication operator. It is also known as 'AND' operator. We may define the 'AND' operator by listing all possible combination of A and B and the resulting value of C in the equation A.B=C. From truth table 2 we may observe that C is equal to 1 only when both the input variables A and B are 1, otherwise it is 0. The equation A.B=C is normally read as "A and B equals C".

TABLE 2
Truth table for Logical AND (1) operator

INPUTS		OUTPUT
A •	B	A.B=C
0	0	0
0	1	0
1	0	0
1	1	1

4. Complementation : The two operations defined so far (OR and AND) are binary operations because operations are performed on two variables. The complementation operation is a unary operation which is defined on a single variable. The symbol '-' is normally used for complementation operator. It is also called 'NOT' operator. Thus we write $\overline{A}$, meaning "take the complement" or (A+B), meaning "take the complement of A+B". The completion of a variable is the reverse of its value. This of A=0 then A=1 then $\overline{A}$=0. The truth table for logical 'NOT' operator is shown in the table 3.

TABLE 3
Truth table for Logical NOT(-) operator :

INPUT	OUTPUT
A	$\overline{A}$
0	1
1	0

5. Operator precedence : Does A + B. C mean (A + B).C or A+(B.C)? The two generate different values for A=1, B=0 and C=0, then we have (1+0), 0=0 and 1+(0-0)=1, which differ. Hence it is necessary to define operator precedence in order to correctly evaluate Boolean expressions. The sequence of boolean operators is as follows :
(i)   The expression is seemed from left to right.
(ii) Expressions enclosed within parentheses are evaluated first.
(iii) All complement (NOT) operations are performed next.
(iv) All '.' (AND) operations are performed after that.
(v)   Finally all '+' operations are performed in the end.

Postulates of Boolean Algebra :-
Postulate 1.
(a) A = 0 iff A is not equal to 1. ("Iff' means 'if and only if')
(b) A = 1 iff A is not equal to 0.

Postulate 2.
(a) x + 0 = x
(b) x.1 = x

Postulate 3. (Commutative law)

(a) x + y = y+x
(b) x.y = y.x

Postulate 4. (Associative law)
(a) x + (y+z) = (x+y) +z
(b) x.(y.z) = (x.y).z

Postulate 5. (Distributive law)
(a) x.(y+z) = x.y.+x.z
(b) x+y.z = (x+y).(x+z)

Postulate 6.
(a) x + $\bar{x}$ =1
(b) x. $\bar{x}$ = 0

Principle of Duality :
In Boolean Algebra, there is a precise duality between the operators 1 (AND) & + (OR) and the digits 0 and 1. From the table 4 we can see that the second row of the table is obtainable from the first row and vice-versa, simply by interchanging '+' with '.' and '0' by '1'. This important property is called the principle of duality in Boolean algebra.

Table 4

	Column-1	Column-2	Column-3
Row 1	1 + 1 = 1	1+ 0 = 0 + 1 = 1	0 + 0 = 0
Row 2	0.0 = 0	0.1 = 1.0 = 0	1.1 = 1

Boolean Function :
A Boolean function is an expression formed with binary variables, the two binary operators OR and AND, the unary operator NOT, parentheses and equal sign. For a given value of the variables, the value of the function can be either 0 or 1. For example, we consider :

W = $x + \bar{y}.z$

Here the variable W is a function of X, and Y and Z. This is written as W=F(X, Y, Z) and the right hand side of the equation is called an expression. The symbols X, Y and Z are called literals of this function.

Table 5 : Truth table for the Boolean Function W = X + $\bar{X}$.Z

x	y	z	W
0	0	0	0
0	0	1	1
0	1	0	0
0	1	1	0
1	0	0	1
1	0	1	1
1	1	0	1
1	1	1	1

Minimization of Boolean function :
When a Boolean function is implemented with logic gates, each literal in the function designates input to a gate and each term is implemented with a gate. Thus for given Boolean function, the minimization of number of literal and the number of terms will result in a circuit with less equipments. To find simpler circuits, one must know how to manipulate Boolean functions to obtain equal and simpler expressions.

Complement of a function :
The complement of a function F is $\bar{F}$ and is obtained by interchanging 0's for 1's and 1's for 0's in the truth table that defines the function. Algebraically, the complement of a function may be derived through DeMorgan's theorems whose generalized forms are as follows :

$$\overline{A_1 + A_2 + A_3 + \ldots + A_n} = \bar{A_1}.\bar{A_2}.\bar{A_3}\ldots\bar{A_n}$$
$$\overline{A_1 A_2 A_3 \ldots A_n} = \bar{A_1} + \bar{A_2} + \bar{A_3} + \ldots + \bar{A_n}$$

These theorems state that the complement of a function is obtained by interchanging the OR and AND operators and complementing each literal.

Canonical forms For Boolean functions :
Minterms and Maxterms. A binary variable may appear either in its normal form (x) or in its complement form ($\bar{x}$). Let us consider two binary variables x and y combined with an AND operation. Since each variable may appear in either form, there are four possible combinations :

$\bar{x}.\bar{y}, \bar{x}.y, x\bar{y}, x.y$

Each of these four AND terms is called a minterm or a standard product. In a similar manner, n variables can be combined to form 2^n minterms. The 2^n different minterms may be determined by a method similar to the one shown in the table 6 below for three variables. The binary number from 0 to 2^{n-1} are listed under the n variables. Each minterm is obtained from an AND term of the n variables, with each variable being primed if the corresponding bit of the binary number is 0 and unprimed it a 1. A symbol for each minterm is also shown in the table and is of the form mj where j denotes the decimal equivalent of the binary number of the minterm designated. In a similar fashion, n variables forming an OR term, with each variable being primed or unprimed, provided 2^n possible combinations called maxterms or standard sums.

Variables			Min. Terms		Max. Terms	
X	Y	Z	Term	Designation	Term	Designation
0	0	0	$\bar{x}.\bar{y}.\bar{z}$	m_0	$\bar{x}+\bar{y}+\bar{z}$	M_0
0	0	1	$\bar{x}.\bar{y}.z$	m_1	$x+y+\bar{z}$	M_1
0	1	0	$\bar{x}.y.\bar{z}$	m_2	$x+\bar{y}+z$	M_2
0	1	1	$\bar{x}.y.z$	m_3	$x+\bar{y}+\bar{z}$	M_3
1	0	0	$x.\bar{y}.\bar{z}$	m_4	$\bar{x}+y+z$	M_4
1	0	1	$x.\bar{y}.z$	m_5	$\bar{x}+\bar{y}+\bar{z}$	M_5
1	1	0	$x.y.\bar{z}$	m_6	$\bar{x}+\bar{y}+z$	M_6
1	1	1	$x.y.z$	m_7	$\bar{x}+\bar{y}+\bar{z}$	M_7

Sum of Products : A sum of products expression is a product term (minterm) or several product terms (minterms) logically added (OR ed) together.
The following steps are followed to express a Boolean function in its sum-of-products form:
1. Construct a truth table for the given Boolean function.
2. Form a minterm for each combination of the variables which produces a 1 in the function.
3. The desired expression is the sum (OR) of all the minterms obtained in step 2.

Product-of-sums : A product-of-sums expression is a sum of terms (maxterms) or several sum terms (maxterms) logically multiplied (ANDed) together.
The following are the steps followed to express a Boolean function in its product-of-sums form.
(i) Construct a truth table for the given Boolean function.
(ii) Form a maxterm for each combination of the variables
(iii) The desired expression in the product (AND) of all the maxterms obtained

in step 2.

Convert Between Canonical forms.
The complement of a function expressed as the sum of minterms equals the sum-of-minterms missing from the original function. This is because the original function is expressed by those minterms that make the function equal to 1, while its complement is 1 for those minterms for which the function is zero.

Logic Gates and its utility :
All the operations within a computer are carried out by means of combinations of signals passing through standard blocks of built-in-circuits that are known as logic gates. In other word, a logic gate is simply an electronic circuit which operates on one or more input signals these logic gates are the building blocks of all the circuits in a computer.

Computer circuits are built up using combinations of different types of logic gates to perform the necessary operations. There are several types of gates, but we shall discuss about some of them which are most important for operation.

OR Gate : An OR Gate is the physical realization of the logical addition (OR) operation. It is an electronic circuit which generates an output signal of 1 if any of the input signal in also 1. Two or more switches connected parallel behave as on OR gate. There will be no output only when both the switches are in the iff(o) state.

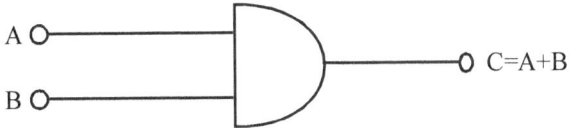

INPUTS		OUTPUT
A	B	C=A+B
0	0	0
0	1	1
1	0	1
1	1	1

Block diagram symbol and truth table for an OR gate.

AND GATE : An AND Gate is physical realization of the logical multiplication (AND) operation. It is an electronic circuit that generates an output signal of 1 only if all input signals are also 1.

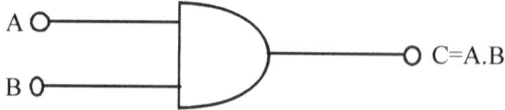

INPUTS		OUTPUT
A	B	C=A.B
0	0	0
0	1	0
1	0	0
1	1	1

Block diagram symbol and truth for an AND Gate

NOT GATE : A NOT gate is a physical realization of the complementation operation. it is an electronic circuit which generates an output signal which is the reverse of the input signal. A NOT gate is also called invertor because it inverts the input. A NOT gate always has a single input.

A ○───▷○─── $\overline{A}$

INPUT	OUTPUT
A	$\overline{A}$
0	1
1	0

Figure : Block diagram symbol and truth table for a NOT gate and Two NOT gates in series.

NAND GATE : A NAND gate is a complemented AND gate. The output will be a 1 if any one of the input is 0 and will be a 0 only when all the inputs are 1. The truth table and the block diagram symbol is shown below. The symbol ↑ is usually used to represent NAND operation in Boolean expression. Thus A ↑ B = $\overline{A} \cdot \overline{B}$ = $\overline{A} + \overline{B}$

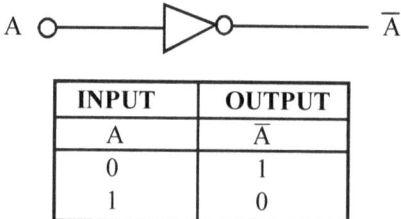

INPUTS		OUTPUT
A	B	C=A+B
0	0	1
0	1	1
1	0	1
1	1	0

Figure : Block diagram symbol and truth table for a NAND gate.

NOR GATE : A NOR gate is a complemented OR gate. That is the output of a NOR gate will be 1 only when all inputs are 0 and it will be a 0 if any input represents a 1.

The truth table and the block diagram symbol for a NOR gate are shown in figure below. The symbol '↓' = $\overline{A} + \overline{B} = \overline{A} \cdot \overline{B}$

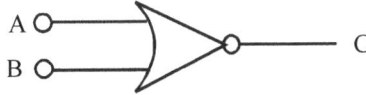

INPUTS		OUTPUT
A	B	C=A.B
0	0	1
0	1	0
1	0	0
1	1	0

Logic Circuits : Logic gates are interconnected to form gating, or logic, networks which are called as combination logic circuits. For these logic circuits, the Boolean algebra expression can be derived by systematically progressing from input to output on the gates.

Expressions to Logic Circuits?
The reverse problem of constructing a logic circuit for a given Boolean expression is also not difficult. The three logic gates AND, OR and NOT are said to be logically complete because any Boolean expression may be realized using only these gates.

Universal NAND gate : We have seen that AND, OR and NOT gates are logically complete in the sense that any Boolean function may be realized using those three gates.

However, the NAND gate, which was introduced in the previous section, is said to be universal gate because it is alone sufficient to implement any Boolean function.

The implementation of Boolean functions with NAND gates may be obtained by means of a simple block diagram manipulation technique. The method requires that two other logical diagrams be drawn prior to obtaining the NAND logic diagram. The following steps are to be carried out in sequence.

Step 1 : From the given algebraic expression, draw the logic diagram with AND, OR and NOT gates. A ssume both the normal (A) and ($\bar{A}$) inputs are available.

Step 2 : Draw the second logic diagram with the equivalent NAND logic substituted for each AND, OR and NOT gate.

Step 3 : Remove any two cascaded inverters from the diagram since double inversion does not perform any logical function. Also remove inverts connected to single external inputs and complement the corresponding input variable. The new logic diagram so obtained is the required NAND gate implementation of the Boolean function.

Universal NOR gate

The NOR function is the dual of the NAND function. For this reason, all procedures and rules for NOR logic form a dual of the corresponding procedures and rules developed from NAND logic. Like NAND gate, the NOR gate is also universal because it is alone sufficient to implement any Boolean function.

Similar to the NAND logic diagram, the implementation of Boolean function with NOR gate may be obtained by carrying out the following steps in sequence:

Step 1: For the given algebraic expression, draw the logic diagram with AND, OR and NOT gates. Assume that both the normal (A) and complement (A) inputs are available.

Step 2 : Draw a second logic diagram with equipment NOR logic substituted for each AND, OR, and NOT gate.

Step 3 : Remove any two cascaded inverters from the diagram since double inversion does not perform any logical function. Also remove inverts connected to single external inputs and complement the corresponding input variable. The new logic diagram so obtained is the required NAND gate implementation of the given Boolean function.

Combinational Circuit

The design of combinational circuits starts from the verbal outline of the

problem and ends in a logic circuit diagram. The procedure involves the following steps :
(i) State the given problem completely and exactly.
(ii) Interpret the problem and determine the available input variables and required output variable.
(iii) Assign a letter symbol to each input and output variables.
(iv) Design the truth table that defines the required relations between inputs and output.
(v) Obtain the simplified Boolean function for each output.
(vi) Draw the logic circuit diagram to implement the Boolean function.

Half-adder and full-adder
The first three operations produce a sum whose length is one digit, but when both argend and addend pits are equal to 1, the binary sum consists of two digits. The higher significant bit of this result is called a carry. When the argend and addend numbers contain more significant digits, the carry obtained from the addition of two bits is added to the next higher order pair of significant bits. A combinational circuit that performs the addition of two bits is called a half-adder. One that performs the addition of three bits is called a full-adder. The name of the former stems from the fact that two half-adders can be employed to implement a full-adder.

Q.1 Prove the following by (i) truth table (ii) by deduction
$a + \bar{a}b = a + b$

(i) **Truth table method :** The following table shows that L.H.S. is equal to R.H.S.

(ii) **Deduction Method :** By successive application of various postulates of Boolean algebra, we get

a	b	$\bar{a}b$	$a+\bar{a}b$	$a+b$
0	0	0	0	0
0	1	1	1	1
1	0	0	1	1
1	1	1	1	1

L.H.S. $= a + \bar{a}b = (a+\bar{a})(a+b) = 1 \cdot (a+b) = a + b =$ R.H.S.

Q.2 Prove that $\bar{\bar{a}} = a$.
By successive application of various postulates of Boolean Algebra, we get
R.H.S $= a \qquad\qquad\qquad = a + a.(\bar{a}) = (\bar{\bar{a}}) + (a.\bar{a})$

$= a + \overline{(\overline{a})}.a = \overline{(\overline{a})} + 0$ $\qquad = a + \overline{(\overline{a})}.a + 0 = \overline{(\overline{a})}$
$= a + \overline{(\overline{a})}.a + (\overline{(\overline{a})}.\overline{a}) = $ L.H.S.
$= a + \overline{(\overline{a})}.(a+\overline{a})$ $\qquad = a + \overline{(\overline{a})}.1$
$= a + \overline{(\overline{a})}$ $\qquad\qquad = \overline{(\overline{a})} + a$
$= (\overline{(\overline{a})} + a).1$ $\qquad\qquad = (\overline{(\overline{a})}+a).(\overline{(\overline{a})}+\overline{a})$

Q3. Describe gating network corresponding to the statement formula

(i) $(x.y) \overline{(z.y)} + \overline{(x+y).z}$

(ii) $(x+y) \overline{(u.w)} + (x.y) + \overline{w}$

(iii) $\overline{(u.v)} (w+x) + \overline{(u+v)} (w.x)$

(iv) $(z+x+y) + \overline{(z.u)} (x.y)$

(v) $\overline{(x+y)} (z.u) + (\overline{x.y}) (z+u)$

(vi) $\overline{(x+y)}.z + \overline{x}.(\overline{y}+z)$

(vii) $(x.y) + (y.z) + (z.x)$

(i) $(x.y) \overline{(z.y)} + \overline{(x+y).z}$
The gating network corresponding to the given statement formula is as follows:
-

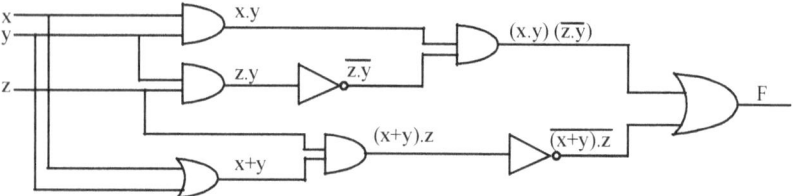

Where $F = (x+y) \overline{(z.y)} + \overline{(x+y).z}$

(ii) $(x+y) \overline{(u.w)} + (x.y).\overline{w}$
The gating network corresponding to the given statement formula is as follows:
-

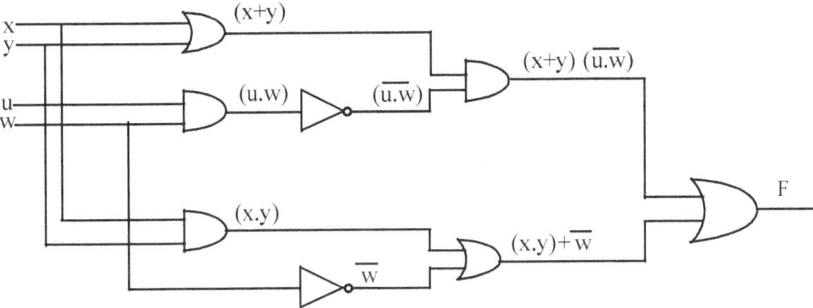

Where F = (x+y) $\overline{(u.w)}$ + (x.y)+$\overline{w}$

(iii) $\overline{(u.v)}$ (w+x) + $\overline{(u+v)}$ (w.x)

The gating network corresponding to the given statement formula is as follows:
-

Where F = $\overline{(u.v)}$ (w+x) + $\overline{(u+v)}$ (w.x)

(iv) (z+x+y) + $\overline{(u.w)}$ + (x.y) + $\overline{w}$

The gating network corresponding to the given statement formula is as follows:
-

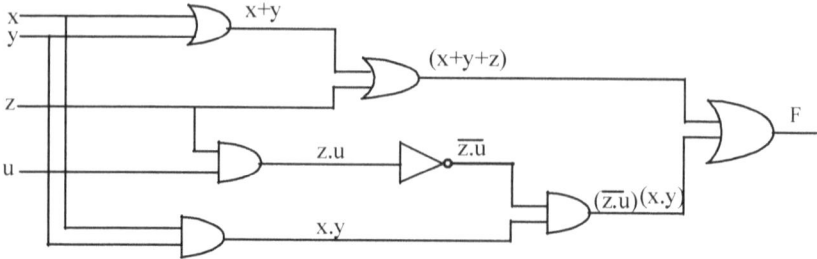

Where F = (z+x+y) + $\overline{(z.u)}$ (x.y)

(v) $\overline{(x+y)}$ (z.u) + $\overline{(x.y)}$ (z+u)

The gating network corresponding to given statement formula is as follows: -

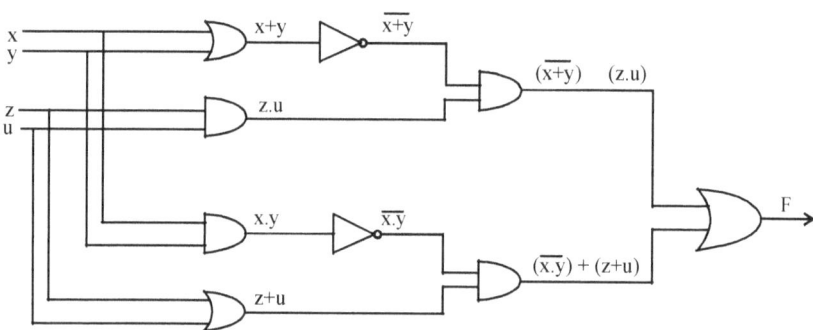

Where F = $\overline{(x+y)}$ (z.u) $\overline{(x.y)}$ (z+u)

(vi) $\overline{(x+y)}$ .z + $\overline{x}$ $(\overline{y}+z)$

The gating network corresponding to given statement formula is as follows: -

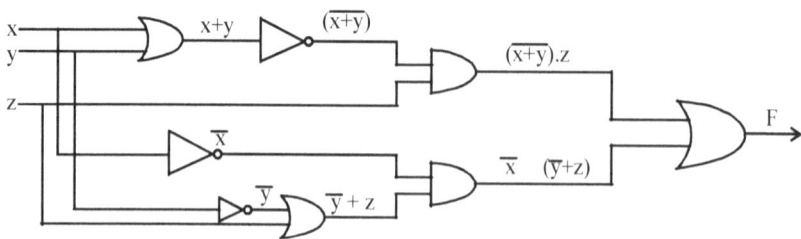

Where F = $\overline{(x+y)} \cdot z + \overline{x} \, (\overline{y}+z)$

(vii) $(x.y) + (y.z) + (z.x)$

The gating network corresponding to given statement formula is as follows: -

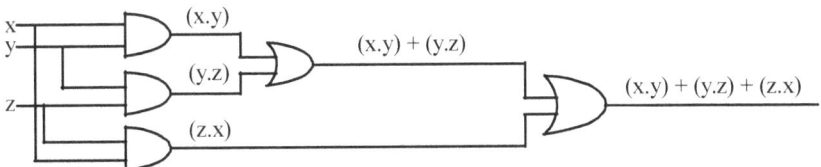

Q.4 Describe the gating network corresponding to statement formula
$(\overline{x+y})(z.u) + (\overline{x.y})(z+u) = R$

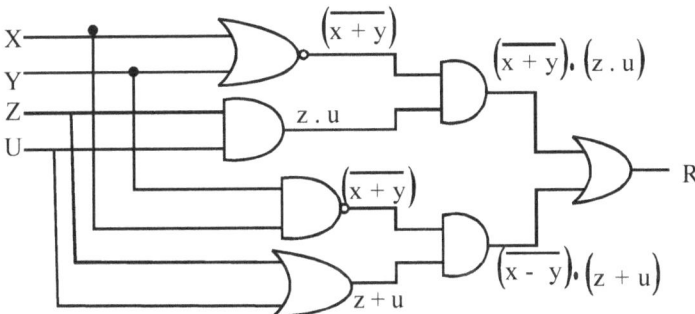

Q.5 Describe gating network corresponding to the statement formula
$(z+x+y) + (\overline{z.u})(x.y)$.

R = (Z + X + Y) + ($\overline{ZU}$) (XY)

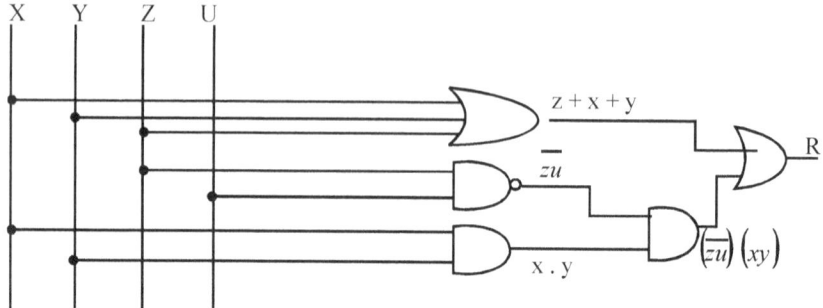

Q.6 Describe gating network corresponding to the statement formula :
$(\overline{u.v})(w+x) + (\overline{u+v})(w.x)$
$R = (\overline{u.v})(w+x) + (\overline{u+v})(w.x)$

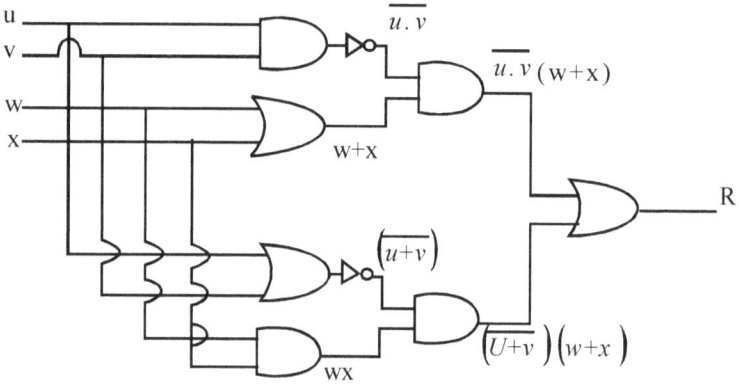

Q.7 Describe gating network corresponding to the statement :
$(x+y)(\overline{u.w}) + (x+y) + \overline{w}$
Gating network corresponding to the statement

$F = (x+y)\overline{(u.w)} + (x+y) + \overline{w}$

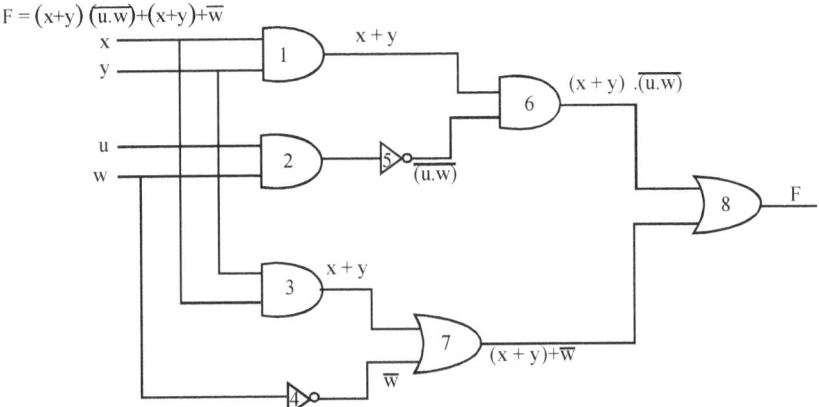

So the final diagram is :-

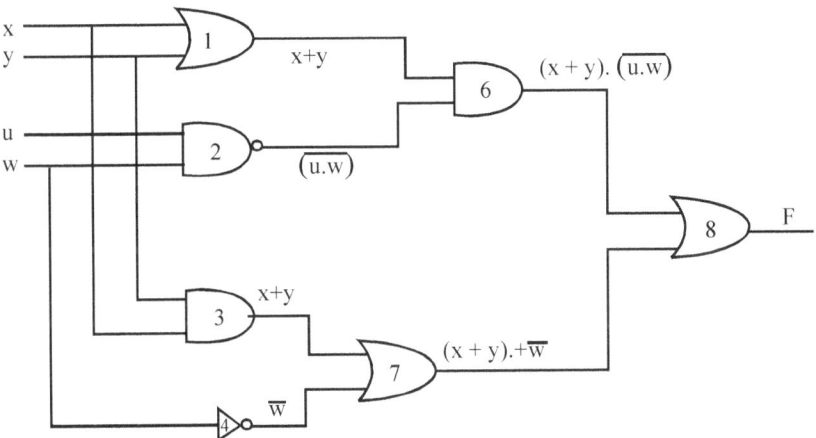

Q.8 Describe gating network corresponding to the statement formula :
$(x.y)(\overline{z.y}) + (\overline{x+y}).z$

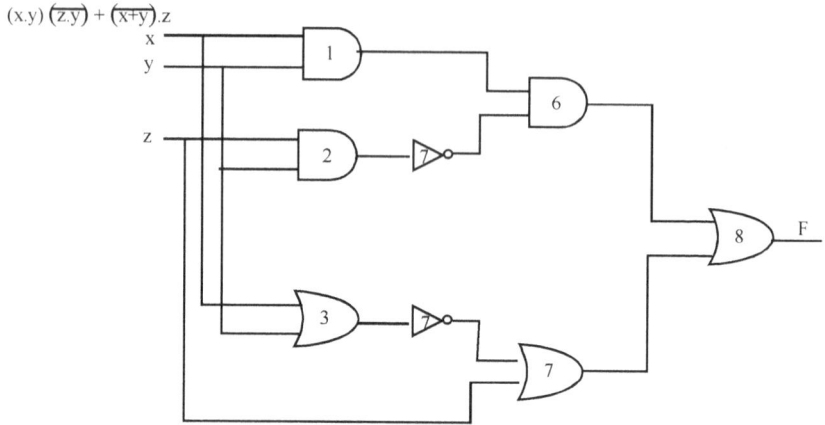

So, updated network is.

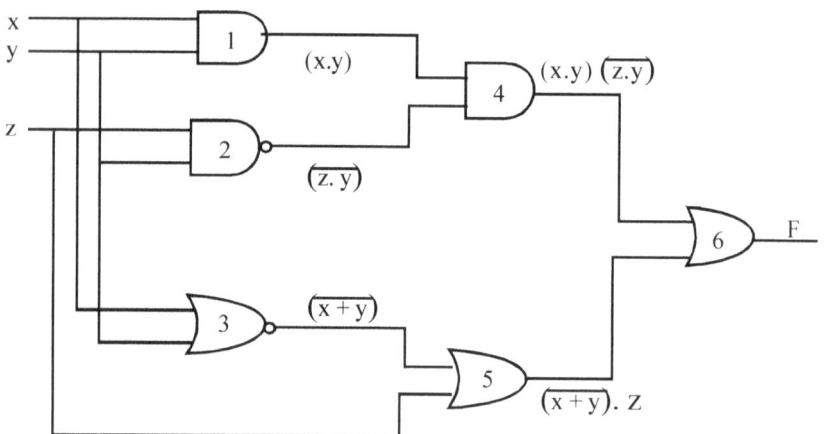

So now output of
1 is (x,y)
2 is (y,z)
3 is (z+y)'
So now according to problem output of gate 1 and 2 are ANDed to get result as (x.y) (y.z)' and output of 3 and 2 are ANDed to have result (x+y)'.z

Q.9 Describe the gating network corresponding to the statement formula:

$(\overline{x+y}).(w.x)+(\overline{u.w}).(w+y)$

Following gating network is of above formula

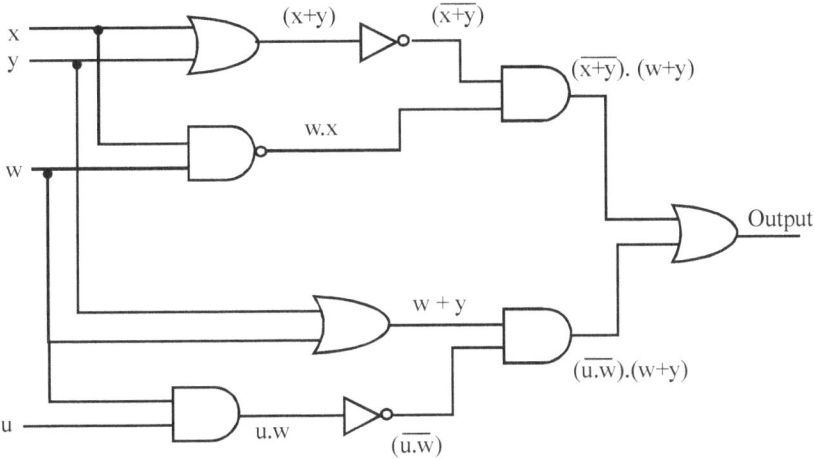

Q.10 Describe a gating network corresponding to the statement formula :

$(\overline{x+y}).z + \overline{x}.(\overline{y}+z)$

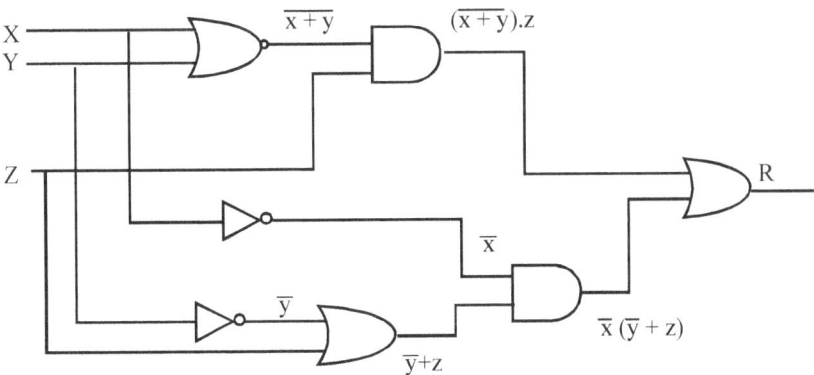

Q.11 Describe the gating network corresponding to the statement formula

$(\overline{x+y}).z + (y+z).(\overline{z+x})$

Here is network corresponding to the $(\overline{x+y}).z + (y+z).(\overline{z+x})$

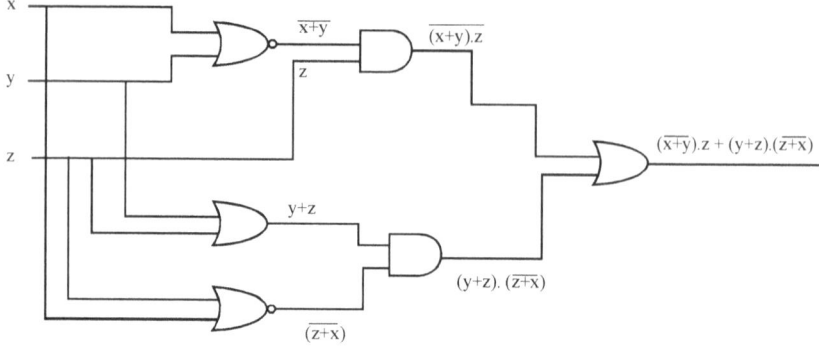

Q.12 Simplify the Boolean expression $x(x_1, x_2, x_3) = (x_1 \wedge x_2) \vee ((x_1 \wedge x_2) \wedge x_3) \vee (x_2 \wedge x_3)$.

We can write
$x(x_1,x_2,x_3) = ((x_1 \wedge x_2) \vee (x_1 \wedge x_2) \wedge x_3)) \vee (x_2 \wedge x_3)$
$= (x_1 \wedge x_2) \vee (x_2 \wedge x_3)$ (by absorption law)
$= x_2 \wedge (x_1 \vee x_3)$ (by Distribution law)
This is the simplest form of the given expression.

Q.13 Let $\beta = \{0,1\}$ consist of the bits 0 and 1. Show that β is a Boolean algebra, i.e., that the bits 0 and 1 form a two-element Boolean algebra.

Ans. Firstly observe that the information about the output of the three elementary gates, for different value of inputs, can also be written as follows:
$0 \wedge 0 = 0 \wedge 1 = 1 \wedge 0 = 0, 1 \wedge 1 = 1$:
$0 \vee 0 = 0, 0 \vee 1 = 1 \vee 0 = 1 \vee 1 = 1$:
$0' = 1, 1' = 0$

Clearly then both the operation # and # are the binary operations on β and $': \beta \to \beta$ is a unary operation. Also, we may take 0 for o and 1 for I in the definition of a Boolean algebra.

Now, by looking at the logic tables of the three elementary gates, we can see that all the five laws b1-b5 are satisfied. Thus β is a Boolean algebra.

Q.14 Find the Boolean expression for the output of the logic circuits given below.

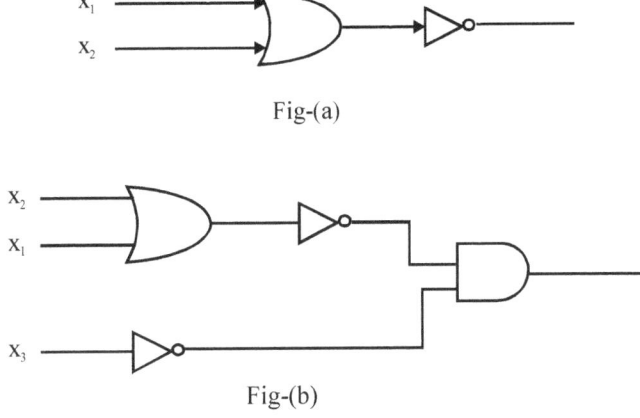

Fig-(a)

Fig-(b)

(a) Here x_1 and x_2 are inputs to an or-gate, and so, we take $x_1 \vee x_2$ as input to the NOT-gate next in the chain which, in turns yields $(x_1 \vee x_2)'$ as the required output expression for the circuits given in (a).

(b) Here x_1 and x_2 are the inputs to an AND-gate, so, the expression $x_1 \wedge x_2$ serve as an inputs to the NOT-gate, being next in the chain.

This given the expression $(x_1 \wedge x_2)'$ which serve as one inputs to the extreme right AND-gate. Also, since x_3 is another input to this AND-gate (Coming out of a NOT-gate), we get the expression $(x_1 \wedge x_2)' \wedge x'_3$ as the final output expression which represents the circuit given in (b)

Q.15 Find the logic circuit corresponding to the expression $x'_1 \wedge (x_2 \vee x_3)$

We know that the circuit representing expressions x_1 and $x_2 \vee x'_3$ are as show in fig.

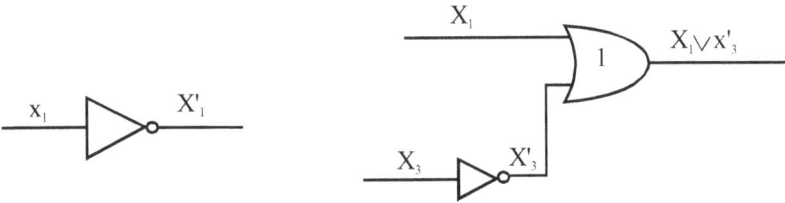

Thus, the expression $x'_1 \vee (x_2 \vee x'_3)$, being connected by the symbol $\wedge$, gives the circuit corresponding to it as given in following fig.

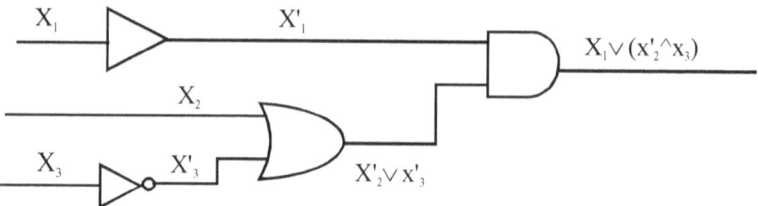

Q.16 Construct the logic and obtain the logic table for the expression $x_1 \vee (x'_2 \wedge x_3)$.

The circuit represented by the expression $x_1 \vee (x'_2 \wedge x_3)$ is as given in fig.

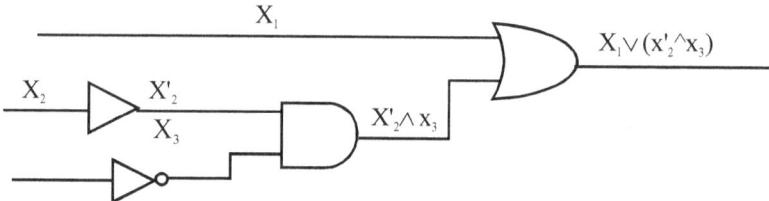

The logic table of this expression is as given below.

X_1	X_2	X_3	X'_2	$X'_2 \wedge X_3$	$X_1 \vee (x'_2 \wedge x_3)$
0	0	0	1	0	0
0	0	1	1	1	1
0	1	0	0	0	0
1	0	0	1	0	1
0	1	1	0	0	0
1	1	0	0	0	1
1	0	1	1	1	1
1	1	1	0	0	1

Q.17 Compute the logic table for the following circuit :

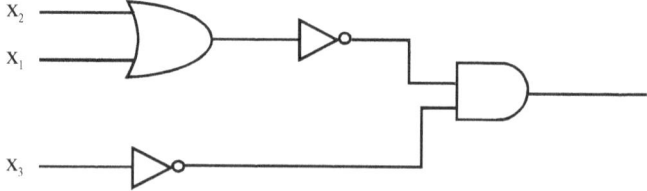

Since the output expression representing the circuit given in E8(b) is found to be $(x_1 \wedge x_2)' \wedge x_3$, the logic table for this circuit is as given below.

X_1	X_2	X_3	$X_1 \wedge X_2$	$(X_1 \wedge X_2)'$	X'_3	$(X_1 \wedge X_2)' \wedge X'_3$
0	0	0	0	1	1	1
0	0	1	0	1	0	0
0	1	0	0	1	1	1
1	0	0	0	1	1	1
0	1	1	0	1	0	0
1	1	0	1	0	1	0
1	0	1	0	1	0	0
1	1	1	1	0	0	0

Q.18 **Find all the values of the Boolean function f : $\beta_2 \to \beta$ defined by the Boolean expression $(x_1 \wedge x_2) \vee (x_1 \wedge x'_3)$**

Because the expression $(x_1 \wedge x_2) \vee (x_1 \wedge x'_3)$ involves three variable, the corresponding Boolean function, f(say) is a three function, i.e. $f = B_3 \to b$. It is defined by
$f(e_1, e_2, e_3) = (e_1 \wedge e'_3)$, e_1, e_2 and $e_3 \in B$.
Now, we can verify that the value of f in tabular form are as given in the following table.

E_1	E_2	E_3	$E_1 \wedge e_2$	E'_3	$E_1 \wedge e'_3$	$F(e_1,e_2,e_3)=(e_1 \wedge e_2)$ $\vee (e_1 \wedge e'_3)$
0	0	0	0	1	0	0
0	0	1	0	0	0	0
0	1	0	0	1	0	0
1	0	0	0	1	1	1
0	1	1	0	0	0	0
1	1	0	1	1	1	1
1	0	1	0	0	0	0
1	1	1	1	0	0	1

Q.19 **Show that the Boolean expressions $X = (x_1 \vee x_2) \vee (x_1 \wedge x_3) \vee$ and $Y = x_1 \wedge (x_2 \vee x'_3)$ are equivalent over the two-element Boolean algebra $\beta = \{0,1\}$**

X_1	X_2	X_3	X'_3	$X_2 \vee X'_3$	$G(x_1,x_2,x_3)=x_1 \wedge (x_2 \vee x'_3)$
0	0	0	1	1	0
0	0	1	0	0	0
0	1	0	1	1	0
1	0	0	1	1	0
0	1	1	0	1	0
1	1	0	1	1	1
1	0	1	0	0	0
1	1	1	0	1	1

Q.20 In the previous example, show that $X(e_1,e_2) \forall e_1, e_1 \in B$.

Firstly, let us evaluate the given expression $X(x_1,x_2)$ over the two-element Boolean algebra $B=\{0,1\}$, as follows :

$X(0,0)$ = $(0'\wedge 0) \vee (0'\wedge 0) \vee (0 \wedge 0)$
= $(1 \wedge 1) \vee (1 \wedge 0) \vee (0 \wedge 0)$
= $1 \vee 00 \vee 0 = 1 = f(0,0)$:

$x(1,0)$ = $(1'\wedge 0') \vee (1'\wedge 0) \vee (1 \wedge 0)$
= $(0 \wedge 1) \vee (0 \wedge 0) \vee (1 \wedge 0)$
= $0 \vee 0 \vee 0 = 0 = f(1,0)$:

$X(0,1)$ = $(0'\wedge 1') \vee (0'\wedge 1) \vee (0 \wedge 1)$
= $(1 \wedge 0) \vee (1 \wedge 1) \vee (0 \wedge 1)$
= $0 \vee 1 \vee 0 = 1 = f(0,1)$:

$X(1,1)$ = $(1'\wedge 1) \vee (1'\wedge 1) \vee (1 \wedge 1)$
= $(0 \wedge 0) \vee (0 \wedge 1) \vee (1 \wedge 1)$
= $0 \vee 0 \vee 1 = 1 = f(1,1)$

in thus follows that $X(e_1,e_2)=f(e_1,e_2)$ e_1,e_2 $B = \{0,1\}$

Q21. Describe a getting network corresponding to the statement formula:

$$\overline{(x+y)}. z + \overline{x}. \overline{(y+z)}$$

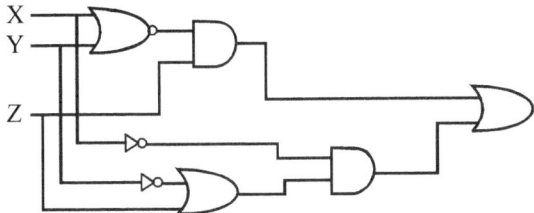

Q22. Describe getting network corresponding to the statement formula :

$(\overline{u.v})(w + x) + (\overline{u + v})(w.x)$
$(\overline{u.v})(w + x) + (\overline{u + v})(w.x)$

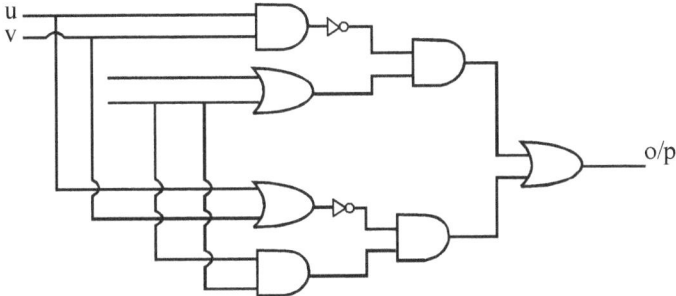

Q23. Describe the gating network corresponding to given statement formula :

$(\overline{x + y}) \cdot z + \overline{x} \cdot (\overline{y} + z)$

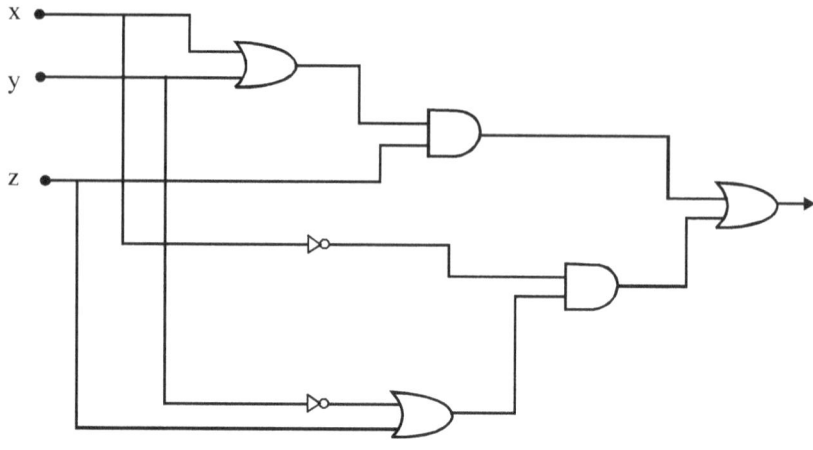

Q24. Describe getting network corresponding to the statement formula.

$(z + x + y) + (\overline{z.u})(x.y)$.

$R = (Z+X+Y) + (\overline{ZU})(XY)$

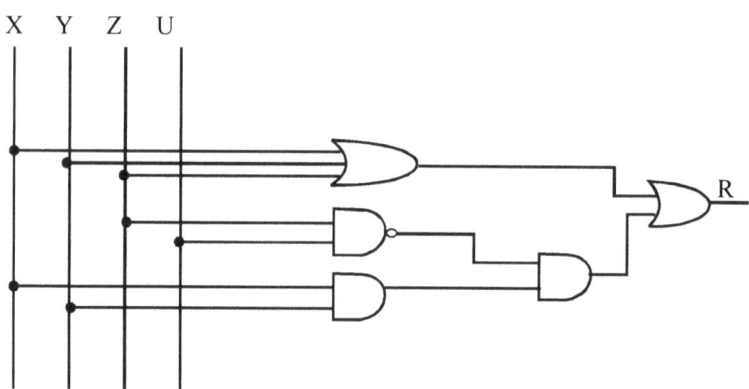

Q25. In a Boolean Algebra B, for x1, x2 and x3 ∈ find whether the following three expressions are equivalent or not :

(i) $(x_1 \wedge x_2) \vee (x_1' \wedge x_3)$
(ii) $(x_1 \vee x_2) \wedge (x_1 \vee x_3) \wedge x_2 \vee x_3$
(iii) $(x_1 \vee x_2) \wedge (x_1' \vee x_3)$

(i) x_1, x_2 and $x_3 \in B$ Where B is a Boolean algebra.
(i) $(x_1 \vee x_2) \vee (x_1 \wedge x_3)$

x_1	x_2	x_3	$x_1 \wedge x_2$	x_1'	$x_1' \wedge x_3$	$(x_1 \wedge x_3) \vee (x_1' \wedge x_3)$
0	0	0	0	1	0	0
0	0	1	0	1	1	1
0	1	0	0	1	0	0
0	1	1	0	1	1	1
1	0	0	0	0	0	0
1	0	1	0	0	0	0
1	1	0	1	0	0	1
1	1	1	1	0	0	1

(ii) $(x_1 \vee x_2) \wedge (x_1 \vee x_3) \wedge x_2 \vee x_3$

			a	b	c		
x_1	x_2	x_3	$x_1 \vee x_2$	$x_1 \vee x_3$	$a \wedge b$	$a \wedge b \wedge x_2$	$c \vee x_3$
0	0	0	0	1	0	0	0
0	0	1	0	1	0	0	1
0	1	0	1	1	1	1	1
0	1	1	1	1	1	1	1
1	0	0	1	0	0	0	0
1	0	1	1	1	1	0	1
1	1	0	1	0	0	0	0
1	1	1	1	1	1	1	1

(iii) $(x_1 \vee x_2) \wedge (x_1 \wedge x_3)$

x_1	x_2	x_3	x_1'	$x_1' \vee x_2$	$x_1 \vee x_3$	$(x_1' \vee x_3) \wedge (x_1 \vee x_3)$
0	0	0	1	0	1	0
0	0	1	1	0	1	0
0	1	0	1	1	1	1
0	1	1	1	1	1	1
1	0	0	0	1	0	0
1	0	1	0	1	1	1
1	1	0	0	1	0	0
1	1	1	0	1	1	1

So all the three expressions are not equivalent

Q26. In a Boolean R, show that a ∨ (1+a) = 1 and a . (1+a) = 0 for all a.

(i) In a Boolean ring R,
Show that a $\vee$ (1+a) = 1
In a Boolean Ring, a $\oplus$ 1 = 1 a = a'.
So a $\vee$ (1+a)
= a $\vee$ a

i.e. either of a or a' is surely going to be 1.
So a $\vee$ a' = 1

(ii) a.(1+a) = 0
a.(1+a)
= a.a'
= 0.

Hence proved.

Q27. Define and explain with examples the concept of a finite state machine. What are transition diagrams ? Draw the transition diagram of a serial binary adder.

#: Explain the basic ideas behind a state finite machine with suitable example.

#: How does a finite state machine function?

Finite State Machine :

A sequential machine or a finite state machine is a system M = (Q, Σ, P, δ, λ) where Q, Σ, P are **finite** sets of states, input symbols and output symbols. We require that Q ∩ Σ = Q ∩ P = φ Here

δ   : Q Σ → Q
and λ : Q x Σ → P

are function called the next state and output functions respectively. The machine is supposed initially to be in a state q_0.

The Basic Ideas Behind a State Finite Machine :

As the block diagram shows, the reading head of the machine reads input symbols, sequentially from an input tape which is divided into equal squares containing one symbol each. Depending upon the current state q and the symbol read, its writing head, writes an output symbol on the output tape, and updates its state to the next. In this new state (which may be the old one) it is ready to read the next symbol from the input tape. If it reads a symbol a_j from the input tape while in a state q_i, then the output is given by $\lambda(q_i, a_j) \in p$ and the next state is $\delta(q_i, a_j) \in Q$. For the case of the serial binary adder considered in the preceding section.

Q = {s_0, s_1}, Σ = {(0, 0), (0, 1), (1, 0), (1, 1)} P = {o, 1} and the functions

δ and λ are given by

$\delta [s_0, (0, 0)] = \delta [s_0, (0, 1)] = \delta [s_0, (1, 0)] = s_0, \delta [s_0, (1, 1)] = s_1$
$\delta [s_1, (0, 0)] = s_0, \delta [s_1, (0, 1)] = \delta [s_1, (1, 0)] \delta [s_1, (1, 1)] = s_1$
and $\lambda [s_0, (0, 0)] = \lambda [s_0, (1, 1)] = 1, \lambda [s_0, (0, 1)] = \lambda [s_0, (1, 0)] = 0$
$\lambda [s_0, (0, 0)] = \lambda [s_1, (1, 1)] = 1, \lambda [s_1, (0, 1)] = \lambda [s_1, (1, 0)] = 0$

The machine is started in state s_0.

Transition Diagrams :

It is convenient for visual purposes, to depict the working of such a machine by means of a directed graph with labelled directed edges. Such a graph is called the **transition diagram** of the machine. The notes are each labelled by the states. From each node, an edge emanates corresponding to each input symbol. Thus given any state q_i and input symbol a_j, if $\delta(q_i, a_j) = q_k$ and $\delta(q_i, a_j) = p_m$, then there is a directed edge from the node labelled by the state q_i to that labelled by q_k. This edge is labelled by the input a_j and output p_m.

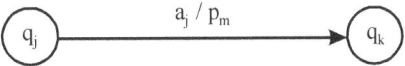

The transition diagram contains the sum total of all the functional information about the machine in the sense that the sets Q, Σ, the maps δ, λ and the subset of P occurring as λ- images (which is all that is needed) may be recovered from this diagram. For example the transition diagram of the serial binary adder is given as

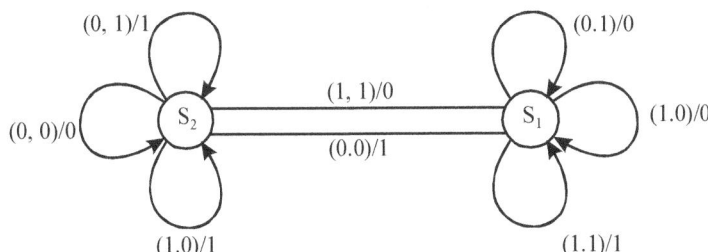

Fig. Transition Diagram of a Serial Binary Adder

Finite State Machine function :

Now what do we do with such a machine ? The machine just not only product an output symbol corresponding to an input symbol. In fact if a finite sequence or string of input symbols is given to it, it processes them one by one to produce a finite sequence of output symbols.

For any set A, we denote by A* the set of all finite strings of elements of A.

$$A^* = \{a_i \ldots a_n \mid a_i \in A, n \geq 0\}$$

Here the members of a string may be distinct or repeated and its length may be any non-negative integer. It is supposed to contain an empty string $\in$ not containing any symbol and which has length 0. Now A* contains A in the form of string of length 1; $\{\in\} \subseteq A^*, A \subseteq A^*$

We define powers of A as the following subsets of A* :

A^2 = $\{a_i a_j \mid a_i, a_j \in A\} \subseteq A^*$
A^3 = $\{a_i a_j a_k \mid a_i, a_j, a_k \in A\}$

as sets of strings of length 2, 3 ....
In this notation

$$A^* = \bigcup_{n=0}^{\yen} A^n$$

Where $A^0 = \{\in_0\}$, and $A^1 = A$. The set A* is a semigroup under the operation of juxtaposition (called the catenation operation) of strings and the empty strings behaves as the identity element of this semigroup. This semigroup is infinite if $A \neq \phi$ and cancellation laws hold here, although it is not a group. This semigroup A* is called the free semigroup or free monoid over the alphabet A.

We also note that $A^* = \bigcup_{n=0}^{\yen} = A^* - \{\in\}$ is also a semigroup. We now extend the action and of input symbols on the states to those of input strings as follows: We take $\delta_0 (q, \in) = q.$ and $\delta_1 = \delta$.

Suppose that $a_i \in \Sigma$, for i = 1, 2, ... (need not be all distinct). Let $q1 \in Q$. We denote $\delta(q_1, a_1)$ by q_2, $\delta(q_2, a_2)$ by q_3 etc. so that $(q_i, a_i) = q_{i+1}$. We then define $\delta_2(q_1, a_1, a_2) = \delta[\delta(q_1, a_1), a_2] = \delta(q_2, a_2) = q_3$ in this way we have $\delta_i(q_1, a_1, a_2 \ldots a_i) = q_{i+1}$.

Observe that $\delta_i : Q \times \Sigma^i \to Q$. Since Σ^n is a disjoint union of the $\alpha_s^{0\,i}$ these $\delta_i s$ together define a map

$\delta^* : Q \times \Sigma \to Q$ by

$\delta^* (q, x) = \delta_m (q, x)$ since any $x \in \Sigma^*$ belongs to unique Σ^i viz. Σ^m where m = length of x.

In a similar manner if

$\lambda (q_1, a_1) = p_1, \lambda (q_2, a_2) = p_2, \ldots \lambda (q_i, a_i) = p_i$ then we get maps λ_i :

$Q \times å_1 \to P$, given by

$$\lambda_1 = \lambda_1 \lambda_2 (q_1, a_1, a_2) = \lambda(q_2, a_2) = p_2,$$
$$\lambda_3 (q_1, a_1 a_2 a_3) = \lambda (q_3, a_3) = p_3$$
$$\vdots$$
$$\lambda i (q_1, a_1 \ldots a_n) = \lambda (q_i, a_i) = p_i$$

Again these maps together define $\lambda^* : Q \times \Sigma^+ \to P$ given by $\lambda^* (q, x) = \lambda_m (q, x)$ where m = length of x.

Q28. Describe a plus divider which receives as inputs, bits 0 and 1 produces 1 if and only if the number of 1s on the input tape upto that instance is a non-zero even number.

Thus the machine starts in a state q_0 and the state changes to q_1 as soon as it gets a 1 while the state remains q_0 and long it gets inputs of 0. Again in state q_1, it changes to q_0 if and only if it gets a 1 and otherwise it remains at q_1. The outputs in the first case are 0 on both inputs and in the second case it is 1 one the input 1 and 0 on the input 0.

Therefore state q_1 represents the fact that an odd number of 1s has been read and the next input of 1 changes it to q_0 with a corresponding output of 1. Therefore its transition diagram is

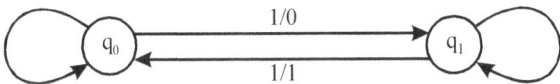

An input machine of the type described above is also known as a Mealy machine. There is another variant in which there is no output but there is a specified subset of the set of states, called the set of accepting states and an input string is said to be accepted if after processing through it the machine is none of the accepting states. Such a machine is called a Moore machine or a finite state acceptor r a finite state automation and is used for recognition of specified class of language over the input alphabet, called the regular languages.

Q29. Given an arbitrary finite state input-output machine formulate an algorithm to reduce the machine to a minimal one. What procedure would you use to identify redundant states ?

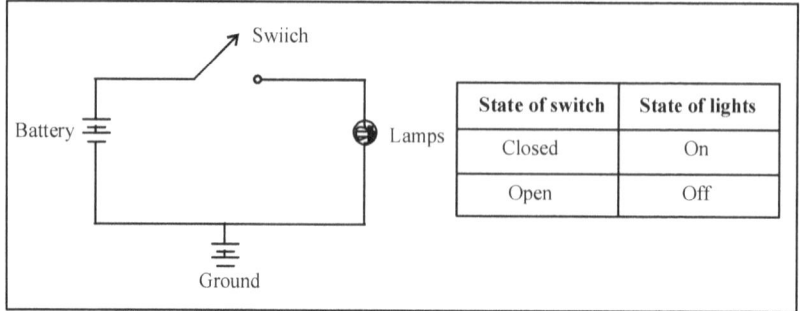

Step 1 : [Initialized row counter] set i ← 0
Step 2 : [Scan next row] set i ← i + i > n then exit.
Step 3 : [Is i in a previous class?] If FIRST [i] ≠ 0 then go the step 2 : Otherwise set k ← i and m ← 0
Step 4 : [Scan row starting at diagonal] Repeat Step 5 and 6 for j = i, i + 1, ..., n.
Step 5 : [All members found?] If j > n then MEMBER [m] ← 0, print class member from output, and go to step 2.
Step 6 : [Is i related to j ?] If R [i, j] = T. Then MEMBER [k] ← j FIRST [j] ← i, k ← j, m ← m + 1, and OUTPUT [m] ← j

Q30. How will you represent states of a simple electric lamp-switch circuit by a truth tables ?

Let P denote the (input) switch and s the (output) indicator lamp. When p is open, no current flows in the circuit and the lamp s is 'off'. When p is closed, s is 'on'.
Let the statements be denoted by
P : The switch p is closed
S : The lamp s is on.
This can be expressed as a truth table or as a table for input-output values in the following manner:

Statue of p	State of s		p(P)	s(S)
Closed	On	or	1	1
Open	Off		0	0

Consider a circuit in which there are two switches p and q in series. The lamp in this case is turned on whenever both the switches p and q are closed. Let
P : The switch p is closed,
Q : The switch q is closed,

S : The light s is on.
From the following it will be clear that P∨Q⇔S.

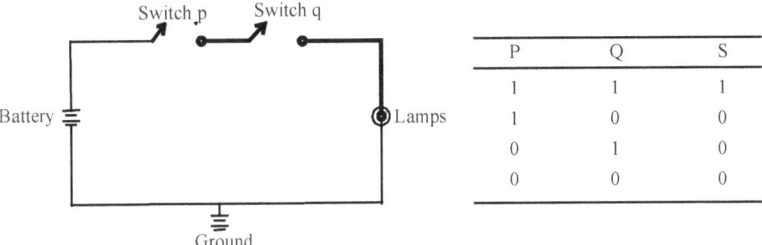

P	Q	S
1	1	1
1	0	0
0	1	0
0	0	0

The above figure shows a two-state device for AND logic.
The following figure and table show the case when two switches are connected in parallel. From the table it will followed that P∨Q⇔S.

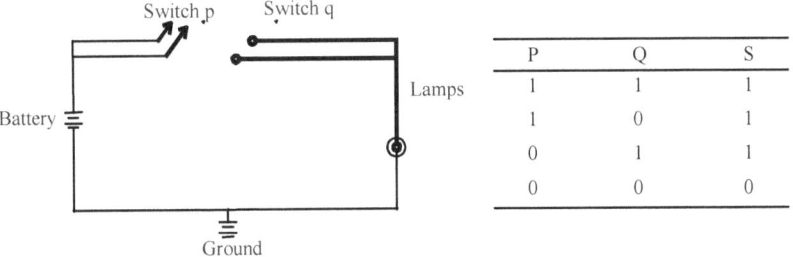

P	Q	S
1	1	1
1	0	1
0	1	1
0	0	0

The above figure shows a two state device for OR logic.
Thus observe that the logical connections ∧ and ∨ correspond to switches connected in series and in parallel respectively.

Q31. Define a two level network. Explain the SOP and POS networks with suitable diagrams.

A two-level network is defined as are network in which the longest path through which information passes from input to output is two gates. A two level network consisting of AND gates at the input stage followed by OR - gates at the output stage is called a sum of product network.
Another type of two-level network is to have OR gates at the input stage and them AND gates at the output stage and such an expression is of the form (a + b). (c + d). This is called a product of sum (OR-AND) network and is shown as :

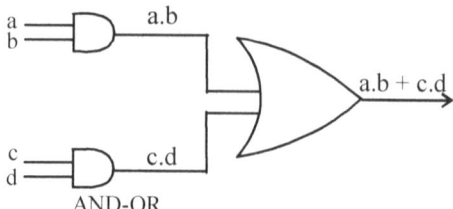

Fig : Sum of Product Network

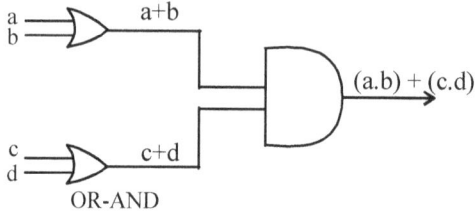

Fig : Product of Sum Network

Q.32 Reduce the following Boolean expressions to a simpler form.

(a) $X(x_1, x_2) = (x_1 \wedge x_2) \wedge (x_1 \wedge x'_2)$;

(b) $X(x_1, x_2, x_3) = (x_1 \wedge x_2) \vee (x_1 \wedge x_2 \wedge x_3) \vee (x_1 \wedge x_3)$

(a) Here we can write

$(x_1 \wedge x_2) \wedge (x_1 \wedge x'_2)$

	$= ((x_1 \wedge x_2) \wedge x_1) \wedge x'_2$	(Associative law)
	$= (x_1 \wedge x_2) \wedge x'_2$	(Absorption law)
	$= x_1 \wedge (x_2 \wedge x'_2)$	(Associative law)
	$= x_1 \wedge O$	(Complementation law)
	$= O$	(Identity law)
	$=$ null expression.	

(b) $(x_1 \wedge x_2) \vee (x_1 \wedge x'_2 \wedge x_3) \vee (x_1 \wedge x_3)$

$= [x_1 \wedge \{x_2 \vee (x'_2 \wedge x_3)\}] \wedge (x_1 \wedge x_3)$ (Distributive law)

$= [x_1 \wedge \{(x_2 \vee x'_2) \wedge x_2 \vee x_3)\}] \wedge (x_1 \wedge x_3)$ (Distributive law)

$=$ (Complementation law)

$= [x_1 \wedge (x_2 \vee x_3)] \wedge (x_1 \wedge x_3)$ (Identity law)

$= [(x_1 \wedge x_2) \vee (x_1 \wedge x_3)] \wedge (x_1 \wedge x_3)$ (Distributive law)

$= [(x_1 \wedge x_2) \wedge (x_1 \wedge x_3)] \vee [(x_1 \wedge x_3) \wedge (x_1 \wedge x_3)]$ (Distributive law)

$= (x_1 \wedge x_2 \wedge x_3) \vee (x_1 \wedge x_3)$ (Idemp. & assoc. laws)

$= x_1 \wedge [x_2 \wedge x_3) \vee x_3]$ (Distributive law)

$= x_1 \wedge x_3$ (Absorption law)

Q33. Construct the logic circuit represented by the Boolean expression $\left(x_1' \wedge x_2\right) \vee (x_1 \vee x_3)$, where x_i $(1 \le i \le 3)$ are assumed to be inputs to that circuitry.

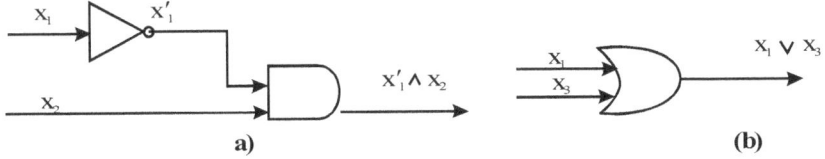

a)   (b)

Logic circuits for the expressions $x_1' \wedge x_2$ and $x_1 \vee x_3$

FINAL RESULT

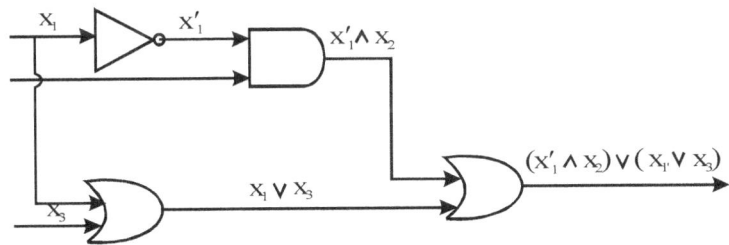

Circuitry for the expression $(x_1' \wedge x_2) \vee (x_1 \vee x_3)$

Q34. Given the expression $(x_1' \vee (x_2 \wedge x_3')) \wedge (x_2 \vee x_4')$, find the corresponding circuit, where x_i $(1 \le i \le 4)$ are assumed to be inputs to the circuitry.

We first consider the circuits representing the expressions $x_2 \wedge x_3'$ and $x_2 \vee x_4'$. They are as show in Fig.13(a)

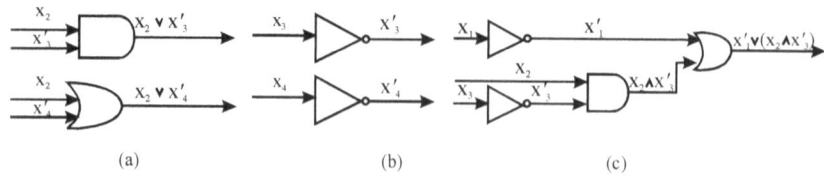

(a) (b) (c)

Construction of a logic circuitry.

FINAL RESULT

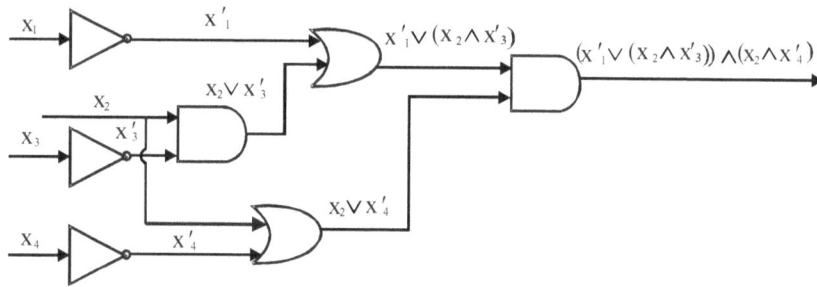

Q35. Design a logic circuit capable of operating a central light bulb in a hall by three switches x_1, x_2, x_3 (say) placed at the three entrance to that hall.

Step 1: Function corresponding to the unspecified circuit.

The bulb is off when all the switches are off.

This demands a situation where $x_1 = x_2 = x_3 = 0$ implies $f(0,0,0)=0$, where f is the function which depicts the functional utility of the circuit to be designed.

The other values of $f(x_1, x_2, x_3)$ are given as in Table 9.

Function of a circuitry for a three-point functional bulb.

X_1	X_2	X_3	$F(X_1,X_2,X_3,)$
0	0	0	0
1	0	0	1
1	1	0	0
1	1	1	1
0	1	0	1
0	1	1	0
0	0	1	1
1	0	1	0

Step 2: A boolean expression to specify that function f. Firstly, we shall obtain the expression in DNF (instead of CNF).

$$X(x_1,x_2,x_3) = \left(x_1 \wedge x_2' \wedge x_3\right) \vee \left(x_1' \wedge x_2 \wedge x_3'\right) \vee \left(x_1' \wedge x_2' \wedge x_3\right) \vee \left(x_1 \wedge x_2 \wedge x_3\right)$$

Step 3: To simplify the expression $X(x_1, x_2, x_3)$ given above.

$$\left(x_1 \wedge x_2' \wedge x_3\right) \vee \left(x_1 \wedge x_2 \wedge x_3\right) = x_1 \wedge \left[(x_2' \wedge x_3) \vee (x_2 \wedge x_3)\right]$$
$$= x_1 \wedge \left[(x_2' \vee x_2) \wedge x_3\right]$$
$$= x_1 \wedge (1 \wedge x_3)$$
$$= x_1 \wedge x_3$$

by using distributive, complementation and identity laws (in that order). Similarly, you can see that

$$(x_1' \wedge x_2' \wedge x_3) \vee \left(x_1 \wedge x_3\right) = \left(x_2' \vee x_1\right) \wedge x_3.$$

A simpler (and equivalent) expression,

$$X(x_1,x_2,x_3) = (x_1' \wedge x_2 \wedge x_3') \vee \left[(x_2' \wedge x_1) \wedge x_3\right],$$

whose Boolean function is same as the function f.

Step 4: A circuit for the expression

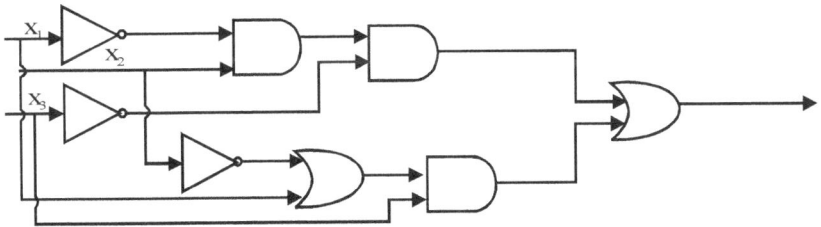

A circuit for the expression $(x_1' \wedge x_2 \wedge x_3') \vee ((x_2' \vee x_1) \wedge x_3)$

Q36. Find the logic circuit corresponding to the expression $x'_1 \wedge (x_2 \vee x'_3)$.

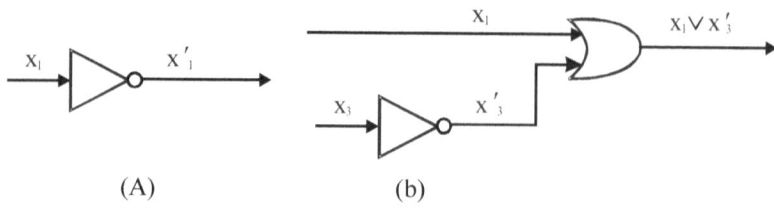

(A)   (b)

FINAL RESULT

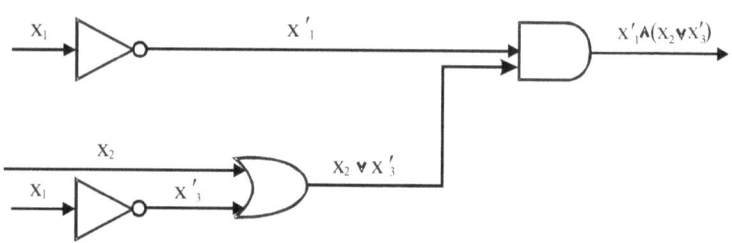

Q37. Find the Boolean expression for the output of the logic circuits given below.

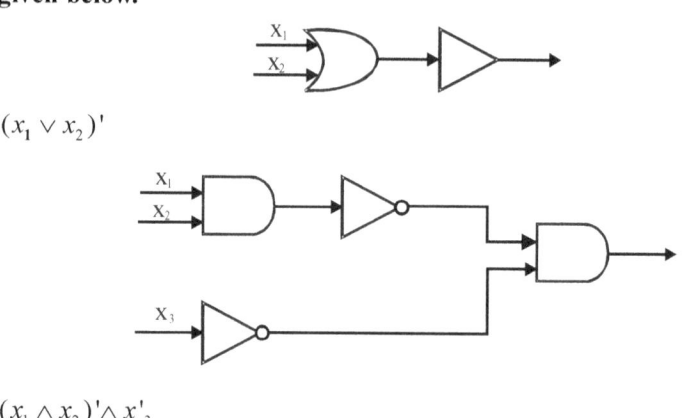

$(x_1 \vee x_2)'$

$(x_1 \wedge x_2)' \wedge x'_3$

Q38. Give an alternate arrangment of the circuit, given in the following figure such that the new circuit has five switches only

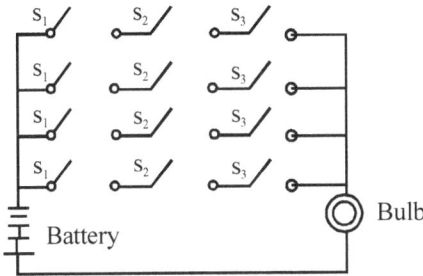

Statement of the various conditions are as-
p : the switch s_1 is closed
q : the switch s_2 is closed
r : the switch s_3 is closed
b : the lamp b is on.
Then ∼ p : the switch s_1 is closed
 ∼ q : the switch s_2 is closed
 ∼ r : the switch s_3 is closed
We see that the bulb b will glow if all three switches s_1, s_2, s_3 are closed or switches s_1, s_2 and s_3 all three are closed or s_1, s_2 and s_3 all three are closed.

Expression

$(p \wedge q \wedge r) \vee [p \wedge q \wedge (\sim r)] \vee [p \wedge (\sim q) \wedge r] \vee [(\sim p) \wedge q \wedge r] \equiv b$
$\Rightarrow [(p \wedge q \wedge r) \vee (p \wedge q \wedge \sim r)] \vee [(p \wedge q \wedge r) \vee (p \wedge \sim q \wedge r)]$
$\vee [(p \wedge q \wedge r) \vee (\sim p \wedge q \wedge r)] \equiv b$
$\Rightarrow [(p \wedge q) \wedge (r \vee \sim r)] \vee [(p \wedge q) \wedge (q \vee \sim q)] \vee [(q \wedge r) \wedge (p \wedge \sim p)]$
$\equiv b$
$\Rightarrow [(p \wedge q) \wedge t] \vee [(p \wedge r) \wedge t] \vee [t \wedge (q \wedge r)] \equiv b$
where t is a tauto log y
$\Rightarrow (p \wedge q) \vee (p \wedge r) \vee (q \wedge r) \equiv b$ (*identity law*)
$\Rightarrow [(p \wedge q) \vee (p \wedge r)] \vee (q \wedge r) \equiv b$ (*associative law*)
$\Rightarrow [p \wedge (q \vee r)] \vee (q \wedge r) \equiv b$ (*distributive of* $\wedge$ *over* $\vee$)

In this equivalent statements, there are only 5 switches, and the depicts the following diagrams

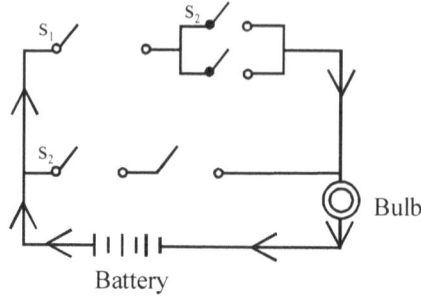

Q39. Make a logic circuit of elementary gates corresponding to the boolean expression : [JUNE05, Q5(a)] [3]

$$(x \vee y \wedge z)' \wedge (r \vee z) \vee x$$

We know that $\wedge \rightarrow$ and

$\vee \rightarrow$ or

$' \rightarrow$ Not

$(x \vee y \wedge z)' \wedge (r \vee z) \vee x$
which may be written as :
$(x+y.z)' \cdot (r + z) + x$

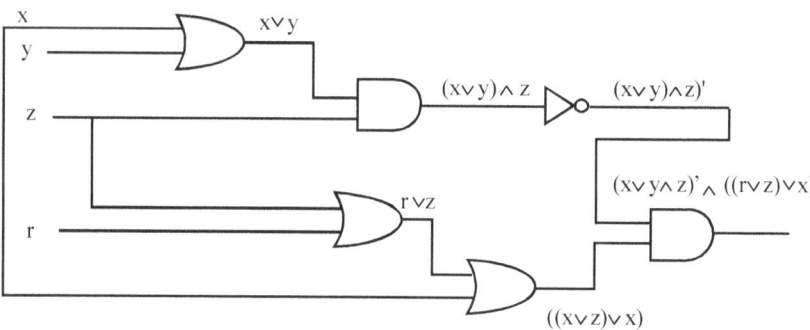

Chapter-4
Sets, Relations and Functions

Set : Collection of well defined elements is called a set and is denoted by capital letters. Elements are placed in middle brackets(curly) separated by commas (,) and written in small letters.

e.g.
A = {a, b, c, d}
A = {Bareilly, Rampur, Shahjahanpur, Lucknow, Kanpur}

Forms of Sets : Sets are formed by mainly two ways
(i) Set builder form (or property method)
(ii) Tabular form (or listing method)

(i) Set builder form : In this way sets are designed by taking property of elements
e.g.
A = {Dravid, Tendulkar, Dhoni, Ganguly} or
A = {x : x is great-batsman of India}
B = {Discrete, Trigonometry} or
B = {x: x is a book of maths}

(ii) Tabular form : In this way sets are arranged by putting elements in any order separated by commas.
e.g.
A = {1, 2, 3, 4, 5}
B = {x, y, z, u, v, w}
Few examples of sets :
(1) Book is set, collection of pages
(2) Sentence is a set, collection of words.
(3) Word is a set collection of letters.
(4) School is a set, collection of students.
(5) City is set of Buildings.
(6) Country is a set, collection of cities.

Finite set : A set having limited elements is called a finite set. e.g. school is a set, collections of students.

e.g. wall is a set, collection of bricks.
Infinite set : A set having elements is called an infinite set.
e.g. collection of drops in sea water, Stars in the sky.
Singleton set : A set which contains only one element is called as singleton set
e.g. Principal in the college, President in a country.

Subset : A set A is said to be a subset of a set B if each element of A is also the elements of B. In this case B is called a superset of A. If A is a subset of B, we represent this by $A \subseteq B$.
e.g. Class is $\subseteq$ school
e.g. $A = \{a, b, c\}$
$B = \{a, b, c, d\}$
$A \subseteq B$.

Equal sets : Two sets A and B are equal if every element of A belongs to B and every element of B belongs to A. We represent this by A=B.
e.g. if $A=\{p,q,r\}$, $B=\{r, q, p\}$ then $A \subseteq B$ and $B \subseteq A$, so that $A = B$.

Power Set : It is a set of all subsets of a set.
e.g. Let x be any set
$x = \{x, y, z\}$
then subsets of x are
$\{\{x\} \{y\} \{z\} \{x,y\} \{y,z\} \{z, x\} \{x, y, z\}\}$
$\therefore$ power set $P(x)$
$\{\varnothing \quad \{x\}, \{y\},\{z\}, \{x,y\}, \{y,z\}, \{z,x\}, \{x,y,z\}\}$

Universal set : Any set which is a superset of all the sets under consideration is known as the universal set and denoted by U.
e.g. if $A = \{1, 2, 3\}$, $B=\{3,4,6,9\}$ and $C=\{0,1\}$, then we can make $U=\{0,1,2,3,4,5,6,7,8,9\}$ or $U = N$, or $U = Z$ as the universal set.
Note that the universal set can be chosen arbitrarily for a given problem. But once chosen, it is fixed for the discussion of that problem.
Note :
(1) Total number of subsets of a set containing n element in it $= 2^n$
(2) If A is a set with n elements, then $|P(A)| = 2^n$, where P(a) is power set of set A.

Operations on Sets :
<u>Union of two sets</u> : The union of two sets A and B is the set of all those elements which are either in A or in B or in both A and B. This set is denoted by $A \cup B$, and read as 'A union B'.

Symbolically, A ∪ B = {x:x ∈ A or x ∈ B} e.g. A = {1, 2, 4, 6}, B = {3, 5}
A ∪ B = {1, 2, 3, 4, 5, 6}
By Vein diagram :

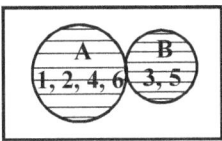

Intersection of Sets : The intersection of sets A and B is the set of all the elements which are common to both A and B. This set is denoted by $A \cap B$, and read as 'A intersection B'.

Symbolically, $A \cap B$ = {x:x ∈ A and x ∈ B};
For example A = {1, 2, 3} and B = {2, 1, 5, 6}, then $A \cap B$ = {1,2}.

Difference of two sets : The difference of two sets A and B is the set of all those elements of A which are not elements of B. Sometimes, it is denoted by A~B or A\B, and is read as 'A complement B'.

Symbolically, A~B = {x:x ∈ A and x ∉ B} and
　　　　　　　B~A = {x:x ∈ A and x ∉ A}

Note 1 : A - B ≠ B - A (Integral)
For example, if A = {4,5,6,7,8,9} and B = {3,5,2,7}, then A~B = {4,6,8,9} and B~A = {3,2}

Note 2 : If A - B = ϕ then sets are disjoint.

Complement of Set : The complement of a set A, is the set U - A and is denoted by A' or A^c i.e. A' = U~A. If U = {1,2,3,4,5}, A = {2,3,4}, A' =U-A = {1,5}

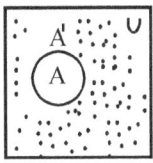

Symmetric difference of sets : The symmetric difference of two sets A and B is the set of all those elements which are in A or in B, but not in both. It is denoted by $A \triangle B$.

i.e., $A \triangle B = (A \sim B) \cup (B \sim A)$.

Note that $A \triangle B = B \triangle A$, i.e. the symmetric difference is commutative.
For example $A = \{1,2,3,4,5\}$ and $B = \{3,5,6,7\}$, then $A \sim B = \{1,2,4\}$ and $B \sim A = \{6,7\}$

$\therefore A \triangle B = \{A \sim B\} \cup (B \sim A) = \{1,2,4,6,7\}$

Properties of Sets : Let A, B, C are three sets. These hold following properties:

1. **Associative Law**
   Union: $A \cup (B \cup C) = (A \cup B) \cup C$
   Intersection: $A \cap (B \cap C) = (A \cap B) \cap C$

2. **Commutative Law**
   Union: $A \cup B = B \cup A$
   Intersection: $A \cap B = B \cap A$

3. **Identity**
   Union: $A \cup \phi = A$
   Intersection: $A \cap U = A$

4. **Complement**
   Union: $A \cup A' = U$
   Intersection: $A \cap A' = \phi$

5. **Distributive properties**
   Union: $A \cup (B \cap C) = (A \cup B) \cap (A \cup C)$
   Intersection: $A \cap (B \cup C) = (A \cap B) \cup (A \cap C)$

De Morgan's Law - Let A and B are two sets then :
1. $(A \cup B)' = A' \cap B'$ and
2. $(A \cap B)' = A' \cup B'$

Another form of (1) and (2) are:

1. $A \sim (B \cup C) = (A \sim B) \cap (A \sim C)$
2. $A \sim (B \cap C) = (A \sim B) \cup (A \sim C)$ where C is another set.

Relations :
Ordered Pairs : A set consisting of two elements a, b with a first element a and b as second element is called an ordered pair and denoted by (a,b).

Cartesian Product of Sets :
If A and B be are two sets, then the set of all ordered pairs (x,y), such that the first members x belongs to A and the second members y belongs to B is called the Cartesian product of the sets A and B, and is denoted by $A \times B$ symbolically
$A \times B = \{(x,y) : x \in A, y \in B\}$
e.g. $A = \{1,2,3\}$, $B = \{4,5\}$
then
$A \times B = \{(1,4),(1,5),(2,4),(2,5),(3,4),(3,5),\}$

Note : 1. $A \times B \neq B \times A$ unless $A = B$
2. If A have elements m and B has elements n then $A \times B$ have elements $m \times n$.

A *Relation* R from a set A to a set B is a subset of $A \times B$. And is denoted by $R \subseteq A \times B$. or $(x, y) \in R$.
Domain A is called the domain of R and B is called the Codomain of R. i.e. $D = \{x : (x, y) \in R, \text{ for } x \in A\}$.
Range The set of second entries of the ordered pairs in a relation is called the range of the relation.
If $(a, b) \in R$, then we write it as a R b and it is read as 'a is in relation to b'.
If $A = B$, then the relation is called a relation defined in A or simply a relation in A.

Properties of a Relation :
(i) Reflexive : A relation R is said to be reflexive if a always belongs to R i.e. $(a, a) \in R, \forall \ a \in A$.

(ii) Symmetric A relation R is said to be symmetric if aRb implies bRa. i.e. if $(a, b) \in R \Rightarrow (b,a) \in R$.

(iii) Transitive : A relation R is said to be transitive if aRb and bRc implies aRc.

(iv) Equivalence Relation A relation R is said to be equivalence if the relation is reflexive, symmetric and transitive.
i.e. $\forall \ a \in R \ (a, a) \in R$, and $(a, b) \in \Rightarrow R \ (a, b) \ R \Rightarrow (b, a) \in R, \ \forall \ a, b \in A$ and $(a, b) \in R$ and $(b, c) \in R \Rightarrow (a,c) \in R \ \forall \ a,b,c \in A$.

(v) Anti-Reflexive Relations : Let R be a relation in a set A. Then R is called an anti-reflexive relation if (a,a) ∈ R for every a ∈ A i.e. a/Ra ∀ a ∈ A.
For e.g. let A = {1, 2, 3, 4}. Then the relation R = {(1,1), {2, 3}, (3, 4)} is not anti-reflexive since (1, 1) ∈ R.

(vi) Anti-symmetric Relations Let R be a relation in a set A, Let R be a subset of A×A. Then R is said to be an anti-symmetric relation if (a, b) ∈ R and (b, a) ∈ R ⇒ a = b.
E.g., Let A be a family of sets and let R be the relation in A defined by 'x' is a subset of 'y'. Then R is anti symmetric Since A ⊆ B and B ⊆ A ⇒ A = B.

Types of relations in a set :

(a) Binary relations in a set : A binary relation R is said to be defined in a set A if for any ordered pair (x, y) ∈ A × A, it is meaning full to say that xRy is true or false.
In other words : R {(x, y) ∈ A × A : xRy is true}.

(b) Inverse Relation Any relation R from the set A to the set B, possesses inverse relation R^{-1} from the set B to Set A is defined as R^{-1} = {(b, a) : (ab) ∈ R}
In other words, the inverse relation R^{-1} consists of those ordered pairs which when reversed belong to R.
E.g. : Let A = {2, 3, 4}, B = {2, 3, 4} and R = {(x, y) : |x-y| = 1} be a relation from A to B. That is, R = {(3, 2), (2, 3), (4, 3), (3, 4)}.
The inverse relation of R is
R^{-1} = {(3, 2), (2, 3), (4, 3), (3, 4)}.
It may be noded that R = R^{-1}.

(c) Void or null Relation Any relation R in a set is said to be void relation if R is a null or empty set. i.e. if R = ϕ.
E.g. : Let A = {2, 3, 7} and let R be defined as "aRb" if and only if a divides b then R = ϕ ⊂ A × A is a void relation.

(d) Identity Relation : A relation R in a set A is said to be identity relation, generally denoted by I_A, if.
I_A = {(x, x) : x ∈ A}.
E.g. : Let A = {2, 4, 6} then I_A = {(2, 2), (4, 4), (6, 6)} is an identify relation in A.

(e) Universal relation : Any relation R is said to be universal relation if R is equal to A × A. i.e. if R = A ×A.
E.g. If A = {1, 2, 3}, then

R = A × A = {(1, 1), (1, 2), (1, 3) (2, 1), (2, 2), (2, 3), (3, 1), (3, 2), (3, 3)} is a universal relation in A.

Some examples of Relations :
1. If R be an equivalence relation in a set A, then R^{-1} is also an equivalence relation in A.
Proof : Let R be an equivalence relation in a set A. Therefore R is reflexive, symmetric and transitive.
Let a, b, and c be any elements of A.
The relation R^{-1} is
(i) Reflexive : (a, a) ∈ R^{-1}, Since for all a, (a, a) ∈ R ⇒ (a, a) ∈ R^{-1}.
(ii) Symmetric : (a, b) ∈ R^{-1} ∈ (b, a) ∈ R^{-1}.
Since, (a, b) ∈ R^{-1} ⇒ (b, a) ∈ R
                           ⇒ (a,b) ∈ R as R is symmetric
                           ⇒ (b, a) ∈ R^{-1}.
(iii) transitive (a, b), (b, c) ∈ R^{-1} ⇒ (a, c) ∈ R^{-1}
Since, (a, b), (b, c) ∈ R^{-1} ⇒ (b, a) (c ,b) ∈ R
                           ⇒ (c, b) (b, a) ∈ R as R is symmetric
                           ⇒ (c, a) ∈ R as R is transitive
                           ⇒ (a, c) ∈ R^{-1}.
∴ R^{-1} is reflexive, symmetric, and transitive.
Hence R^{-1} is an equivalence relation in A.

2. Let A = {x, y, z} Give an example of a relation on A which is
(a) reflexive and symmetric but not transitive.
(b) reflexive and transitive but not symmetric.
(c) symmetric and transitive but not reflexive.

(a) Consider the relation
R_2 = {(x, x), (y, y), (z, z), (x, y) (y, x), (y, z), (z, y)} on A
Here, the relation R_1 and A is reflexive and Symmetric but not transitive (∵ (x, y) ∈ R_1, (y, z) ∈ R_1 but (x, x) ∈ R_1)

(b) Consider the relation
R_2 ={(x, x), (y,y), (z, z), (x,y)} on A
Here, the relation R2 on A is reflexive and transitive but not Symmetric (∵ (x, y) ∈ R_2, (y, x) ∉ R_2)

(c) Consider the relation
R_3 = {(x, y), (y, x), (x, x), (y, y)} on A.
Here, the relation R_3 on A is symmetric and transitive but not reflexive (∵ (z, z) ∉ R_3)

Functions : If there be two non empty sets A and B and f be any rule which associates each $x \in A$ to an unique element of B then the rule denoted by f(x), is called function (mapping) from A to B and denoted by

$f: A \rightarrow B \Rightarrow x \in A, \Rightarrow f(x) = B$. The element f(x) is called the f-image of x, x is called the pre-image of f(x). The set A is said to be domain of the function and the set $\{f(x) : x \in A\}$ is the range of the function denoted by f(A). We shall note that the set A is called the domain of the function f and B is called the co-domain of the function.

Kinds of functions : The kinds of functions are:

(i) Identify function :
If $f : A \rightarrow A : f(x) = x \ \forall \ x \in A$ is called the identify function, and is denoted by **I**.

(ii) Greatest Integer function :
The function f from R to Z, defined by the rule that f maps any real number x to the greatest integer less than or equal to x is known as the greatest integer function or the floor function and is denoted by f(x) = [x], where [x] is the greatest integer $\leq x$. For example, if x = 0.6 then f(x) = [x]=0, if x = 2.3 then f(x) = [x] =2, and if x = -5, then [x]' = -5.

(iii) Absolute Function
Function f: $R \rightarrow R$: f(x) = |x| is known as the modulus (or absolute value) function, where |x| is the absolute value of x. For example, if x = 10 then f(x) = |x| = 10 and if x = -10, then f(x)=|x| = 10.

(iv) Onto Mapping : A mapping f: $A \rightarrow B$ is said to an onto (or surjective) mapping if f(A) = B, that is, the range and co-domain coincide. In this case we say that f maps A onto B. Symbolically : $\{f(x)\}$ = B, $x \in A$
e.g. if A = {1,2,3,4,...}, B = {0,1} and f: $A \rightarrow B$ is defined by f(2m)=0, f(2m+1)=0, where m is a +ve integer, then f is onto mapping, since both the elements 0, 1 of B are f images of the elements of A; 0 is the f-images of 2,4,6, ... of A and 1 is the f-image of 1,3,5..... of A.

(v) One-one mapping : A mapping f: $A \rightarrow B$ is said to be (one-one) mapping if the images of distinct elements of A under F are distinct, i.e. no element of B is the image of more than one element in A. Symbolically, f : $A \rightarrow B$ is one-one if $f(x_1) = f(x_2), \ \forall \ x_1, x \in A$.

(vi) One-one onto (bijective) mapping : A mapping f: $A \rightarrow B$ is said to be bijective (or one-one onto) if f is both injective and surjective, i.e., one-one as well as onto e.g. if A={a,b,c} and B={1,2,3} and f(a)=1, f(b)=2, f(c)=3 then it is one-one onto mapping.

(vii) Into (or injective) function : If the mapping is such that there is at least one element of B, which is not the f-image of any element of A, then f is called mapping of A into B or f is an into mapping.

(viii) Permutation : A bijective mapping f : A $\to$ A is said to be permutation on the set A. Let A = $\{a_1, a_2, ..., a_n\}$, and f be a bijection from A onto A that maps a_i to $f(a_i)$, then we write f as

$$f = \begin{pmatrix} a_1 & a_2 & ...... & a_n \\ f(a_1) & f(a_2) & .... & f(a_n) \end{pmatrix}$$ So, the identity mapping

$$I = \begin{pmatrix} a_1 & a_2 & ..... & a_n \\ a_1 & a_2 & ..... & a_n \end{pmatrix}$$

(ix) Inverse Function : Let f : A $\to$ B be a bijective mapping. Then the mapping g : B $\to$ A which associates to each element b $\in$ B the unique element a $\in$ A, such that f(a) = b, is called the inverse mapping of the mapping f : A $\to$ B. We denote this function g by f^{-1}.

Note that a function f is invertible iff f^{-1} exists iff f is bijective.
Hence, if f: A $\to$ B is a one-one onto mapping then f^{-1}:B $\to$ A exists, and is also 1-to-1.

(x) Equal Function : If f and g are two functions defined on the same domain A and if f(a) = g(a) for every a $\in$ A, then the functions f and g are equal, i.e., f = g.

For example $f(x) = x^2+5$, where x is a real number, and $g(x) = x^2+5$, where x is a complex number. Then the function f is not equal to the function g since they have different domains although $f(x) = x^2+5 = g(x \; \forall \; x \in R)$.

Composition of two functions :
Let f and g be the two functions then the composition of f(x) and g(x), denoted by, fog.
In general (fog) $\neq$ (gof).

For example, if $f(x) = x^2$ and $g(x) = x+1$, then $(fog)(x) = (x+1)^2$ and $(gof)(x) = x^2+1$.
Here we can see that $fog \neq gof$.

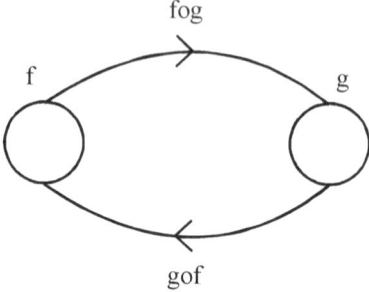

Q.1 Find the power set of the set A = {a,e,i,o,u}
Subsets are
{a} {e} {i} {o} {u} {a,e} {e,i} {o,u} {a,u} {e,u}, {i,u} {a,e,i} {e,i,o} {i,o,u} {a,e,i,o,u}
P(A) = {∅ {a}, {e},{i}, {o}, {u}, {a,e}, {e,i}, {o,u}, {a,u}, {e,u}, {i,u}, {a,e,i}, {e,i,o}, {i,o,u}, {a,e,i,o,u}}

Q.2 Find the dual of
(i) $A \cap (B \cap C) = (A \cap B) \cap C$, and (ii) $(A \cup B) \cap (A \cup C)$.
(i) Dual of $A \cap (B \cap C) = (A \cap B) \cap C$ is $A \cup (B \cup C) = (A \cup B) \cup C$
(ii) Dual of $(A \cup B) \cap (A \cup C)$ is $(A \cap B) \cup B \cap C)$

Q.3 Draw a Venn diagram to represent $A \cup (B \cap C)$.

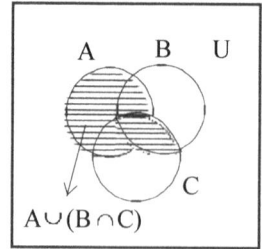

Figure : Horizontal line shows $A \cup (B \cap C)$

Q.4 Check whether $(A \cup B) \cap C = A \cup (B \cap C)$ or not using a Venn diagram.

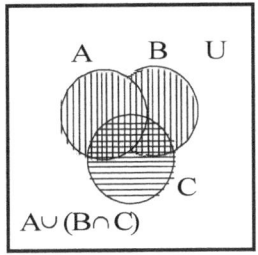
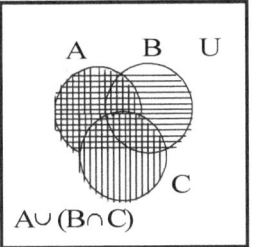

Figure (a)   **Figure (b)**

Shaded area in Figure (a) and Figure (b) is not same so LHS is not equal to RHS in the given problem.

Q5. In a group of 50 foreign tourists. 30 tourists can understand Hindi and 25 understand Tamil. Ten tourists understand neither Hindi nor Tamil. How many tourists understand both Hindi and Tamil?

Fact 1 :   Total foreign to units = 50
Fact 2 :   Hindi knows = 30
Fact 3 :   Tamil knows = 25
Fact 4 :   Neither Hindi nor Tamil = 10

$U = 50$, $x = 30$, $Y = 25$

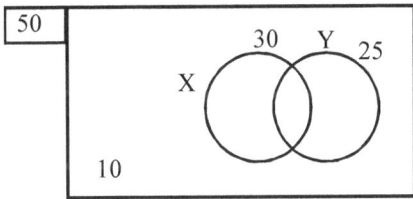

by fact 1 $U = 50$
by fact 2 $X = 30$
by fact 3 $Y = 25$
by fact 4 $4\ XUY = 10 \Rightarrow XUY = 40$
$X \cap Y = ?$

We know that :
$|X \cup Y| = |X| + |Y| - |X \cap Y|$
$|X \cap Y| = |X| + |Y| - |X \cup Y|$
$ = |X| + |Y| - |X \cup Y|$
$ = 30 + 25 - 40$
$ = 15$

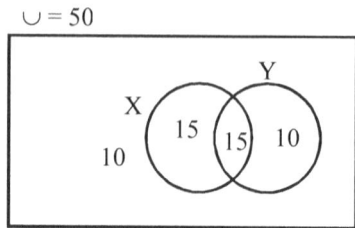

Q6. If in a city 70% of the residents can speak Tamil and 50% can speak Kannada, what percentage of residents can speak both the language, if 10% residents cannot speak any of these two languages?
In question the data is in percentage so let there are 100 residents in a city.
$\Rightarrow \cup = 100$
70% if residents can speak Tamil
$\Rightarrow |T| = 70$
50% can speak Kannada
$\Rightarrow (K) = 50$
If 10% cannot speak any language i.e., Tamil & Kannada.
$\Rightarrow |T \cup K| = 100$
$\Rightarrow |T \cup K| = 100-10 = 90$
How much percentage of residents can speak both language.
$\Rightarrow |T \cap K| = ?$
We know that :
$|T \cup K| = |T| + |K| - |T \cap K|$
$|T \cap K| = |T| + |K| - |T \cup K|$
$= 70 + 50 - 90 = 30$
So 30% of residents of the city can speak both languages.

Q7. In a survey about liking for fruits, it was found that, everyone who was surveyed had a liking for at least one of three fruits namely Apples, Bananas and Oranges. Further 60% liked Apples, 50% liked Bananas and 70% liked Oranges. Further 20% people liked both Apples and Bananas. 25% liked Apples and Oranges and 15% liked both Oranges and Bananas. Find the percentage of surveyed people who like all the three fruits.
Let $\cup = 100$
A = Number of people liked Apple
B = Number of people liked Banana
C = Number of people liked Orange
$||A| = 60;$

|B| = 50;
|C| = 70;
|A∩B| = 20
|A∩C| = 25
|B∩C| = 15
We know that: |A∪B∪C| = |A|+|B|+|C|+|A∩B∩C|
-|A∩B|-|B∩C|-|A∩C|
100 = 60+50+70+|A∩B∩C|
   -20-25-15
100 = 180 - 60 + |A∩B∩C|
100 = 120 + |A∩B∩C|
|A∩B∩C| = -20

Note : Data given in Question seems to be wrong because (-20) cannot be number
of people any how method and formula may be followed for similar problem.

Q8. In a town of 10,000 families, it was found that 40% families buy newspaper A, 20% families buy newspaper B and 10% families buy newspaper C. Further 5% families buy both A and B, 3% buy B and C and 4% buy A and C. If 2% buy all the three newspapers, find the number of families which buy (i) A only (ii) none of A, B and C.

Total families in town = 10,000
Families buying newspaper A = 40%
Families buying newspaper B = 20%
Families buying newspaper C = 10%
Families buying Both A&B = 5%
Families buying Both B&C = 3%
Families buying Both A&C = 4%
Families buying all three = 2%
Definitely families buying none of the newspaper is terms of % = 6%
(as 100- (same of all the combination given above)
So now families purchasing A only are 40%
= $\frac{400}{100}$ × 10,000
= 4000
Families purchasing none of A, B, C are 6%.
= $\frac{6}{100}$ × 100
= 600

Q9. In a class of 100 students, 10 students have opted both Mathematics

and History, 20 students opted neither History nor Mathematics. Further, number of students in History is ten less than number of students in Mathematics. Find number of students opting History and number of students opting Mathematics.

Let A and B denotes the set of students opted Mathematics and History respectively, Now we have

$n(A \cap B) = 10$ i.e. no. of students opted both subjects.

$N(A \cup B) = 100 - 20 = 80$ since 20 students opted neither Mathematics nor history.

We also have $n(B) = n(A) - 10$

Now using :

$n(A \cup B) = n(A) + n(B) - n = (A \cap B)$
$80 = n(A) + n(B) - 10$
or $\quad n(A) + n(B) = 90$
and $\quad n(A) - n(B) = 10$

Solving these equations $2n(A) = 100$
i.e. $\quad n(A) = 50$ and similarly
$50 + n(B) = 90$
$n(B) = 40$
Thus
$n(A) = 50 \quad$ No. of students opted Mathematics
$n(B) = 40 \quad$ No. of students opted History.

Q10. In a class of 120 students 80 students study Mathematics, 45 study history and 20 students neither study history nor study Mathematics. What is the number of students, who study both Mathematics and history?

V = Total Students = 120
M = Student studying mathematics = 80
H = Student studying History = 45
$\overline{M \cap N}$ student studying neither history nor mathematics = 20
$M \cup N$ = Total student - Student who don't study either history or mathematics.
= 120 - 20
- 100

So 100 students studies either Mathematics or history or both.
So,
$N \cup H = N + H - M \cap H$
$M \cap H = M + H - M \cup H$
= 80 + 45 - 100
= 125 - 100
= 25

Q11. In a group of 1000 people, 750 can speak Hindi and 400 can speak Bengali. Find out the number of people who can speak Hindi only and Bengali only?

Let A and B denote the set of people who can speak Hindi and Bengali respectively.

Then
n (A∪B) = 1000 n (A) = 750 n (B) = 400
n (A∩B) = n (A) + ∩(B) - n (A∪B)
= 750 + 400 - 1000'
= 150 Speak both languages
using n (A - B)= n (A) - n (A∩B)
   = 750 - 150
   = 600 Speak Hindi only
and similarly
n(B - A) = n (B) - n (B∩A)
   = 400 - 150
   = 250 Speak Bengali only.

Q12. Draw a Venn diagram to represent the following three facts :
(i)   A ∩ B ≠ ϕ
(ii) D ⊆ B ⊆ C and
(iii) A ∩ D = ϕ

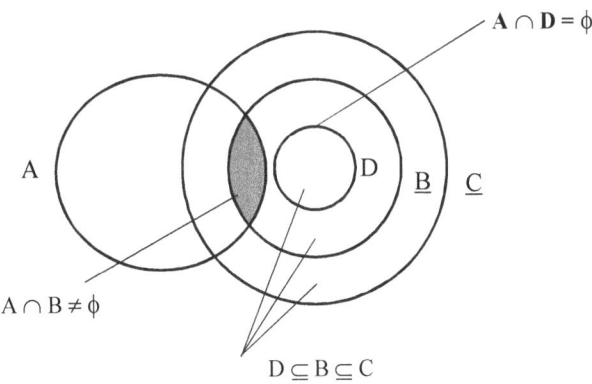

Q13. Draw a Venn diagram to represent the following facts for the sets P, Q, R and S.
(i) P ∩ Q ≠ φ
(ii) S ⊆ Q ⊆ R and
(iii) P ∩ S ≠ φ

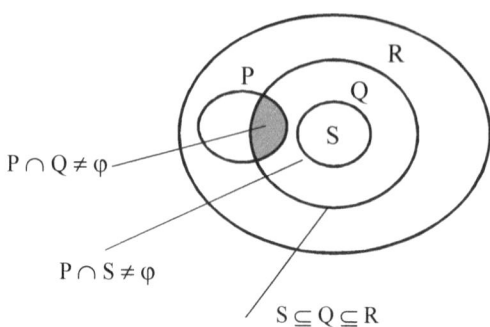

Q14. A = {1, 2, 4, 5}, B = {a, b, c, f} and C = {a, 5} are three given sets. Compute (A∩C) - (A U C) x B where 'U' '-' '∩' and 'x' are well-known set-theoretic operations.

A = {1, 2, 4, 5}
B = {a, b, c, f}
C = {a, 5}
(A∩C) - (A∩C) x B
(A∩C) = 5
(A∩C) x B = {(5, a), (5, b), (5,c), (5, f))}
(A∩C) - (A∩C) x B
{5} - {(5,a), (5, b), (5, c), (5, f)}
{5}

Q15. Do as directed :
(i) Find the power set of the set A = {1, {2,3}}.
A = {1, {2,3}}
Power set of A
{1}, {{2,3}}, {1, {2,3}}

(ii) For sets P = {{1,2},3} and Q = {{1,3}, 2} find P∩Q
For P = {1,2},3}
Q = { {1,3}, 2}
P∩Q = φ

(iii) For S = {x:x is a letter in the word 'wolf'}
T = {x}x is a letter in the word 'follow'}
Find whether S = T
S = {x:x is a letter in word 'wolf'}
∴ S = {'w', 'o', 'l', 'f'}

T = {x : x is a letter of the word 'follow'}
∴ T = {'f', 'o', 'l', 'w'}
∴ S = T

Q16. If A = (14, 15), B = (16,17) and C = (17,18) find (A × B) ∪ (B × C)
A = {14, 15},   B = {16, 17},   C = {17, 18}
A × B = {(14,16), (14,17), (15,16), (15,17)}
B × C = {(16,17), (16,18), (17,17), (17,18)}
(A × B) ∪ (B × C) = {(14,16), (14,17), (15,16), (15,17), (16,17), (16,18), (17,17), (17,18)}

Q17. If P = {a,c,e), Q = (100,101,102), R = (m,c,e,101), compute ((P∪R) - (P∩)) × Q Where '∪', '-', '∩' and '×' are well-known set-theoretic binary operations.
P = {a, c, e}
Q = {100, 101, 102}
R = {m, c, e, 101}
(P∩R) = {a, c, e, m, 101}
(P∪R) - (P∩R) = {a,m,101}
{a, m, 101} × {100, 101, 102}
= {(a, 100), (a, 101), (a, 102), (m, 100) , (m, 101), (m, 102)
(101, 100), (101, 101), (101, 102)}

Q18. If G = {p,q,r,}, H = {20,70,90} K = {r,70,s), then compute the set (G-K) × (K-H), Where '-' and '×' are well-known set-theoretic operation.
G = {p,q,r}
H = {20, 70, 90}
K = {r, 70, 5}
(G-K) X (K-H)
G - K = {p,q}
K-H = {r,s}
(G-K) × (K-H) = {(p,r), (q,r), (q.,s)}

Q19. If A = (3,4,5} B = {a,b} and C = {5,6,7} compute ((A∪C) - (A∩C) × B
(A∪C)   = {3,4,5} ∪ {5,6,7}
           ={3,4,5,6,7}
(A∩C)   = {3,4,5} ∩ {5,6,7}
        = {5}
((A∪C) - (A∩C) = {3,4,5,6,7} - {5}
            = {3,4,6,7}

$((A \cup C) - (A \cap C)) \times B = \{3,4,6,7,\} \times \{a,b\}$
$= \{(3,a), (3,b), (4,a), (4,b), (6,a), (6,b), (7,a), (7,b)\}$

Q20. If A = {a,b,c,} B = {1,2} and C = {#,*} then list all the elements of A × B × C. How many elements are there in your answer?

(A×B) = {a,b,c,} × {1,2}
       = {(a,1), (a,2), (b,1), (b,2), (c,1), (c,2)}
A×B×C = {a,1}, #), ((a,1), *), ((a,2), #), ((a,2), *),
       ((b,1}, #), ((b,1), *), ((b,2) #), ((b,2), *),
       ((c,1}, #), ((c,1), *), ((c,2) #), ((c,2), *)}

Thus there are 12 elements in the set (A×B×C)

Q21. Let A = {a,b,c} and B = {14,15}. List the elements in :
(i)   A × B
(ii) B × A
(iii) A × A
(iv) B × B

A = {a,b,c}
B = {14,15}
(i)   A×B = {(a,14), (a,15), (b,14), (b,15), (c,14), (c,15)}
(ii) B×A = {(14,a), (14,b), (14,c), (15,a), (15,b), (15,c)}
(iii) A×A = {(a,a), (a,b), (b,c), (b,a), (b,b), (b,c), (c,a), (c,b), (c,c)}
(iv) B×B = {(14,14), (14,15), (15,14), (15,14), (15,15)}

Q22. Let A = {a,b} and B = {4,5,6}. List the elements in
(i) A×B   (ii) B×A   (iii) A×A   (iv) B×B

A = {a,b}
B = {4,5,6}
(i)   A×B = {a,b} × {4,5,6}
           = {(a,4), (a,5), (a,6), (b,4), (b,5), (b,6)}
(ii) B×A = {4,5,6} × {a,b}
           = {(4,1), (4,b), (5,a), (5,b), (6,a), (6,b)}
(iii) A×A = {a,b} × {a,b}
           = {(a,a), (a,b), (b,a), (b,b)}
(iv) B×B = {4,5,6} × {4,5,6}
           = {(4,4), (4,5), (4,6), (5,4), (5,5), (5,6), (6,4), (6,5), (6,6)}

Q23. Prove that if R be an equivalence relation in a set A, then R^{-1} is also a equivalence relation in A.

: If R be an equivalence relation in a set A, then prove that R^{-1} is also an equivalence relation in A.

Let R be an equivalence relation in a Set A. Therefore R is reflexive, symmetric and transitive.
Then $R = \{(x, y) \mid x, y \in A\}$ _____ (1)
$\Rightarrow R^{-1} = \{y, x) \mid (x, y) \in R, x, y \in A\}$ _____ (2)
Now we have to prove that R^{-1} is an equivalence relation in the set A.
Now, Since R is reflexive relation
then xRx, $\forall x \in A$
i.e. $(x, x) \in R, \forall x \in A$
$\therefore (x, x) \in R^{-1} \forall x \in A$
Hence R^{-1} is reflexive relation.
Also Since, R is symmetric relation
$\therefore xRy \Rightarrow yRx, \forall x, y \in A$
i.e. $(x, y) \in R \Rightarrow (y, x) \in R \ \forall x, y \in A$
$\therefore (y, x) \in R^{-1}$ and $(x, y) Î R^{-1}, \forall x, y \in A$
Hence R^{-1} is Symmetric relation.
Also, Since R is transitive relation
$\therefore$ for $(x, y) \in R$ and $(y, z) \in R$
$\Rightarrow (x, z) \in R \ \forall, x, y, z \in A$
$\therefore$ for $(x, y) \in R \Rightarrow (y, z) \in R^{-1}$
$(y, z) \in R \Rightarrow (z, y) \in R^{-1}$
and $(x, z) \in R \Rightarrow (z, x) \in R^{-1}$
$\therefore$ for (z, y) & $(y, x) \in R^{-1}$
$\Rightarrow (z, x) \in R^{-1}$
Hence R^{-1} is transitive relation.
Since R^{-1} is reflexive, Symmetric and transitive. Therefore R^{-1} is an equivalence relation.

Q24. Is every relation which is symmetric and transitive on a set A, always reflexive ? Why or why not?

Let R be a symmetric and transitive relation on A. Let a, b $\in$ R and aRb hold.
Since, R is symmetric
$\therefore$ aRb = bRa
or bRa = aRa
Therefore R is reflexive, consequently R is an equivalence relation. But this argument is fallacious.
i.e. R is reflexive if aRa holds for every a $\in$ A. If R is Symmetric and transitive then aRa holds an the assumption that there exists another element b $\in$ A such that aRb holds. It may happen that for a particular element a $\in$ A there exists no element b $\in$ A such that aRb holds.

Q25. For a given relation R in a set A, define and explain with suitable examples the concepts of reflexive closure, and symmetric closure of R.

Consider a relation R an set A $\{1, 2, 3, 4\}$ as
   R = $\{(1, 3), (1, 4), (2, 2), (3, 3), (4, 1)\}$

(i) The relation R is not reflexive since, (1, 1) and (4, 4) $\notin$ R. To obtain the reflexive relation r(R) all we need to do is add the two ordered pairs (1, 1) and (4, 4). Therefore r(R) = $\{(1, 1), (1, 3), (1, 4), (2, 2), (3, 3), (4, 1), (4, 4)\}$

(ii) The relation R is not Symmetric since (1, 3) $\in$ R but (3, 1) $\notin$ R. If we add (3, 1) to R we get the symmetric relation S(R) as
   S(R) = $\{(1, 3), (1, 4), (2, 2), (3, 1), (3, 3), (4, 1)\}$

(iii) The relation R is not transitive either here we have (4, 1) and (1, 3) $\in$ R but (4, 3) $\notin$ R. The scheme for finding t(R) is not so simple as those for r(R) and s(R). Since (4, 1) and (1, 3) $\in$ R and t(R) must be transitive, so t(R) must contain (4, 3) and we put (4, 3) in t(R). That is t(R). That is t(R) = $\{(1, 3), (1, 4), (2, 2), (3, 3), (4, 1), (4, 3)\}$. In general, if there is a chain from x to y, i.e. if there are points $x_1, x_2 ... x_{m-1}$ so that $xRx_1, x_1Rx_2, ... x_{m-1}Ry$ then (x, y) must be in t(R). The relation r(R), s(R) and t(R) are called the reflexive, symmetric and transitive closures of R.

Q26. Give one examples of each of the following :
(i) A relation which is reflexive and symmetric but not transitive.
(ii) A relation which is reflexive and transitive but not symmetric.
(iii) A relation which is reflexive but neither symmetric nor transitive.
(iv) A relation which is symmetric but neither reflexive nor transitive.
(v) A relation which is symmetric and transitive but not reflexive.
(vi) A relation which is transitive but neither reflexive nor symmetric.
(vii) 1 — 1 onto function
(viii) Anti-symmetric relation on a set

(i) A relation which is reflexive and symmetric but not transitive.
Let A be the set of all straight lines in the plane. A relation R is defined on A as lRm iff 'l' lies on the plane of m, $\forall$ l, m $\in$ A
Then the relation R is reflexive, symmetric but not transitive.

(ii) A relation which is reflexive and transitive but not symmetric.
Let A be a family of sets and Let R be the relation in A defined by 'x is a subset of y' i.e.
xRy iff x is subset of y $\forall$ x, y $\in$ A

Then R is a relation which is reflexive, transitive but not symmetric.

(iii) A relation which is reflexive but neither symmetric nor transitive.
Consider A = {1, 2, 3, 4, 5}
and R = {(1, 1), (2, 2), (3, 3), (4, 4), (5, 5), (3, 4), (4, 5)}
Since (1, 1) ∈ R, (2, 2) ∈ R, (3, 3) ∈ R, (4, 4) ∈ R, (5, 5) ∈ R
i.e. xRx, $\forall$ x ∈ A
Therefore R is reflexive
Also (3, 4) ∈ R, but (4, 3) ∉ R $\Rightarrow$ 3R4 but 4R3
Therefore R is not symmetric
also (3, 4) ∈ R and (4, 5) ∈ R, but (3, 5) ∉ R
$\Rightarrow$ 3R4, 4R5 but 3 is not related to 5
Therefore R is not transitive
Hence, R is reflexive but neither symmetric nor transitive.

(iv) A relation which is symmetric but neither reflexive nor transitive.
Consider P = {Set of all straight line in a plane}
and R is a relation perpendicular to P.
i.e. xRy if x $\perp$ y, $\forall$ x, y ∈ x
Clearly, if x $\perp$ y $\Leftrightarrow$ y $\perp$ x
$\Rightarrow$ xRy $\Leftrightarrow$ yRx
Therefore R is symmetric
and let (x, x) ∈ R $\Rightarrow$ x $\perp$ x, which is not possible
$\therefore$ R is not reflexive.
Also, if x $\perp$ y, y $\perp$ z then x $\perp$ z (not possible)
because x $\perp$ y & y $\perp$ z then x $\parallel$ z
Therefore R is not transitive
Hence, R is a relation which is symmetric but neither reflexive nor transitive.

(v) A relation which is symmetric and transitive but not reflexive.
Let I is the set of integers
Now we define a relation R on I, such that
aRb if ab > 0, $\forall$ a, b ∈ I
Then R is a relation, which is symmetric, transitive but not reflexive.

(vi) A relation which is transitive but neither reflexive nor symmetric.
Consider a Universal set U and R is a relation of proper subset.
i.e. ARB iff A $\subset$ B
Clearly, if A $\subset$ B & B $\subset$ D then A $\subset$ D
i.e. ARB, BRD $\Rightarrow$ ARD
Therefore R is transitive

and Let ARA $\Rightarrow$ A $\subset$ A, which is not possible, because a set cannot be proper subset of itself
Therefore R is not reflexive.
Also Let ARB $\Rightarrow$ A $\subset$ B not possible.
and BRA $\Rightarrow$ B $\subset$ A jointly
Therefore R is not symmetric.
Hence R is a relation which is transitive but neither reflexive nor symmetric.

(vii) 1 — 1 onto function
Let $f : z \to z$ be defined by $f(x) = x + 1$, $x \in z$ then every element y in the codomain set z has a pre-image y - 1 in the domain set z.
Therefore $f(z) = z$ and f is an 1 - 1 onto mapping.

(viii) Anti-symmetric relation on a set
Let A be a family of sets and Let R be the relation in A defined by 'x is a subset of y'.
Then R is anti-symmetric since $A \subseteq B$ and $B \subseteq A \Rightarrow A = B$.

Q27. A relation R is defined in the set of natural numbers N as follows:
   x R y if x + 3y = 12. Determine whether
(i) R is reflexive,   (ii) R is symmetric,   (iii) R is transitive
#: Let x, y $\in$ N, the set of natural number. A relation R is defined in N as follows : x R y if and only if x + 3y = 12.
Determine whether R is (i) reflexive (ii) symmetric (iii) anti-symmetric (iv) transitive
(i) Let R be a relation defined by: -
xRy if x + 3y = 12
Let x = 2 $\in$ N, then
xRx $\Rightarrow$ 2 + 3(2) = 8 $\neq$ 12
Hence $\forall$ x $\in$ N, is not related to itself except x = 3
Hence R is not reflexive

(ii) R is Symmetric, iff
(x, y) $\in$ R $\Rightarrow$ (y, x) $\in$ R
i.e. xRy $\Rightarrow$ yRx
i.e. x + 3y = 12 $\Rightarrow$ y + 3x = 1
But it is not necessary always
Hence R is not Symmetric

(iii) Also, R is anti-Symmetric, iff
(x, y) $\in$ R and (y, x) $\in$ R $\Rightarrow$ x = y
i.e. xRy and yRx $\Rightarrow$ x = y

i.e. $x + 3y = 12$ and $y + 3x = 12$
$\Rightarrow x = y$
Which is true
Therefore R is Anti-Symmetric

(iv) we have
$3 + 9 = 12$ and $9 + 3 = 12$ but $3 + 3 \neq 12$ i.e.
3R9 and 9R3 holds but 3R3 does not hold hence R is not transitive

Q28. A relation R is defined in the set of natural numbers N as follows :
x R y if x + 3y = 12,
Determine whether
(i)   R is reflexive
(ii)   R is symmetric
(iii) R is transitive
xRy iff $x + 3y = 12$
(i)   **Reflexive :**
        R is not reflexive as if $x = 1$.
            $1 + 3(1) = 1+3 = 4 \neq 12$
            $\therefore (1,1) \notin R$
            $\therefore$ R is not reflexive.
(ii)   **Symmetric :**
            $(6,2) \in R$
            as $6 + 3(2) = 12$
            Taking case of (2,6)
            $2 + 3(6)$
            $= 2 + 18$
            $= 20 \neq 12$
            $\therefore (2,6) \notin R$
            So R is not symmetric
(iii) **Transitive :**
            $(-6,6) \in R$
            and $(6,2) \in R$
            Now $(2, -6)$
            $2 + 3(-6)$
            $2 + (-18)$
            $-16 \neq 12$
            R is not transitive

Q29. Give one example of each of the following :

(i) a relation which is reflexive but neither symmetric nor transitive.
(ii) a relation which is symmetric but neither reflexive nor transitive.
Let R on A X A, Where A = (x,y,z)
(i)   {(x,x), (y,y, (z,z), (x,y), (y,z)}
      (x,x) + (y,y) + (z,z) all are present ⇒ reflexive
      (x,y) is present + (y,x) is not present
      (x,z) is present + (z,y) is not present not ⇒ symmetric
      (x,y) + (y,z) are present but (x,z) not present
      ⇒ not transitive.

(ii) {(x,x), (x,y), (y,x), (y,z), (z,y)}
      only (x,x) is present & (y,y) & (z,z) are not present
      ⇒ not reflexive
      (x,y), (y,z) & (x,z) are present
      ⇒ transitive
      (x,x), (y,y), (z,z) not present
      ⇒ not reflexive
      (x,y) present by (y,x) not present
      ⇒ not symmetric

Q30. Distinguish between relations and function.
Function is a special type of relation i.e. Relation is a generalized concept and function is a case of it.
A relation R from A to B is a subset of A x B, relation is represented by set of ordered pairs (x,y) ⇒ x R y i.e. x is related to y. Function are also represented by set of ordered pairs and a member (a,b) ⇒ f(a) = b i.e., b is result of f(a) denoted by f: A→B.

Q31. Let A{a, b, c, d}, B={1,2,3} and R={(a,b2), (b,1), (c,2), (d,1)}. Is R a function? Why?
R is a function because each element of A is assigned to a unique element of B.

Q32. Every function is a relation. Is every relation a function? Why?
Not every relation is a function. For example, this relation does not satisfy the property that,
a) Each element of A must have assigned one element in B.
b) If a ∈ A is assigned b ∈ B and a ∈ A is assigned b' ∈ B then b=b'.
That is why relations those who don't satisfy above properties are not a function.

Q33. What is hashing function and why is it important?

Hashing function is a function, which produces a number after accepting a KEY value as its argument. Ideally for every 'key' value the hash function should produce a unique result. This kind of function is used in Direct File Organization where a bulk of data records are required to be stored in such a way that they (any of them) can be accessed with same amount of time. So using this technique record is stored at the address computed by hash function and when required, retrieved directly from that function.

In practical situation hash function uses mod and produces result within a certain range and hence may be used for sub area selection where to store and from where to access.

Q34. Let f : R → R be defined by
f(x) = 3x + 2
Find whether f is (i) one-one and (ii) onto function. Further, state the conditions for the inverse function f⁻¹ to exist. Are these conditions satisfied in this case?

Given f: R → R is defined by
   f(x) = 3x + 2

(i) Is f one-one?
A function f: A → B is said to be one to one is different elements in domain A have distinct images. This means f is one-to-one if f(a) = f(a') implies a = a'. The graph of f(x) = 3x + 2 is as shown below (Drawn for a range of values of x i.e. 0, 1, 2, ...)
Obviously, f is one-to-one since, all horizontal lines can intersect it at most one point. There are no two distinct pairs (a_1, b) and (a_2, b) in the graph of f(x) = 3x + 2.

(ii) Is f(x) onto function?
The function f(x) = 3x + 2 also onto function because each horizontal line must intersect its graph at least once.

(iii) Conditions for the inverse functions
A function f : A → B is invertible if and only if the function is both one-to-one and onto. Each element of A corresponds to a unique element of B and vice-versa.
The conditions for inverse function are satisfied in case of f : R → R, where f(x) = 3x + 2. This is because it is both one-to-one and onto.

Q35. For any two integers x, y we define the binary operation $\otimes$ in I as follow: $x \otimes y = x + y + 1$
Find out whether

(i) ⊗ is closed in the set of even integers
(ii) ⊗ is closed in the set of odd integers
(iii) ⊗ is commutative in integers
(iv) ⊗ is associative in integers

 # : The symbol ⊗ is a binary operation on integers such that for any two integers x and y
$x \otimes y = x + y + 1$
Show that the set of even integers is not closed under ⊗, but set of odd integers is closed under ⊗.
$x, y \in I$
(i) $x \otimes y = y \otimes x \ \forall x, y \in I$
(ii) $(x \otimes y) = (y \otimes x) \ \forall + x = + y \in I$
(iii) $(x \otimes y) \otimes e = x \otimes (y \otimes e) \ \forall e = I \ x \Leftrightarrow y$
(iv) $x \otimes (y \otimes z) = (x \otimes y) \otimes z \ \forall x, y, z \in 1^+$

Q36. Let D(625) be the set of all positive integral divisors of 81. Then show that D(625) under the binary relation 'divides' is a poset. Is the poset totally ordered?

Since D(625) is the set of all positive divisors of 81 we have to show that D(625) under the binary relation 'divides' is a poset.
Suppose that R is a relation on the given set D (625). Then
(i) for any a ∈ D(625), we have aRa.
(ii) If aRb and bRa, then a = b
(iii) If aRb and bRc than aRc.
Now D(625) = {1, 5, 25, 125, 625}
This set satisfies the above three properties and so, it is a poset. Now Every pair of element of D(625) i.e. {1, 5, 25, 125, 625} are compatible and since
$\frac{1}{5}, \frac{5}{25}, \frac{25}{125}, \frac{125}{625}$. Hence D(625) is totally ordered.

Q37. Let f(x) = 1/x and g(x) = x³+2. Find the following functions, where x ∈ R.
(i)   (f+g)(x)
(ii) (f-g)(x)
(iii) (fg)(x)
(iv) (f/g)(x)

(i) $(f+g)(x) = \frac{1}{x} + x^3 + 2$

(ii) $(f-g)(x) = \frac{1}{x} - (x^3+2)$

(iii) $(f.g)(x) = \left(\dfrac{1}{x}\right)(x^3+2)$

(iv) $(f/g)(x) = \dfrac{1}{x(x^3+2)} \; \forall x \in R$.

Q38. Let $f(x) = \sqrt{x+1} \; \forall \; x \geq -1$ and $g(x) = x^3 \; \forall \; x \in R$. Define the following functions. Also give their domains.

i) (f+g)
ii) (f-g)
iii) (fg)
iv) (f/g)
v) (f o g)

i) $(f+g)(x) = \sqrt{x+1} + x^3 \; \forall \; x \geq -1$

ii) $(f-g)(x) = \sqrt{x+1} - x^3 \; \forall \; x \geq -1$

iii) $(f.g)(x) = \sqrt{x+1} \; x^3 \; \forall \; x \geq -1$

iv) $(f/g)(x) = \forall \; \sqrt{x+1}/x^3 \; \forall \; x \geq -1 \;, x \neq 0$

v) $(fog)(x) = f(x^3) = \sqrt{x^3+1} \; \forall \; x \geq -1.$

Q39. Let $f : R \rightarrow R$
$f(x) = x^2,$
$g : R \rightarrow R$
$g(x) = \cos x$ find fog, and gof and show that fog $\neq$ gof
fog $(x) = f[g(x)]$
$= f[\cos x]$
$= (\cos x)^2$ ....(i)
and gof $(x) = g[f(x)]$
$= g[x^2]$
$= \cos x^2$ ....(ii)
from (i) and (ii) we see that fog $\neq$ gof

Q40. Let $f : R \rightarrow R,$
$g : R \rightarrow R$
$h : R \rightarrow R$

are such that $f(x) = x^2$, $g(x) = \tan x$ $h(x) = \log x$, find $[ho(gof)]x$, If $x = \sqrt{\dfrac{\pi}{2}}$

ho(gof)x = h [(gof)x]
= h [g {f(x)}]
= h [g (x²)]
= h [tanx²]
= log tan x²

= log tan $\frac{\pi}{4}$

= log 1
= 0

Q41. The identity function I on R is defined by $f(x) = x^2+3x+1$ and $g(x) = 2x-3$, Find formulae for functions.
(i) fof (ii) gof   (iii) gog   (iv) fof
(i) fog = f(g(x)) = f(2x-3)
= (2x-3)²+3(2x-3)+1
= 4x²-6x+1

(ii) gof = g(f(x1))
= g (x²+3x+1)
= 2 (x²+3x+1)-3
= 2x² + 6x -1

(iii) gog = g (g(x))
= g (2x-3)
= 2(2x-3)-3
= 4x-9

(iv) fof = f(f(x))
= f(x²+3x+1)
= (x²+3x+1)² + 3(x²+3x+1) + 1
x⁴+9x²+6x+1+2x² (3x+1)+3x²+9x+4
= x⁴ + 6x³ + 14x² + 15x + 5

Q42. Find the product fog of the permutations $f = \begin{pmatrix} 1 & 2 & 3 & 4 & 5 \\ 3 & 4 & 2 & 1 & 5 \end{pmatrix}$ and $g = \begin{pmatrix} 1 & 2 & 3 & 4 & 5 \\ 2 & 4 & 1 & 5 & 3 \end{pmatrix}$. Also write fog as a product of transpositions. Check whether fog is even.

$$f = \begin{pmatrix} 1 & 2 & 3 & 4 & 5 \\ 3 & 4 & 2 & 1 & 5 \end{pmatrix}$$

$$g = \begin{pmatrix} 1 & 2 & 3 & 4 & 5 \\ 2 & 4 & 1 & 5 & 3 \end{pmatrix}$$

$$fog = \begin{pmatrix} 1 & 2 & 3 & 4 & 5 \\ 5 & 1 & 4 & 2 & 3 \end{pmatrix}$$

for is having following cycle (1 5 3 4 2)

So, product of transposition is (1, 5) (1, 3), (1, 4), (1, 2)

Here, it is having 4 transposition so, it is even.

Q.43 For the following two permutations $f = \begin{pmatrix} 1 & 2 & 3 & 4 & 5 & 6 \\ 4 & 5 & 6 & 3 & 1 & 2 \end{pmatrix}$

and $g = \begin{pmatrix} 1 & 2 & 3 & 4 & 5 & 6 \\ 5 & 6 & 4 & 2 & 1 & 3 \end{pmatrix}$. **Find the product f.g. and express f as a product of cycles and then as a product of transpositions.**

Product f.g. says first perform f and then g. So,

$$fg = \begin{pmatrix} 1 & 2 & 3 & 4 & 5 & 6 \\ 2 & 1 & 3 & 4 & 5 & 6 \end{pmatrix}$$

Product of cycles :

$$f = \begin{pmatrix} 1 & 2 & 3 & 4 & 5 & 6 \\ 4 & 5 & 6 & 3 & 1 & 2 \end{pmatrix}$$

f = (1 4 3 6 2 5)
Product of transposition
Transposition product of 2 cycle
f = (1, 4), (3) (16) (12) (15)

Q.44 For the following two permutations : $f = \begin{pmatrix} 1 & 2 & 3 & 4 & 5 & 6 \\ 3 & 4 & 5 & 6 & 1 & 2 \end{pmatrix}$ **and**

$g = \begin{pmatrix} 1 & 2 & 3 & 4 & 5 & 6 \\ 2 & 3 & 5 & 6 & 4 & 1 \end{pmatrix}$. Find the product f.g. and express f and g each as product of cycles. Then express each of f and g as product of transpositions.

$$f \circ g = \left[\begin{array}{l} g = \begin{pmatrix} 1 & 2 & 3 & 4 & 5 & 6 \\ 2 & 3 & 5 & 6 & 4 & 1 \end{pmatrix} \\ f = \begin{pmatrix} 1 & 2 & 3 & 4 & 5 & 6 \\ 3 & 4 & 5 & 6 & 1 & 2 \end{pmatrix} \end{array} \right]$$

$$\Rightarrow \left[\begin{array}{l} g = \begin{pmatrix} 1 & 2 & 3 & 4 & 5 & 6 \\ 2 & 3 & 5 & 6 & 4 & 1 \end{pmatrix} \\ \downarrow \downarrow \downarrow \downarrow \downarrow \downarrow \\ f = \begin{pmatrix} 2 & 3 & 5 & 6 & 4 & 1 \\ 4 & 5 & 1 & 2 & 6 & 3 \end{pmatrix} [\textit{Suffled}] \end{array} \right]$$

$$\Rightarrow f \circ g = \begin{pmatrix} 1 & 2 & 3 & 4 & 5 & 6 \\ 4 & 5 & 1 & 2 & 6 & 3 \end{pmatrix}$$

f = product of cycles

f(1) = 3, f(3) = 5, f(5) = 1 $\Rightarrow$ [1, 3, 5] cycle
f(2) = 4, f(4) = 6, f(6) = 2 $\Rightarrow$ [2, 4, 6] cycle
f = (2, 4, 6) o (1, 3, 5)
g = $\Rightarrow$ product of cycles.

Q45. Which of the following statements are true ? Give reasons for your answer. [JUNE05, Q3(b)] [8]
(i) {0, φ, IGNOU} is a set.
(ii) P (m + n, r) = P (m, r) + P (n, r) for m, n, r ∈ N.
(iii) The Pigeon-hole principle states that r + 1 objects can be placed in r boxes only.
(iv) The contrapositive of the statement "if Manju is unwell, she will not go to school", is "if Manju is well then she will go to school".

(i) {0, φ, IGNOU} is a set because 0, φ and IGNOU are taken as elements. False because set is formed by collecting elements of same type.

(ii) $^{m+n}P_r = {}^mP_r + {}^nP_r$ for m, n, r∈N : False because :
$$P(m+n,r) > P(m,r) + P(n,r) \ \forall \ m,n,r \in N.$$
(iii) False, because the Pigeon Hole Theorem states that there are r boxes and (r+1) objects, then there will be a box with more than one objects in it.
(iv) True

Chapter-5
Counting Principles

Multiplication Principle : According to it " the number of ways in which the whole task can be performed are $n_1, n_2, n_3, n_4 .... n_k$ where 1, 2, 3.........k are the subtasks."

Addition Principle : According to it "when sub tasks are mutually exclusive i.e. disjoint (no effect of performance of tasks of previous or next task) then no. of ways performing the subtasks 1, 2, 3, ..., k is given by $n_1 + n_2 + ... n_k$"

Permutations : It is an arrangement in definite order of number of objects taken when some or all at a time. Number of permutations of n things taken at a time is denoted by the symbol ^nP_r
where (n > r)

Circular Permutation and Linear permutation
Let x, y, z are three dissimilar things. When all arranged indifferent ways (3! permutations) Such permutations are termed as linear permutations. But when three things are placed round a circle or other closed curve, then only 2! permutations will obtained, then this type of permutation is called cyclic permutation or circular permutation. Reason for 2! permutations is that one of three elements is first placed on circle and the remaining two elements can be arranged in 2! ways. If there are n things then there are (n-1) ways.

Combinations : It is a selection of some or all of a number of different things. In it order of selection is immaterial and notation used is ^nC_r

and $^nC_r = \dfrac{n!}{r!(n-r)!}$

$^nC_r = \dfrac{^nP_r}{r!}$

Binomial Theorem :

$(x+a)^n = {}^nC_0 x^n + {}^nC_1 x^{n-1} a + {}^nC_2 x^{n-2} a^2 + {}^nC_3 x^{n-3} a^3 + \ldots + {}^nC_n a^n$

$(x-a)^n = {}^nC_0 x^n + {}^nC_1 x^{n-1}(-a) + {}^nC_2 x^{n-2}(-a)^2 + {}^nC_3 x^{n-3}(-a)^3 + \ldots + {}^nC_n(-a)^n$

General Terms : $T_{r+1} = \dfrac{n(n-1)\ldots\ldots(n-r+1)}{r!} x^{n-r} a^r$

$(1-x)^n = 1 + nx + \dfrac{n(n-1)}{2!} x^2 + \dfrac{n(n-1)(n-2)}{3!} x^3 + \ldots\ldots$

$(1-x)^n = 1 - nx + \dfrac{n(n-1)}{2!} x^2 \ldots\ldots\ldots + (-1)^n x^n$

$e^x = 1 + x + \dfrac{x^2}{2!} + \dfrac{x^3}{2!} + \ldots\ldots\ldots\infty$

Some Important formulae

${}^nP_r = \dfrac{n!}{(n-r)!}$

${}^nc_r = {}^nc_{n-r}$

${}^nc_o = 1$

${}^nP_r = n(n-1)(n-2)\ldots\ldots(n-r+1)$
${}^nP_r = n \cdot {}^{n-1}P_{r-1}$
${}^nP_r = r \cdot {}^{n-1}P_{r-1} + {}^{n-1}P_r$
${}^nP_n = n!$
$0! = 1$
$(-r)! = \infty$

Special Notes :

(i) The no. of permutations of n dissimilar things taken r at a time when one particular thing always occurs is $r \cdot {}^{n-1}P_{r-1}$

(ii) The no. of permutations of n dissimilar things taken r at a time when one particular thing is never taken is ${}^{n-1}P_r$.

(iii) The number of permuatations of n objects, taken r at a time, where $0 \le r \le n$, is given by

${}^nP_r = \dfrac{n!}{(n-r)!}$

(iv) Suppose there are n objects classified into k distinct types, with m_1 identical objects of the first type, m_2 identical objects of the second type, ..., and m_k identical objects of the kth type, where $m_1+m_2....+m_k = n$. Then the number of distinct arrangements of these n objects, denoted by P (n;m_1, m_2,.....m_k) is $\dfrac{n!}{m_1!m_2!....m_k!}$

(v) The no. of permutations of n dissimilar things taken 'r' at a time when each thing can be repeated once, twice, ..., upto r times is n^r.

(vi) The no. of permutations of n different things taken r at a time in circular is

$$\dfrac{^nP_r}{r}$$

(vii) The numbers of ways in which (m+n+p) things can be divided into groups containing m, n, p things respectively $\dfrac{(m+n+p)!}{m!n!p!}$

(viii) Let n and r be natural numbers. Then the number of solutions in natural numbers, to the equation $x_1+x_2+......+x_n = r$, is $^{n+r-1}C_r$. Equivalently, the number of ways to choose r objects from a collection of n objects, with repetition allowed, is $^{(n+r-1)}C_r$.

(ix) For all positive integers n and all r such that
$^{n+1}C_r = {^nC_r} + {^nC_{r-1}}$

This formula is also known as Pascal Formula.

Experiment : An experiment is a clearly defined procedure that produces one of a given set of outcomes. The set of all outcomes is called the sample space of the experiment.

For example **(i)** the experiment could be checking the weather to see if it is raining or not on a particular day. The sample space here would be (raining, not raining)

(ii) If the outcomes are the sequence of heads and tails observed, then the sample space is {HH, HT, TH, TT}

Event : A subset of the sample space of an experiment is called an event. For example, for an experiment consisting of tossing 2 coins, with sample space {HH, HT, TH, TT}, the event that two heads do not show up is the subset {HT, TH, TT}

Impossible and Sure Events : Suppose X is a sample space of an experiment with N outcomes. Then, the events are all the 2^N subsets of X. The empty set ϕ is called the impossible event, and the set X itself is called the sure event.

Equally likely events : all the outcomes of an experiment are equally likely, that is, there is nothing to prefer one case over the other. For example, in the experiment of coin tossing, we assume that the coin is unbiased. This means that 'head' and 'tail' are equally likely in a toss. The toss itself is considered a random mechanism ensuring 'equally likely' outcomes. Of course, there are coins that are 'loaded', which means that one side of the coin may be heavier discussions we shall always assume that our sample space is finite.

Probability : The probability of the event A, represented by P(A), is $\dfrac{n(A)}{n(X)}$

Some standard results :
(i) As $n(\phi) = 0$, it follows that $P(\phi) = 0$.

(ii) By definition, $P(X) = \dfrac{n(X)}{n(X)} = 1$.

(iii) If A and B are two events, then $n(A \cup B) = n(A) + n(B) - n(A \cap B)$. Therefore,
    $P(A \cup B) = P(A) + P(B) - P(A \cap B)$

(iv) Addition Theorem in Probability : If A and B are two mutually exclusive events, then the probability of their union is the sum of the probabilities of A and B, i.e. if $A \cap B = \phi$, then $P(A \cup B) = P(A) + P(B)$.

(v) Suppose A is an event. Then the probability of A^c (Also denoted by A'), the event complementary to A, or the event 'notA' is 1-P(A) i.e.,
    $P(A^c) = 1-P(A)$
    The reason is that the events A and A^c are mutually exclusive and exhaustive i.e., $A \cup A^c = X$ and $P(A) + P(A^c) = 1$.

(vi) (The generalised addition theorem) : If the events $A_1, A_2, ...A_m$ are pairwise disjoint (i.e. mutually exclusive), then $P(U_i A_i) = \sum_i P(A_i)$

The Generalized Pigeonhole Principle : If nm+1 objects are distributed among in boxes, then at least one box will contain more than n objects.

Proof : We prove this by contradiction. Suppose all the m boxes have at most n objects in them. Then the total number of objects is at most nm, a contradiction. Hence, the theorem.

Some Theorems

Theorem 1: If a finite set S is partitioned into s subsets, then at least one of the subsets has $\frac{|S|}{k}$ or more elements.

Proof: Let $A_1, \ldots, A_k$ be a partition of S. (This means that $A_i \cap A_j = \phi$ for $i \neq j$ and

$S = A_1 \cup A_2 \cup \ldots \cup A_k$). Then the average value of $|A_i|$ is $\frac{1}{k}[|A_1| + \ldots + |A_k|] = \frac{|S|}{k}$.

So the largest A_i has at least $\frac{|S|}{k}$ elements.

Theorem 2: Consider a function $f: S \to T$, where S and T are finite sets satisfying $|S| > r|T|$. Then at least one of the sets $f^{-1}(t)$, $t \in T$, has more than r elements. ($f^{-1}(t)$ denotes the inverse image of the set $\{t\}$, i.e., $f^{-1}(t) = \{x \in S : f(x) = t\}$.)

Proof: The family $\{f^{-1}(t) : t \in T\}$ partitions S into k sets with $k \leq |T|$. By Theorem 3(below), some set in this family, say $f^{-1}(t')$, has a least $\frac{|S|}{k}$ members. Since $\frac{|S|}{k} \geq \frac{|S|}{T} > r$ by our hypothesis, $f^{-1}(t')$ has more than r elements.

Theorem 3: Suppose we put an infinity of objects in a finite number of boxes. Then at least one box must have an infinity of objects.

Proof: If every box contains only a finite number of objects, then the total number of objects must be finite. Hence the theorem.

Theorem 4: (The inclusion-exclusion formula): Let $A_1, A_2, \ldots, A_n$ be n sets in a universal set U consisting of N elements. Let S_k denote the sum of the sizes of all the sets formed by intersecting k of the A_is at a time. Then the number of elements in none of the sets $A_1, A_2, \ldots, A_n$ is given by

$\left|\overline{A}_1 \cap \overline{A}_2 \cap \overline{A}_n\right| = N - S_1 + S_2 - S_3 + \ldots + (-1)^k S_k + \ldots + (-1)^n S_n$.

Proof: The proof is on the same lines of the counting argument given in the 'sports club' example. If an element is in none of the A_is, then it should be counted only once, as part of 'N' in the RHS of the formula above. It is not counted in any of the S_ks since it is in one of the A_is.

Next, an element in exactly one A_i, say A_r, is counted once in N, and once in S_1,

and in none of the other S_ks. so the nect count is 1-1=0.
Finally, take an element x in exactly m of the A_is. This is counted once in N, m times in S_1, C(m, 2) times in S_2 (since x is in C(m,2) intersections $A_i \cap A_j$)...., C(m,k) times in S_k for k≤m. x is not counted in any S_k for k > m. So the net count of x in the RHS of the formula is
1-C(m,1) + C(m,2) - ..... +$(-1)^k$ C (m,k) + ... + $(-1)^m$ C(m, m) =0

So the only elements that have a net count of 1 in the RHS are those in $\bigcap_{i=1}^{n} \overline{A}_i$. The rest have a net count of 0. Hence the formula.

Theorem 5 : The number of functions from an m-element set onto a k-element set is

$\sum_{i=0}^{k} (-1)^i C(k,i)(k-i)^m$, where $1 \leq k \leq m$.

Proof : We will apply the inclusion-exclusion principle for this prove. Let we define the objects to be all the functions (not just the onto functions) from M, an m-element set, to K, a k-element set. For these objects, we will define A_i to be the set of all f : M → K for which the ith element of K is not in f(M). Then what we want is $|\overline{A}1 \cap \ldots\ldots\ldots\overline{A}_k|$.

The total number of functions from M to K is k^m. Also, the number of mappings that exclude a specific set of i elements in K is $(k-i)^m$, and there are C(k,i) such sets. There fore
$|A_i| = (k-1)^m$, $|A_i \cap A_j| = (k-2)^m$, and so on.
Now by applying inclusion-exclusion formula we get
$|\overline{A}1 \cap \ldots\ldots\ldots\overline{A}_k|$ = k^m - C (k,1) $(k-1)^m$ + C(k,2) $(k-2)^m$ - ... + $(-1)^{k-1}$C(k,k-1)1^m
Hence the results.

Theorem 6 : Suppose $A_1, A_2,..., A_n$ are n events in a probability space, then

$P(A_1 \cup A_2 \cup \ldots \cup A_n) = \sum_{r=1}^{n}(-1)^{r+1} \sum_{1 \leq i_1 < i_2 < \ldots\ldots\ldots i_r \leq n} (A_{i1} \cap A_{i2} \cap \ldots \cap A_{ir})$

Proof : We have that $A_1 \cup A_2 \cup ... \cup A_n$ means that at least one of the events $A_1, A_2,..., A_n$ occurs. Now, let the ith property be that on outcome belongs to the event A_i. By De Morgan's law, $\overline{A}_1 \cap \overline{A}_2 \cap ... \cap \overline{A}_n$ is the complement of $A_1 \cup A_2 \cup .... \cup A_n$. But the principle of inclusion-exclusion gives :

$|\bar{A}_1 \cap \bar{A}_2 \cap \ldots \cap \bar{A}_n| = N - \sum (-1)r \sum_{1 \le i_1 < i_2 < \ldots i_r \le n} |A_{i_1} \cap A_{i_2} \cap \ldots \cap A_{i_r}|$,

where N is the total number of outcomes.
Now, we divide throughout by N and note that
$P(A_1 \cup A_2 \cup \ldots \cup A_n) = 1 - P(\bar{A}_1 \cap \bar{A}_2 \cap \ldots \cap \bar{A}_n)$, to get theorem

Some Solved Examples of various types

Q.1 If m and n are positive integers, show that $(m+n)! \geq m! + n!$.
$(m+n)! = (m+n)(m+n-1) \ldots (m+1) m!$.
$\Rightarrow (m+n)! - m! = \geq m^n + n! \geq m! [n! + m^n - 1]$
$\Rightarrow (m+n)! - m! - n! \geq n! (m! - 1) + m! (m^n - 1) \geq 0$.

Q.2 How many ways are there to rank n candidates for the job of chief engineer? In how many rankings will Ms. Sheela be in the second place.
A ranking is an ordering of the n candidates. This can be done in $P(n,n) = n!$ ways. The total number of rankings in which Sheela is in 2nd place in $P(n-1, n-1) = (n-1)!$.

Q.3 Consider seven people seated about a round table. How many circular arrangements are possible if at least one of them will not have the same neighbours in any two arrangements?
The two distinct arrangements in Fig.2 show that each has the same neighbours.

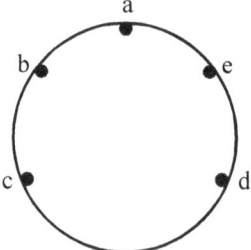 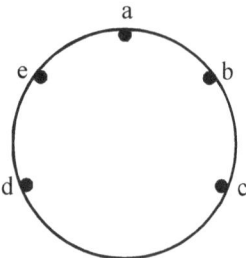

Hence, the total number of circular arrangements $= (7-1)! \times \frac{1}{2} = 360$.

Q.4 If there are 7 men and 5 women, how many circular arrangements are possible in which women do not sit adjacent to each other?
Ans. The seven men can be seated first. This can be done in 6! ways. The women can sit in between two men. There are seven such places. So, the women can sit in $P(7,5)$ ways. Hence the answer is $6! \times P(7,5) = 6! \times {}^7P_5 =$

$$61 \times \frac{7!}{(7-5)!} = \frac{6!\,7!}{2!}$$

Q.5 How many distinct words can be formed from the letters in TANTALISING ? Explain the answer briefly.
Total number of letters = 11
We see that in 'TANTALISING' word T is twice, A is twice, N is twice and L, S & G are once written.

$$\therefore \text{Total number of permutations} = \frac{11!}{2!2!2!2!}$$

$\therefore \dfrac{11!}{8}$ distinct words can be possible.

Q.6 Show that a total 83160 11 letter words can be made from the letters of the word. ABCRADABARA.
Here A is used 5 times, B is used 2 times, R is used 2 times, and C and D are used once. So, that number of words can be made.

$$= \frac{11!}{5!.2!.2!}$$
$$= \frac{11 \times 10 \times 9 \times 8 \times 7 \times 6 \times 5!}{2 \times 2 \times 5!}$$
$= 990 \times 84$
$= 83160.$

Q.7 How many permutations are there of the letters, taken all at a time, of the words (I) ASSESSES (II) PATTIVEERANPATTI ?
In the word 'ASSESSES' we have alphabet A once, B twice and S five times. Thus the numbers of permutations is $8!/1!2!5! = 168$
In the word 'PATTIVEERANPATTI', R, N and V occur once, P, E and I occur thrice. A three and T four times. Thus the required number of permutations is $16!/1!1!2!2!2!3!4! = 9.10$.

Q.8 How many 6-letter words, not necessarily meaningful can be formed from the letters of CARACAS?
Total number of letters = 7, we see that C is two times, A is 3 times, R is once and S are once. If order is not a concern, we consider the solutions of:
$c+a+r+s = 6$, $0 \leq c \leq 2$, $0 \leq a \leq 3$, $0 \leq r, s \leq 1$.

We convert this to the equivalent problem
$x + y + z + t = 1$, where $x = 2-c$, $y = 3-a$, $r = 1-z$, $s = 1-t$

The number of solutions of this are $c(4+1-1, 1) = 4$
There are $(1,0,0,0)$, $(0,1,0,0)$, $(0,0,1,0)$ and $(0,0,0,1)$
The corresponding solution in (c,a,r,s) are $(1,3,1,1)$, $(2,2,1,1)$, $(2,3,0,1)$, $(2,3,1,0)$

Now order becomes important to us. Applying theorem 2, the required number is

$$\frac{6!}{1 3!1!1!} + \frac{6!}{2!2!1 1 1!} + 2\left(\frac{6!}{2!3!1!0!}\right) = 420$$

Q.9 In a ten-question true-false exam, a student must achieve six correct answer to pass. If she selects her answer randomly, what is the probability that she will pass?

The solution is same as the probability of getting at least 6 heads in 10 tosses of a true coin. Hence the answer is:

$$\frac{c(10,6)}{2^{10}} + \frac{c(10,7)}{2^{10}} + \frac{c(10,8)}{2^{10}} + \frac{c(10,9)}{2^{10}} + \frac{c(10,10)}{2^{10}}$$

$$= \frac{^{10}C_6}{2^{10}} + \frac{^{10}C_7}{2^{10}} + \frac{^{10}C_8}{2^{10}} + \frac{^{10}C_9}{2^{10}} + \frac{^{10}C_{10}}{2^{10}}$$

$$= \frac{(210 + 120 + 45 + 10 + 1)}{1024}$$

$$= \frac{193}{512}$$

Q.10 How many permutations can be made out of the letters of the words ASSASSINATION taken all together?

There are 13 letters of which 4 are S, 3 are A, 2 are I and 2 are N.

no. of permutations = $\dfrac{13!}{4!3!2!2!}$

Q.11 In how many ways a garland can be prepared with 7 unlike flowers?

As there is no distinction as regards clockwise or anticlockwise circular permutations

The required no. = $\dfrac{1}{2}$ (7-1)!

$$= \frac{1}{2} \times 6 \times 5 \times 4 \times 3 \times 2 \times 1$$
$$= 360$$

Q.12 Find the no. of arrangement that can be made out of the letters of the words
(i) Independence   (ii) Mathematics   (iii) ALGEBRA

(i) The word Independence have 12 letters in which N are 3, D are 2, E are 4, and rest are different

$\therefore$ total permutations $= \dfrac{12!}{3!2!4!} = 1663200$

(ii) The word Mathematics has 11 letters of which 2 are M, 2 are A, 2 are T and the rest are different.

$\therefore$ required permutations $= \dfrac{11!}{2!2!2!} = 4989600$

(iii) The word ALGEBRA contains 3 vowels A, A, E and 4 consonants L, G, B, R which are different

Vowels can be arranged in $\dfrac{3!}{2!}$ ways

and consonants is 4!

$\therefore$ Total no. of ways $= \dfrac{3!}{2!} \times 4! = 72$

Q.13 Find the number of distinct sets of 5 cards that can be dealt from a deck of 52 cards.

The required number is ${}^{52}C_5 = \dfrac{52!}{5!47!} = \dfrac{52 \times 51 \times 50 \times 49 \times 48}{5 \times 4 \times 3 \times 2 \times 1} = 2{,}598{,}960$

Q.14 Suppose a valid computer password consists of 8 characters, the first of which is the digit 1, 3 or 5. The rest of the 7 characters are either English alphabets or a digit. How many different passwords are possible?
First of all the initial character can be chosen in ${}^3C_1$ ways. Now, there are 26 alphabets and 10 digits to choose the rest of the characters from, and repetition is allowed. So, the total number of possibilities for these characters is $(26+10)^7$ Therefore, by the multiplication principle, the number of passwords possible are $= {}^3C_1 \times 36^7$

Q.15 At a certain office, a committee consisting of one male and one female worker is to be constituted from among 12 men and 15 men workers. In how many distinct ways can this be done?

This can be done in $^{12}C_1 \cdot {}^{15}C_1$ way

Total no. of ways = $^{12}C_1 \times {}^{15}C_1$

$= \dfrac{12}{11(12-1)!} \times \dfrac{15!}{11(15-1)!}$

$= \dfrac{12 \times 11!}{11!} \times \dfrac{15 \times 14!}{14!}$

$= 12 \times 15$
$= 180$

Q.16 In how many ways can a prize winner choose any 3 CDs from the 'Ten Best' list?

Total no. of ways = $^{10}C_3 = \dfrac{10!}{3!(10-3)!}$

$= \dfrac{10 \times 9 \times 8 \times 7!}{6 \times 7!}$

$= 120$ Ans.

Q.17 How many different 7-person committees can be formed, each containing 3 women and 4 men, from a set of 20 women and 30 men?

The total number of ways are $^{20}C_3 \times {}^{30}C_4$

$= \dfrac{20!}{3!(20-3)!} \times \dfrac{30!}{4!(20-4)!}$

$= \dfrac{20 \times 19 \times 18 \times 17!}{6 \times 17!} \times \dfrac{30 \times 29 \times 28 \times 27 \times 26!}{24 \times 26!}$

$= 31, 241, 700$ Ans.

Q.18 In how many ways can a prize winner choose three books from a list of 10 best sellers, if repeats are allowed?

Here, note that a person can choose all three books to be the same title.
$^{10+3-1}C_3 = {}^{12}C_3 = 220$

Q.19 Determine the number of integer solutions to the equation $x_1 + x_2 + x_3 + x_4 = 7$, where $x_i \geq 0$ for all i=1, 2, 3, 4.

The solution of the equation corresponds to a selection, with repetition, of size 7 from a collection of size 4. Hence, there are $^{4+7-1}C_7 = 120$

Q.20 What is the sum of the coefficients of all the terms in the expansion of $(a+b+c)^7$?

The required answer is $\sum \dfrac{7!}{r!s!t!}$ where the summation is over all non-negative integers r, s, t adding to n. But it is also the value of $\sum \dfrac{7!}{r!s!t!} a^r b^s c^t$ for $a = b = c = 1$

So the answer is $(1+1+1)^7 = 3^7$

Q.21 If $^nC_r = {}^nC_{r-1}$ and $^nP_r = {}^nP_{r+1}$ then find n and r

$^nC_r = {}^nC_{r-1}$ (we have)

$^nC_r = {}^nC_{n-(r-1)}$

$\therefore r = n - (r - 1)$

$r = n - r + 1$

$n = 2r-1$ ....(i)

Again $^nP_r = {}^nP_{r+1}$

$\dfrac{n!}{(n-r)!} = \dfrac{n!}{n-(r+1)!}$

$\dfrac{1}{(n-r)!} = \dfrac{1}{(n-r-1)!}$

$\dfrac{1}{(n-r)(n-r-1)!} = \dfrac{1}{(n-r-1)!}$

$\dfrac{1}{(n-r)} = 1$

$n - r = 1$

$n = r + 1$ ....(ii)

from (i) and (ii) $r = 2, n = 3$

Hence n=3 and r=2

Q.22 How many diagonals can be drawn in a polygon of n sides?

We know that a polygon of n sides has n angular points, therefore no. of straight lines obtained by joining any two of n points is $^nC_2$. But these lines include the n sides of the polygon which are not diagonals.

Hence the no. of diagonals

$= {}^nC_2 - n = \dfrac{n(n-1)}{2} - n$

$$= \frac{n(n-3)}{2}$$

Q.23 How many sums can be made of 4 one rupee note, 6 five rupee note and 3 tenners?
Total No. of sums
$= (4 + 1) (6 + 1) (3 + 1) - 1$
$= 5 \times 7 \times 4 - 1$
$= 139$

Q.24 In how many ways can 2 men be selected out of 13 mens?
Required no. $= {}^{13}C_2$
$= 78$

Q.25 Find the mid term in the expansion of $(x-1/x)^{10}$
No. of term in the expansion $= 10 + 1 = 11$ which is odd
$\therefore$ Mid terms will be $T(\frac{11+1}{2})^{th}$ term $= T_6$

$\therefore T_6 = T_{5+1} = {}^{10}C_5 (x)^{10-5} \left(-\frac{1}{x}\right)^5$

$= -{}^{10}C_5$
$= -252$

Q.26 If a, b, c and d are the coefficients of any four consecutive terms in the expansion of $(1+x)^n$ being a +ve integer then prove that $\frac{a}{a+b} + \frac{c}{c+d}$

$= \frac{2b}{b+c}$

Let $(r+1)^{th}$ be any term. It's coefficient is ${}^nC_r$ and $(r-1)^{th}$ term as a then
$a = {}^nC_{r-2}$, $b = {}^nC_{r-1}$, $c = {}^nC_r$, $d = {}^nC_{r+1}$

$\therefore a + b = {}^nC_{r-2} + {}^nC_{r-1} = {}^{n+1}C_r$
$b + c = {}^nC_{r-1} + {}^nC_r = {}^{n-1}C_r$
and $c + d = {}^nC_r + {}^nC_{r+1} = {}^{n-1}C_{r+1}$

$\therefore \frac{a}{a+b} = \frac{{}^nC_{r-2}}{{}^{n+1}C_{r-1}} = \frac{n!}{(r-2)!(n-r+2)!} \cdot \frac{(r-1)!(n-r+2)!}{(n+1)!}$

$$= \frac{r-1}{n+1}$$

Similarly $\frac{b}{b+c} = \frac{r}{n+1}$ and $\frac{c}{c+d} = \frac{r+1}{n+1}$

$$\therefore \frac{a}{a+b} + \frac{c}{c+d} = \frac{r-1}{n+1} + \frac{r+1}{n+1} = \frac{2r}{n+1} = \frac{2b}{b+c} \quad \text{(proved)}$$

Q.27 Sum the series

$$1 + \frac{3}{4} + \frac{3.5}{4.8} + \frac{3.5.7}{4.8.12} + \ldots$$

$1 + \frac{3}{4} + \frac{3.5}{4.8} + \frac{3.5.7}{4.8.12} + \ldots$

$$= 1 + \left(-\frac{3}{2}\right)\left(-\frac{1}{2}\right) + \frac{\left(-\frac{3}{2}\right)\left(-\frac{3}{2}-1\right)}{1.2}\left(-\frac{1}{2}\right)^2 + \ldots$$

$$= \left(1 - \frac{1}{2}\right)^{-3/2}$$

$$= \left(\frac{1}{2}\right)^{-3/2}$$

$$= 2^{3/2}$$

$$= 2\sqrt{2}$$

Q.28 A die is rolled once. What are the probabilities of the following events?
(i) getting an even number
(ii) getting at least 2
(iii) getting at most 2
(iv) getting at least 10

Let the events are denoted by A, B, C and D, then we have X = {1, 2, 3, 4, 5, 6},
A = {2, 4, 6}, B = {2, 3, 4, 5, 6}, C = {1, 2}, and D = ϕ.
Hence, P(A) = 3/6, P(B) = 5/6, P(C) = 2/6, P(D) = 0

Q.29 A coin is tossed n times. What is the probability of getting exactly r heads?

If H and T represent head and tail, respectively, then X consists of sequences of length n that can be formed using only the letters H and T. Therefore $n(X)=2^n$. The event A consists of those sequences in which there are precisely r Heads. So, $n(A) = {}^nC_r$. Hence, the required probability is $\dfrac{{}^nC_r}{2^n}$

Q.30 If a five-digit number is chosen at random, what is the probability that the product of the digits is 20?

If X is the collection of all 5-digit numbers, than $n(X) = 9.10^4 = 90000$. Now, 20 can be factored in only two ways, viz. 1.1.1.4.5 and 1.1.2.2.5, as the product of five factors. Of course, these factors can be permuted to give all possible cases for A. The numbers 5, 4, 1, 1, 1 can be permuted in 5!/1!1!3!=20 ways, and the numbers 5, 2, 2, 1, 1 can be permuted in 5!/1!2!2! = 30 ways. So, n(A) = 20 + 30 = 50

Q.31 Suppose A and B are mutually exclusive events such that P(A) = 0.3 and P(B) = 0.4. What is the probability that
(i) A does not occur?
(ii) A or B occurs?
(iii) Either A or B does not occur?
(i) $P(A^c) = 0.7$
(ii) $P(A \cup B) = 0.7$
(iii) $P(A^c \cup B^c) = P[(A \cap B)^c] = P(\phi^c) = P(X) = 1$

Q.32 A, B, C and D are four candidates for a chairperson's post. Suppose that A is twice as likely to be elected as B, B is thrice as likely as C, and C and D are equally likely to be elected. What is the probability of election of each candidate?

The relative weightages of A, B, C and D are 6.3, 1, 1, respectively. So, $P(A) = \dfrac{6}{11}$, $P(B) = \dfrac{3}{11}$, $P(C) = \dfrac{1}{11} = P(D)$.

Q.33 In a ten-question true-false exam, a student must achieve six correct answers to pass. If she selects her answers randomly, what is the probability that she will pass?

The answer is same as the probability of getting at least 6 heads in 10 tosses of a true coin. Hence, the answer is

$$= \frac{{}^{10}C_6}{2^{10}} + \frac{{}^{10}C_7}{2^{10}} + \frac{{}^{10}C_8}{2^{10}} + \frac{{}^{10}C_9}{2^{10}} + \frac{{}^{10}C_{10}}{2^{10}}$$

$$= \frac{1}{2^{10}} \left[{}^{10}C_6 + {}^{10}C_7 + {}^{10}C_8 + {}^{10}C_9 + {}^{10}C_{10} \right]$$

$$= \frac{(210 + 120 + 45 + 10 + 1)}{1024}$$

$$= \frac{193}{512}$$

Q.34 **What is the probability that a leap year selected at random will have 53 sundays?**
A leap year have total 366 days and has 52 complete weeks and two days extra. These two days may be
i) Monday and Tuesday
ii) Tuesday and Wednesday
iii) Wednesday and Thursday
iv) Thursday and Friday
v) Friday and Saturday
vi) Saturday and Sunday
vii) Sunday and Monday

Out of these 7 cases, the last two are favourable because there is Sunday in each
∴ n(S) = 7   n(E) = 2

∴ $P(E) = \frac{n(E)}{n(S)} = \frac{2}{7}$

Q.35 **A coin is tossed n times what is the possible ways that the head will present an odd number of times.**
On tossing a coin the no. of possible ways are 2 since either head (H) or tail (T) may appear
therefore the total no. of ways of tossing a coin n times
= 2 x 2 x 2 x ..... x n factors
= 2^n
∴ n(S) = 2^n
The head will appear an odd no. of times if it occurs once or 3 times, or 5

times, 7 times and so on
∴ the no. of favourable ways = N(E)
N(E) = $^nC_1 + {}^nC_3 + {}^nC_5 + \ldots$
= 2^{n-1} ($\because {}^nC_1 + {}^nC_3 + \ldots = 2^{n-1}$)

∴ $P(E) = \dfrac{n(E)}{n(S)} = \dfrac{2^{n-1}}{2^n} = \dfrac{1}{2}$

Q.36 **If 10 points are chosen in an equilateral triangle of side 3 cms., show that we can find two points a distance of at most 1 cm.**

By drawing lines parallel to the sides and through the points trisecting each side, we can divide the equilateral triangle into 9 equilateral triangles of side 1 cm. Thus, if 10 points are chosen, at least two of them must lie in one of the 9 triangles.

Q.37 **On 11 occasions of a pair of persons from a group of 5 was called for a function. Show that some pair of persons must have attended the function at least twice.**

5 persons can be paired in $^5C_2$ = 10 ways. Hence, if pairs are invited 11 times, at least one pair must have been invited twice or more times, by the pigeonhole principle.

Q.38 **Four persons were found in a queue, independently, on 25 occasions. Show that at least on two occasions they must have been in the queue in the same order.**

Four persons can be arranged in a line 4!=24 ways. Hence, if we consider 25 occasions, at least on two occasions the same ordering in the queue must have been found, by the pigeonhole principle.

Q.39 **If any set of 11 integers is chosen from 1,......, 20, show that we can find among them two numbers such that one divides the other.**

Consider the following grouping of numbers :
{1,2,4,8,16}, {3,9,18}, {5,15}, {6, 12}, {7,14}, {10,20}, {11}, {13}, {17}, {19}

There are 10 groupings, exhausting all the 20 integers from 1 to 20. If 11 numbers are chosen it is impossible to select at most one from each group. So two numbers have to be selected from some group. Obviously one of them will divide the other.

Q.40 **If 100 balls are placed in 15 boxes, show that two of the boxes must have the same number of balls.**

Suppose $x_1, x_2, ..., x_{15}$ are the number of balls in the boxes, listed in increasing order, assuming that all these numbers are different. Then, clearly, $x_i \geq i - 1$ for i=1, 2, ..., 15. But then $\sum_{i=1}^{15} x_i \geq 14.15/2 = 105$.

But the total number of balls is only 100, a contradiction. Thus, the x_is cannot all be different.

Q.41 Let A be a fixed 10-element subset of {1, 2, ..., 50}. Show that A possesses two different 5-element subsets, the sum of whose elements are equal.

Let H be the family of 5-element subsets B of A. For each B in H, let f(B) be the sum of the numbers in B. Obviously, we must have
$f(B) \geq 1 + 2 + 3 + 4 + 5 = 15$, and $f(B) \leq 46 + 47 + 48 + 49 + 50 = 240$
Hence, $f : H \to T = \{15, 16, ..., 240\}$

Since $|T| = 226$ and $|H| = {}^{10}C_5 = 252$, H contains different sets with the same image under f, that is different sets, the sums of whose elements are equal.

Q.42 The positive integers are grouped into 100 sets. Show that at least one of the sets has an infinity of even numbers. Is it necessary that at least one set should have an infinity of even numbers and an infinity of odd number?

The 100 collections can be considered as containers. There are an infinity of even numbers. When these even numbers are distributed into 100 containers, at least one container must have an infinity of them.

Q.43 How many solutions are there to the equation $x + y + z + w = 20$, where x, y, z, w are positive integers such that $x \leq 6$, $y \leq 7$, $z \leq 8$, $w \leq 9$?

To use inclusion-exclusion, we let the objects be the solutions (in positive integers) of the given equation. A solution is in A_1 if x > 6, in A_2 if y>7, in A_3 if z>8, and in A_4 if w>9. Then what we need is $|\bar{A}_1 \cap \bar{A}_2 \cap \bar{A}_3 \cap \bar{A}_4|$.

Now, to find the total number of positive solutions to the given equation, we rewrite it as $x_1+y_1+z_1+w_1=16$, where $x_1=x+1$, $y_1= y+1$, $z_1 = x+1$, $w_1 = w+1$. Any non-negative solution of this equation will be a positive solution of the given equation. So, the number of positive solutions is
N = C (16+4-1, 16)
= C (19,3)
Similarly, $|A_1| = C(13,3)$, $|A_2| = C(12,3)$, $|A_3|=C(11,3)$.
$|A_4| = C(10,3)$, $|A_1 \cap A_2| = C(6,3)$, $|A_2 \cap A_3| = C(5,3)$, and so on. Note that for

a solution to be in 3 or more A_is, the sum of the respective variables would exceed 20, which is not possible. By inclusion-exclusion, we obtain

$\left| \bar{A}_1 \cap \bar{A}_2 \cap \bar{A}_3 \cap \bar{A}_4 \right|$ = C(19,3) - C(13,3) - C(12,3) - C(11,3) - C(10,3) +C(6,3) + C(5,3) + C(4,3), + C(4,3) + C(3,3) = 217

Q.44 Eight people enter an elevator. At each of four floors it stops, and at least one person leaves the elevator. After four floors, the elevator is empty. In how many ways can this happen?

The number of functions from an 8-element set (The set of people) onto a set of 4-elements (the set of floors). This number is

$$\sum_{i=0}^{4} C(4,i)(4-i)^8 = 4^8 - 4.3^8 + 6.2^8 - 4.1^8$$

Q.45 How many six-digit numbers contain exactly three different digits?

We can choose three digits in $^{10}C_3$ = 120 ways.
The number of 6-digit numbers, using all the three digits, is the same as the number of functions from a 6-set onto a 3-set. This number is
$3^6 - 3.2^6 + 3.1^6 = 540$
Hence, the answer is 120.540=64800. This will include numbers starting with 0 also.

Q.46 What is the probability that a 13-card hand has at least one card in each suit?

If A_i is the choice of cards, none of which are from the ith suit, for i=1, 2, 3, 4 then $|A_i|$ = C(39,13), $|A_i \cap A_j|$ = C(26,13), and C($A_i \cap A_j \cap A_k$) = C(13,13). So, $|\cap A_i|$ = C(52,13)-4C(39,13)+C(4,2)C(26,13)-C(4,3)C(13,13)

Hence, the required probability is $\dfrac{|\cap \bar{A}_i|}{C(52,13)}$.

Q.47 What is the probability that a number between 1 and 10,000 is divisible by neither 2, 3, 5 nor 7?

If A, B, C, D are the integers divisible by 2,3,5,7, respectively, then

$\left| \bar{A} \cap ... \cap \bar{D} \right| = 10,000 - \left[\dfrac{10000}{2}\right] - \left[\dfrac{10000}{3}\right] - \left[\dfrac{10000}{5}\right] - \left[\dfrac{10000}{7}\right]$
$+ \left[\dfrac{10000}{6}\right] + \left[\dfrac{10000}{15}\right] + \left[\dfrac{10000}{35}\right] + \left[\dfrac{10000}{14}\right] + \left[\dfrac{10000}{21}\right] - \left[\dfrac{10000}{7}\right]$

$-\left[\dfrac{10000}{30}\right]-\left[\dfrac{10000}{42}\right]-\left[\dfrac{10000}{105}\right]-\left[\dfrac{10000}{70}\right]+\left[\dfrac{10000}{210}\right]$

= 2285, where [x] denotes the greatest integer $\leq$ x.

Hence, the required probability is $\dfrac{2285}{10000}=0.23$

Q48. A sequence of then bits (0's and 1's) is randomly generated. What is the probability that at least one of the bits is 0? [DEC05, Q2(a)]

Let P(E) be the event that at least one of the bit (0's and 1's) is 0 and then $P(\overline{E})$ will be the event that at least one of the bit is 1

n = 10 (sample space)

$\therefore P(E) = 1 - P(\overline{E}) \qquad\qquad P(\overline{E}) = \dfrac{1}{2^{10}}$

$= 1 - \dfrac{1}{2^{10}}$

$= \dfrac{1}{1024}$

$= \dfrac{1024-1}{1024}$

$= \dfrac{1023}{1024}$

$\therefore$ Probability that selected bit is 0 (zero) = $\dfrac{1023}{1024}$

Q49. Find the number of permutations of the word ATTENDANT.
[DEC05, Q2(b)]

The word ATTENDANT have 9 letters of which 2 are A, N are 2, T are 3 and the rest are different, hence required number of permutations :

$= \dfrac{9!}{2!2!3!} = \dfrac{9\times 8\times 7\times 6\times 5\times 4\times 3!}{2\times 2\times 3!}$

$= 9\times 8\times 7\times 6\times 5$

$= 15120$

CHAPTER-6
PARTITIONS AND DISTRIBUTION

Partition (In view of sets) : Let S be a non empty set and A, B, C.... be non empty subsets of the set S, then the Set P given by P= {A, B, C,..........} is called a partition of the set S, provided (i) $A \cup B \cup C = S$, any two subsets of S, say A and B $\in$ P,
$A \cap B = \phi$
e.g. Let S = {1, 2, 3, 4, 5, 6, 7} and its subsets,
   A = {1, 5}, B = {2, 4, 7}, C = {3, 6}
then P = {A, B, C} is a partition of S, because :
   (i) Each element of P is a non empty set
   (ii) $A \cup B \cup C = S$
   (iii) $A \cap B = \phi, B \cap C = \phi, A \cap C = \phi$

Integer Partition : Any representation of $n \in N$ as a sum of positive integers in non-increasing order is called a partition (or integer partition) of n. Each such partition can be written in the form $n = p_1 + p_2 + ... + p_k$ where $p_1 \leq p_2 \leq .... \leq p_k$
Here $p_1, p_2, ...p_k$ are called the parts of the partition, and the number of parts of the partition is k.

Striling number of second kind : Suppose $n \geq m$. The number of distributions of an distinguishable objects into m indistinguishable containers such that no container is empty is represented by S^m_n. This number is called the Striling number of the second kind.

Some Important points :
(i) $S^m_n = 0$ if $n < m$ for, if the number of containers exceeds the number of ojbects, then it is impossible to have all the containers non-empty.
(ii) $S^n_n = 1$, since there is only one way of putting n distinguishable objects in n indistinguishable boxes so that no box is empty.

(iii) $S_n^1 = 1$.

Some important statement of Theorems (not proof) for problems :

Theorem 1 : $P_n^1 + P_n^2 + \ldots + P_n^k = P_{n+k}^k$, $P_n^1 = 1$, for $1 \le k \le n$, that is, the number of partitions of n with at most k parts is the same s the number of partitions of n+k with exactly k parts.

Theorem 2 : $S_n^m = \dfrac{1}{m!} \sum_{k=0} (-1)^k C(m, m-k)(m-k)^n$, n>m.

Theorem 3 : If $1 < m \le n$, then $S_{n+1}^m = S_n^{m-1} + mS_n^m$

Theorem 4 : $S_{n+1}^m = \sum_{k=0}^{n} C(n,k) \cdot S_k^{m-1}$

Theorem 5 : The number of ways of distributing n distinguishable objects into m indistinguishable containers is $S_n^1 + S_n^2 + \ldots + S_n^m$, where $n \ge m$. (Note that here we do not insist that no container is empty)

Theorem 6 : $P_n^1 + P_n^2 + \ldots + P_n^k = P_{n+k}^k$, $P_n^1 = P_n^n = 1$, for $1 \le k \le n$, that is, the number of partitions of n with at most k parts is the same as the number of partitions of n+k with exactly k parts.

Proof : Let we have $P_n^1 = 1 = P_n^n$

Let M be the set of partitions of n having k for less parts. Let us consider each partition belonging to M as a k-tuple after adding as many zeroes as necessary. Now by definition of mapping we write:

$$(P_1, P_2, \ldots P_m, \underbrace{0, 0, \ldots 0}_{\text{(K-m) times}}) \mapsto (P_1+1, P_2+1, \ldots P_m+1, \underbrace{1, 1, \ldots 1}_{\text{(K-m) times}}), m \le k$$

from M into the Set M' of partitions of n+k into exactly k parts. This mapping is bijective, since
(i) two distinct k-tuples in M are mapped onto two distinct k-tuples in M';
(ii) every k-tuple in M' is the image of a k-tuple of M. This is because if $(p_1, p_2, \ldots, p_k)$ is a partition of n+k with k parts, then it is the image of $(p_1 - 1, p_2 - 1, \ldots, p_k - 1)$ under the above mapping.

Therefore, $|M| = P_n^1 + \ldots + P_n^k = |M'| = P_{n+k}^k$, and the theorem is proved.

Note that $P_n^k = 0$ if n<k, since there is no partition of n with k parts if n<k.

Also, $P_n^n = P_n^1 = 1$

The formula in Theorem 1 is an identity which allows us to find P_n^r from values of P_m^k, where m < n, k ≤ r. This is why it is also called a recurrence relation for P_n^k.

Theorem 1 is very useful. For instance, to verify your count in E2, you can use it because $P_{10}^5 = P_5^1 + P_5^2 + \ldots + P_5^5 = 7$.

From Theorem 1, the P_n^ks may be calculated recursively as shown below in the Table :

Table : P_n^k for $1 \leq n, k \leq 6$

k \ n	1	2	3	4	5	6
1	1	0	0	0	0	0
2	1	1	0	0	0	0
3	1	1	1	0	0	0
4	1	2	1	1	0	0
5	1	2	2	1	1	0
6	1	3	3	2	1	1

In the above table, the second entry in the row corresponding to n = 4 is P_4^2. By Theorem 1, $P_4^2 = P_2^1 + P_2^2$, which is the sum of the entries in the row corresponding to n = 2. Similarly, P_6^3 is the sum of the entries in the row corresponding to n=3.

Some Solved Examples :
Q.1 Show that $S_n^2 = 2^{n-1} - 1$

S_n^2 is the number of partitions of an n-set into two non-empty classes. For this we have to select members of one class. This can be any non-empty subset of the n-set other than the entire st. But the total number of subsets is 2^n. Hence, the required answer is $(2^n-2)/2 = 2^{n-1}-1$. We have to divide by 2 as the two classes are unordered.

Q.2 In how many ways can 1000 one-rupee notes be bundled into a maximum of 20 bundles?

$P^1_{1000} + P^{20}_{1000} + P^{20}_{1020}$

Had the requirement been that there be exactly 20 bundles, then the number would have been P^{20}_{1000}

Q.3 In how many ways can an employer distribute 100 on-rupee notes among 6 employees so that each gets at least one note ?
This is the number of positive solutions of $x_1 + \ldots + x_6 = 100$
So, the required number is $^{100-1}C_{100-6} = {}^{99}c_{94} = 71,523,144$.

Q.4 Show that the number of positive solutions of the equation $x_1 + x_2 + \ldots + x_n = m$ is $^{m-1}C_{m-n}$
If a positive solution is $x_1, x_2, \ldots, x_n$, then it can be written as $X_1+1, X_2+1, \ldots, x_n+1$, where the X_i's are non-negative. Thus, the required number is the number of non-negative solutions of $X_1 + X_2 + \ldots + X_n + n = m$, which is
$^{n+m-n-1}C_{m-n} = {}^{m-1}C_{m-n}$

Q.5 Find the number of ways of placing n people in n-1 rooms, no room being empty

This is S_n^{n-1}. This can be done by putting one person each in n-2 rooms and 2 persons in 1 room. This can be done in $^nC_2$ ways. So $S_n^{n-1} = {}^nC_2$

Q.6 Find the number of m-letter words with distinct letters, all taken from an alphabet with n letters, where n≥m. Is this different from the number of injective mappings from an n-element set, where n≥m? Give reasons for your answer.
If the alphabet has n letters, the m-letter words with distinct letters can be formed in $n(n-1)(n-2)\ldots(n-m+1) = P(n, m)$ ways.
Now, in an injective mapping, images of distinct elements should be distinct. There are n possible images for the first element of the m-set, n-1 possible images for the second, and so on. Hence, the number of such mappings is also $P(n,m)$

Q.7 There are 4 women and 5 men. A committee of three, a president, a vice-president, and a secretary, has to be formed from them. In how

many ways can this be done if
i) the vice-president should be a woman?
ii) exactly one out of the vice-president and the secretary should be a woman?
iii) there is at least one woman in the committee?

(i) We can choose a woman for vice president in 4 ways. To fill the remaining 2 positions we can select 2 from the remaining 8 persons in 8 x 7=56ways. Hence, the required number is 4 x 56=224.

(ii) If the vice-president is a woman (Chosen in 4 ways), others can be selected in 5 x 4 = 20 ways. Similarly, if the woman is a secretary, the others can be chosen in 20 ways. Hence, by the addition and multiplication principles, the answer is 20 x 4 + 20 x 4 = 160.

(iii) Without any restriction, three can be selected in 9 x 8 x 7 = 504 ways. If no woman is to be selected, then it can be done in 5 x 4 x3 = 60 ways. The complement of this = 504-60=444.

Q.8 How many five-digit numbers are even? How many five-digit numbers are composed of only odd digits?
The total number of even numbers is 9 x 10 x 10 x 10 x 5 = 45,000 since the last digit can only by 0, 2, 4, 6, or 8.
The number of 5-digit numbers composed of only odd digits (i.e. 1, 3, 5, 7, 9) is clearly 5^5 = 3125.

Q.9 Find the number of three-letter words that can be formed using the letters of the English alphabet. How many of them end in x? How many of them have a vowel in the middle position?
The 26 letters are distinguishable objects. We have to fill them in three distinguishable containers, viz., the first, second, and third positions of a three-lettered word. The solution is 26^3.
If the last letter is to be x, the number is only 26^2 x 1.
If the middle letter is a vowel, then by the multiplication principle, the answer is 26 x 5 x 26.

Q.10 Use table given along to find the values of P^k_7, $1 \leq k \leq 6$.
$P^1_7 = 1 = P^7_7$

k\n	1	2	3	4	5	6
1	1	0	0	0	0	0
2	1	1	0	0	0	0
3	1	1	1	0	0	0
4	1	2	1	1	0	0
5	1	2	2	1	1	0
6	1	3	3	2	1	1

$P_7^2 = P_5^1 + P_5^2 = 1 + 2 = 3$, from Table.

$P_7^3 = P_4^1 + P_4^2 + P_4^3 = 1 + 2 + 1 = 4$, from Table.

Similarly, $P_7^4 = P_3^1 + P_3^2 + P_3^3 + P_3^4 = 3, P_7^5 = P_2^1 + P_2^2 = 2$ and $P_7^6 = P_1^1 = 1$

Q.11 Write down all the partitions of 7. Also find P_7^4 and P_7^5

Possible partitions of 7 are

Number of parts	Partitions
1	7
2	1+6, 2+5, 3+4
3	1+1+5, 1+2+4, 1+3+3, 2+2+3
4	1+1+1+4, 1+1+2+3, 1+2+2+2
5	1+1+1+1+3, 1+1+1+2+2
6	1+1+1+1+1+2
7	1+1+1+1+1+1+1

From the table, we see that $P_7^4 = 3$, $P_7^5 = 2$.

Q.12 Calculate S_3^2 and S_4^2

$S_3^2 = S_2^1 + 2'.S_2^2 = 1 + 2' \ 3$, and

$S_4^2 = S_3^1 + 2S_3^2 = 1 + 2 \times 3 = 7 \qquad \because \left(S_{m+1}^m = S_n^{m-1} + m.S_n^m\right)$

Q.13 In how many ways can 20 students be grouped into 3 groups?

This can be done in $S_{20}^1 + S_{20}^2 + S_{20}^3$ ways.

Now, we get this number to be

$$1+\frac{1}{2}\sum_{k=0}^{2}(-1)^k C(2,2-k)(2-k)^{20}+\frac{1}{6}\sum_{k=0}^{3}(-1)^k(3,3-k)(3-k)^{20}$$
= 581, 130, 734.

Q.14 In how many ways can 20 identical books be placed in 4 identical boxes?

The answer is $P_{20}^1 + P_{20}^2 + P_{20}^3 + P_{20}^4 = P_{24}^4$

Q15. Give all partitions of 6 and find P_6^3   [JUNE05, Q1(e)]   [4]

No. Of parts	Particularts
1	6
2	1+5 2+4 3+3
3	1+1+4 1+2+3 2+2+2
4	1+1+1+3 1+1+2+2
5	1+1+1+1+2
6	1+1+1+1+1+1

$P_6^3 = P_3^1 + P_3^2 + P_3^3 = 3$

CHAPTER-7

BASIC SYMBOLS

LOGIC

$P \vee Q$	P or Q
$P \wedge Q$	P and Q
$\rceil P$	not P
$P \to Q$	If P, then Q
$P \leftrightarrow Q$	P if and only if Q
$P \equiv Q$	P & Q are logically equivalent
$\forall$	for all
$\exists$	there exists
$\therefore$	therefore
P Q	P XOR Q
$P \uparrow Q$	P nand Q
$P \downarrow Q$	P nor Q

PROPOSITION	READ AS
$\rceil P$	NOT P
$P \wedge Q$	P AND Q
$P \vee Q$	P OR Q
$P \to Q$	IF P THEN Q
$P \leftrightarrow Q$	P IF AND ONLY IF Q
$P \vee Q$	P XOR Q
$P \uparrow Q$	P nand Q
$P \downarrow Q$	P nor Q

BOOLEAN ALGEBRA

$x + y$	x or y
$x \bullet y$	x and y
$\overline{x}$	not of x
$x \oplus y$	x exclusiveOR y
$a \vee b$	a join b
$a \wedge b$	a meet b
l.e.m. (a,b)	least common multiple of a and b
g.c.d. (a,b)	greatest common divisor of a and b
D(n)	Set of divisiors of numbers n

x, y →	$x \bullet y$	AND gate
x, y →	$x + y$	OR gate
x →	$\overline{x}$	NOT gate
x, y →	$\overline{x+y}$	NOR gate
x, y →	$\overline{x \bullet y}$	NAND gate

B_n Boolean Algebra

SET

$\{x, x_2, \ldots x_n\}$	set containing elements $x_1, x_2, \ldots x_n$
$\{x \mid p(x)\}$	set containing those elements x satisfying property $p(x)$
$x \in X$	x is an element of set X
$x \notin X$	x is not an element of X
$\|X\|$ or $n(X)$	Cardinality of set-X
$X \cup Y$	X union Y
$\bigcup_{i=1}^{i=n} X_i$	union of sets $X_1, X_2, \ldots X_n$
$X \cap Y$	x intersect Y
$X - Y$ or X/Y	set difference
X'	complement of X
(x, y)	ordered pair
$(x_1, x_2, \ldots x_n)$	n tuple
$X \times Y$	Cartesian product of X and Y
$X \subset Y$	X is proper subset
$X \not\subset Y$	X is not proper subset of Y
$X \subseteq Y$	X is subset of Y
$X \not\subseteq Y$	X is not subset of Y
$X \supset Y$	X is proper superset of Y
$X \not\supset Y$	X is not proper super of Y
$X \supseteq Y$	X is superset of Y
$X \not\supseteq Y$	X is not superset of Y
$X \triangle Y$	Set symmetric difference
ϕ	Empty set
$\max \{x_2, x_2 \ldots x_n\}$	largest element of set $\{x_1, x_2 \ldots x_n\}$
$\min \{x_1, x_2 \ldots x_n\}$	smallest element of set $\{x_1, x_2 \ldots x_n\}$
$P(X)$	Power set of X
U	Universal set
xRy	(x,y) is in R (x is related to y by the relation R)
x$\not{R}$y	(x,y) is not in R (x is not related to y by the relation R)
R^*	solution set of a relation R.
R^{-1}	inverse relation
$R_2 o R_1$	composition of R_1 and R_2

[x]　　　　　　　equivalence of class of X
X/R　　　　　　a partition of set X determined by the equivalence relation R on X.
≤　　　　　　　 partial order relation

FUNCTIONS & PERMUTATION

f : X→Y　　　function from X to Y
f(x)　　　　　image of x under mapping f
f　　　　　　 function/mapping/transformation
f⁻¹　　　　　 inverse of function f

$\begin{pmatrix} a_1, a_2 \dots\dots\dots a_n \\ p(a_1), p(a_2) \dots\dots p(a_n) \end{pmatrix}$ permutation of a set A = $\{a_1, a_2, \dots a_n\}$

NOTE : Electronic switches may also termed as logic gates.
∧ means conjunction i.e. (and operation)
∨ means disjunction i.e. (or operation)
⇒ means implies
⇔ means implies and reimplies
⌐ | ~ means negation
Note : ∧ means meet and ∨ means join

Gullybaba.com

Simply Scan QR Codes to Jump at Our Latest Products

HELP BOOKS

TYPED ASSIGNMENTS

HAND WRITTEN ASSIGNMENTS

READYMADE PROJECTS

CUSTOMIZED PROJECTS

COMBOS OF BOOKS/ ASSIGNMENTS

Note: The above QR Codes can be scanned and open through QR Code Scanner Application/App of your smart mobile Phone.

SOLVED PAPERS
MCS-13

MCS-013 : DISCRETE MATHEMATICS
JUNE-2005

Note : *There are five questions in this paper. Question number 1 is* **compulsory.** *Attempt any* **three** *questions from the rest.*

Q1(a). What is a conditional proposition ? Give the truth table of such a statement. Further, give one example each of a conditional statement and a statement which is not conditional. [4]

The statement $P \Leftrightarrow Q$ is called conditional proposition, where P and Q are also two statements.

P	Q	P$\Rightarrow$Q
T	T	T
T	F	F
F	T	T
F	F	T

where $Q \Rightarrow P$ is called converse of 'P $\Rightarrow$ Q'
$\neg P \Rightarrow \neg Q$ is called inverse of 'P $\Rightarrow$ Q'
$\neg P \Rightarrow \neg Q$' is called the contropositive of 'P $\Rightarrow$ Q'

Example : There are 2 shops next to each other. One has a sign board that says 'Good pens are not cheap and other has a sign board that says cheap pens are not good. This may be written as :

G $\Rightarrow \neg$C, where G means first statement and C be second statement
    C $\Rightarrow \neg$G

II Part 1(a)

Let p : x + y = xy, where x, y $\in$ R
    q : x $\not< $ 0 $\forall$ x $\in$ Z

here p is true but q is false. This is a statement which is not conditional. Another example may be :
        Ram is God and he is brave.

Here no need to use the word brave for Ram, because God is almighty and brave. Godness of Ram does not depend on braveness.

(b) Using mathematical induction, show that 2n < n! for n ≥ 4. [4]

Let P(n) : 2n < n! for n ≥ 4
If n = 4, P(4) : 2 × 4 < 4!

$$8 < 24 \qquad (\because 4! = 4 \times 3 \times 2 \times 1 = 24)$$

which is true i.e. P(4) is true.
Therefore, P(k) is true i.e. P(k) : 2K < K!
Now we have to show P(K^+) i.e. P(K+1) is true

$\because$ (K+1)! = (K+1) K! > (K+1)2K

= 2K(K+1) > 2(K+1) $\forall$ K ≥ 4

$\therefore$ P(K+1) is true. Therefore, the given statement is true for every value of n, n ∈ N, hence 2n < n!, n ≥ 4 proved.

(c) Find the boolean expression corresponding to the following circuit :

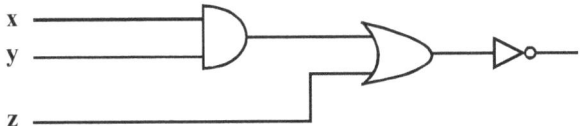

Also obtain the CNF of this expression . [4]
Here the first output is obtained from AND gate i.e. x ∧ y
This is in turn serves as input to OR gate and resultant is (x ∧ y) ∨ z

which enters in NOT gate and becomes $((x \wedge y) \vee z)'$

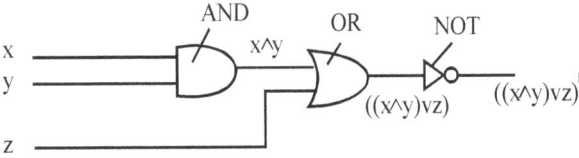

$\therefore$ final output C is as, C = $((x \wedge y) \vee z)'$

CNF is $((x \wedge y) \vee z)'$

$\Leftrightarrow ((x \wedge y)' \wedge z)$

$\Leftrightarrow ((x \vee y) \wedge z)$

Now arrangement of gates will be as :

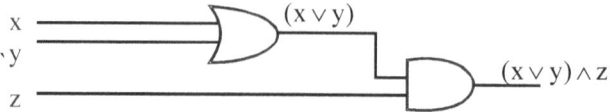

(d) What is a Cartesian product ? Give the geometric representation of the cartesian product of A and B, there A = {2, 3, 4} and B = [1, 4]. [4]

<u>Cartesian Product</u> (def^h) see in Chapter 4 GPH
Now, A = {2, 3, 4}, B = {1, 4}
A × B = {(2,1) (2,4), (3,1), (3,4), (4,1)(4,4)}
<u>Geometrical representation</u>:

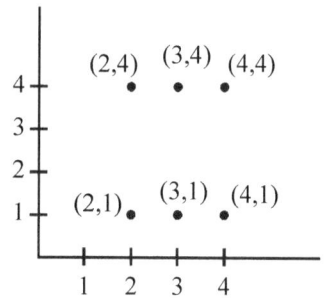

(e) Give all partitions of 6 and find P_6^3 [4]

No. Of parts	Particularts
1	6
2	1+5 2+4 3+3
3	1+1+4 1+2+3 2+2+2
4	1+1+1+3 1+1+2+2
5	1+1+1+1+2
6	1+1+1+1+1+1

$P_6^3 = P_3^1 + P_3^2 + P_3^3 = 3$

Q2(a) Out of a set of 7 men and 6 women, a high level committee of four

persons it to be formed consisting of one President, two Vice Presidents and one secretary. In how many ways can this committee be formed in each of the following situations ?
(i) At least one Vice President should be a woman.
(ii) Only one out of the President and the Secretary should be a man.
(iii) The president should be a woman. [5]

(i) Number of ways in which one Vice President should be selected which is woman :

$$= {}^6C_1 \times {}^{12}C_3 + {}^6C_2 \times {}^{11}C_2$$

$$= \frac{6!}{1!(6-1)!} \times \frac{12!}{3!(12-3)!} + \frac{6!}{2!(6-2)!} \times \frac{11!}{2!(11-2)!}$$

$$= \frac{6 \times 5!}{5!} \times \frac{12 \times 11 \times 10 \times 9!}{6 \times 9!} + \frac{6 \times 5 \times 4!}{2 \times 4!} \times \frac{11 \times 10 \times 9!}{2 \times 9!}$$

$= 6 \times 220 + 15 \times 55$
$= 1320 + 825$
$= 2145$

(ii) Number of ways for selection such that there would be only one out of the President and Secretary should be man :

$$= 2\left[{}^7C_1 \times {}^6C_1 \times {}^{11}C_2 \right]$$

$$= 2 \times \left[\frac{7!}{1!6!} \times \frac{6!}{1!5!} \times \frac{11!}{2!9!} \right]$$

$= 2 \times 7 \times 6 \times 55$
$= 4620$

(iii) Number of ways so that the President should be a woman $= {}^6C_1 \times {}^{12}C_3$

$$= \frac{6!}{1!5!} \times \frac{12!}{3! \times 9!}$$

$$= \frac{6 \times 5!}{5!} \times \frac{12 \times 11 \times 10 \times 9!}{6 \times 9!}$$

$= 6 \times 2 \times 11 \times 10-$
$= 1320$

(b) Explain the difference between a pair of mutually exclusive events and a pair of independent events. Your explanation should include an example of each kind. [5]

Mutually exclusive : Two events E_1 and E_2 of a sample space are mutually exclusive when it is not possible for them to happen simultaneously, for example, let a die be thrown once the event E_1 of getting an even number is : $E_1 = \{2,4,6\}$
The event E_2 of getting an odd no. is $E_2 = \{1,3,5\}$
Since $E_1 \cap E_2 = \varphi$ the two events are mutually exclusive.

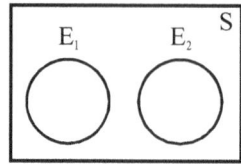

Independent Events : If E_1 and E_2 are two events such that the outcome of E_1 does not affect, nor is affected by outcome of other events E_2 then these two events are said to be independent.

Let there are 4 black and 5 white balls in a bag. If one ball is drawn at random from bag is replaced in the bag before drawing the second ball, then drawing of second ball is independent of first ball.

Q3(a). For any two propositions p and q show that [2]
$\sim (p \lor q) \equiv \sim p \land \sim q$

Table - 1

p	q	p∨q	~(p∨q)
T	T	T	F
T	F	T	F
F	T	T	F
F	F	F	T

Table - 2

p	q	~p	~q	~p∧~q
T	T	F	F	F
T	F	F	T	F
F	T	T	F	F
F	F	T	T	T

From table (1) and (2) we see that ~(pvq) = ~p ∨ ~q proved.

Q3(b). Which of the following statements are true ? Give reasons for your answer. [8]
(i) {0, φ, IGNOU} is a set.
(ii) P (m + n, r) = P (m, r) + P (n, r) for m, n, r ∈ N.
(iii) The Pigeon-hole principle states that r + 1 objects can be placed in r boxes only.
(iv) The contrapositive of the statement "if Manju is unwell, she will not go to school", is "if Manju is well then she will go to school".

(i) {0, φ, IGNOU} is a set because 0, φ and IGNOU are taken as elements. False because set is formed by collecting elements of same type.

(ii) $^{m+n}P_r = {}^mP_r + {}^nP_r$ for m, n, r ∈ N : False because :
$$P(m+n,r) > P(m,r) + P(n,r) \ \forall \ m,n,r \in N.$$
(iii) False, because the Pigeon Hole Theorem states that there are r boxes and (r+1) objects, then there will be a box with more than one objects in it.
(iv) True

Q4(a). Prove or disprove that $\sqrt{11}$ is rational. [5]

We have to prove that $\sqrt{11}$ is irrational but we suppose that $\sqrt{11}$ is a rational number and equal to p/q where q ≠ 0, and there is no factor common to it.

$\therefore \sqrt{11} = \dfrac{p}{q} \Rightarrow p = \sqrt{11} \ q$

$\Rightarrow p^2 = 11 \ q^2$ ....(1)

We see in RHS of (1) 11 is a factor of $11q^2$ and which is an odd integer, therefore, p^2 is also odd. We see p^2 will be odd only when p is odd, and so let p = 11 k where k is only integer. Put this p in (1)

$(11k)^2 = 11q^2$
$121k^2 = 11q^2$
$\therefore q^2 = 11k^2$ which is also an odd number.
$\therefore$ q is an odd number

Now, we see that p and q are both odd integers i.e. there is a common factor 11 $\therefore$ p and q are not indivisible but we have supposed that p and q are indivisible, so there is contradiction, therefore $\sqrt{11}$ be never rational i.e. $\sqrt{11}$ is an irrational number. Hence proved.

(b) What is the duality principle ? Find the dual of

(i) ~ $(x \wedge y) \vee z$;
(ii) $(x \vee y) \wedge (x \wedge z)$.

Duality Principle : Two compounded statements S_1 and S_2 are said to be duals of each other if one can be obtained from other by replacing $\wedge$ by $\vee$ and $\vee$ by $\wedge$. The connections $\wedge$ and $\vee$ are also called dual of each other.

(i) ~$(x \wedge y) \vee z$
 Dual statement is ~ $(x \vee y) \wedge z$
(ii) $(x \vee y) \cap (x \wedge z)$
dual statement is $(x \wedge y) \vee (x \vee z)$

Q5(a). Make a logic circuit of elementary gates corresponding to the boolean expression : [3]

$(x \vee y \wedge z)' \wedge (r \vee z) \vee x$

We know that $\wedge \rightarrow$ and

$\vee \rightarrow$ or

$' \rightarrow$ Not

$(x \vee y \wedge z)' \wedge (r \vee z) \vee x$
which may be written as :
$(x+y.z)' . (r + z) + x$

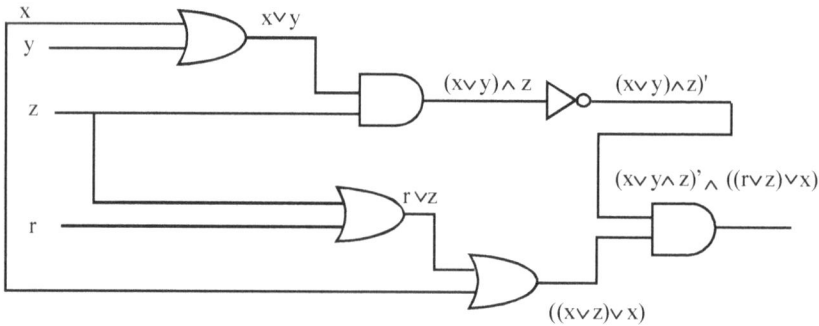

(b) If there are 5 men and 4 women, how many circular arrangements are possible in which women don't sit adjacent to each other ? [2]

The given men can be seated first. This can be done in $(5-1) = 4$ ways = 24 ways. The women can sit in between two men. Then there are fives such places so the women can sit in $5P_4$ ways
∴ Total ways = $4! \times 5P_4$

$$= 24 \times \frac{5!}{(5-4)!}$$
$$= 24 \times 120$$
$$= 4880 \text{ Ans.}$$

(c) In how many ways can 15 students of MCA and 10 students of BCA be grouped into 4 groups? [5]

Total students = 10+15 = 25

No. of ways for selection of 4 groups from 25

Students = $^{25}C_4$

$$= \frac{25!}{4!21!} = \frac{25 \times 24 \times 23 \times 22 \times 21!}{24 \times 21!}$$
$$= 25 \times 23 \times 22$$
$$= 12650$$

MCS-013 : DISCRETE MATHEMATICS
DEC-2005

Note : *There are five questions in this paper. Question number 1 is **compulsory**. Attempt any **three** questions from the rest.*

Q.1 (a) Write the negation of the following statements :
(i) For all x, $x^2 < x$.
(ii) There exists x such that $x^2 = 2$.

(i) for all x, $x^2 < x$
$\quad\quad$ P : $x^2 < x$
$\quad\quad$ ~p : $x^2 > x$ $\quad \forall$ i.e. x be +ve or -ve, x^2 always remains the positive
(ii) p : $x^2 = 2$
$\quad\quad$ ~p : $x^2 \neq 2$, when x $\neq +\sqrt{2}$ or $-\sqrt{2}$

(b) Construct the circuit that produces the following output :
$\quad$ **x' $\wedge$ (y $\vee$ z')'**

Let output is denoted by C = x' $\wedge$ (y $\vee$ z')'

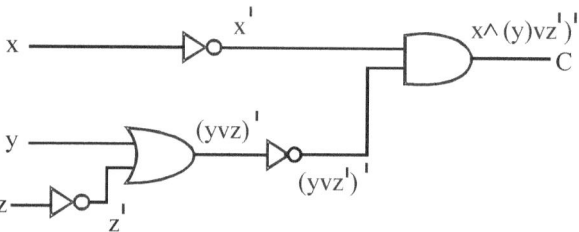

(c) Let A = {1, 2, 3, 4, 5}. Construct a relation R from A to A such that R is reflexive and symmetric but not transitive.

R = {a, b) : a = b^2, a, b $\in$ A}

(d) Prove by induction that $n^3 - n$ is divisible by 3 for all positive integers.
P(n) : n^3-n is divisible by 3
Let n = 2 $\quad\quad$ ($\because$ n $\geq$ 2)
$(2)^3 - 2 = 8-2 = 6$ divided by 3
$\therefore$ P(2) is true.
$\therefore$ The given statement is true for n=k

∴ P(K) : K^3-K is divisible by 3.
It will be true for n = k+1, let us check
∴ P(K) is true
∴ P(K) : $K^3 - K = 3m$ (let m, being any integer)

$P(K^+) = (K+1)^3-(K+1)$
$= (K+1)\{(K+1)^2-1\}$
$= (K+1)\{K^2+1+2K-1\}$
$= (K+1)(K^2+2K)$
$= K^3+2K^2+K^2+2K$
$= K^3+3K^2+2K$
$= \mathbf{K^3-K+3K^2+3K}$
$= (K^3-K)+3(K^2+K)$
$= \mathbf{P(K)+3(K^2+K)}$ **is true**

Since I part of given statement is divisible by 3 because P(K) is true, and part II is multiple of 3 which is always divisible by 3 confirmly.
∴ $P(K^+)$ is true i.e. P(K+1) is true.

∴ We conclude that the given statement is true for every value of n
∴ P(n) is true $\forall$ n $\in$ N, hence proved.

(e) Determine all the integer solutions to
$x_1 + x_2 + x_3 + x_4 = 9$, where $x_i \geq 1$, i = 1, 2, 3, 4.
Equation is $x_1+x_2+x_3+x_4 = 9$, $x_i \geq 1$, i = 1, 2, 3, 4
The solution of the equation corresponds to a selection with repetition of size 9 from a collection of size 4.
Hence there are = $^{4+9-1}C_9$

$= {}^{12}C_9$

$= \dfrac{12!}{9!(12-9)!}$

$= \dfrac{12\times11\times10\times9!}{9!\,3!}$

$= \dfrac{12\times11\times10}{6}$

$= 220$

Q.2(a) A sequence of then bits (0's and 1's) is randomly generated. What is the probability that at least one of the bits is 0?

Let P(E) be the event that at least one of the bit (0's and 1's) is 0 and then $P(\overline{E})$ will be the event that at least one of the bit is 1

n = 10 (sample space)

$\therefore P(E) = 1 - P(\overline{E})$ $\qquad P(\overline{E}) = \dfrac{1}{2^{10}}$

$= 1 - \dfrac{1}{2^{10}}$

$= \dfrac{1}{1024}$

$= \dfrac{1024 - 1}{1024}$

$= \dfrac{1023}{1024}$

$\therefore$ Probability that selected bit is 0 (zero) $= \dfrac{1023}{1024}$

(b) Find the number of permutations of the word ATTENDANT.

The word ATTENDANT have 9 letters of which 2 are A, N are 2, T are 3 and the rest are different, hence required number of permutations :

$= \dfrac{9!}{2!2!3!} = \dfrac{9 \times 8 \times 7 \times 6 \times 5 \times 4 \times 3!}{2 \times 2 \times 3!}$

$= 9 \times 8 \times 7 \times 6 \times 5$

$= 15120$

(c) Write the contrapositive real number, there is a number y such that $y^2 = x$.

Contraposition statement is $y^2 \neq x$

Q.3(a) Give five points inside a square whose side has length 2, prove that two are within a distance of $\sqrt{2}$ to each other.

MCS-13 GPH Solution Book 151

We divide the square in to 4 (r) squares of side length 2 and apply pigeon hole theorem, since thee are 5 points, two will lie in the smaller square (same) and since the side length is 2, then the greatest distance between two points in the small square is the length of the diagonal is $\sqrt{2}$. Hence proved.

(b) Prove that $((p \vee q \to r) \wedge (\sim p)) \to (q \to r)$ is a tautology.

p	q	r	p∨q	(p∨q-->r)	~p	(p∨q-->r)∧(~p)	q-->r	((p∨q)-->r)∧(~p)--->(q-->r)
T	T	T	T	T	F	F	T	T
T	T	F	T	F	F	F	F	T
T	F	T	T	T	F	F	T	T
T	F	F	T	F	F	F	T	T
F	T	T	T	T	T	T	T	T
F	T	F	T	F	T	F	F	T
F	F	T	F	T	T	T	T	T
F	F	F	F	T	T	T	T	T

We see that in the last column there is T, hence

$((p \vee q \to r) \wedge (\sim p)) \to (q \to r)$ is a **tautology**, proved.

Q.4(a) A committee of three individuals decides a proposal. Each individual votes either yes or no. The proposal is passed if it receives at least two yes votes. Design a circuit that determines whether the proposal passes.

For solving the given problem by circuit designing method, we may adopt gates like And, OR, NOT, ...etc. Let individuals are denoted by x, y and z.

Value of variables x, y, z become 1 when first, second and third individual votes and 0 when they do not votes, variables follows value 0 respectively. The conclusion may be given by C,

    C =   proposal will pass if it receives at least two votes
i.e. C =   xy + yz + zx
or C = $(x \wedge y) \vee (y \wedge z) \vee (z \wedge x)$

Circuit diagram is given below:

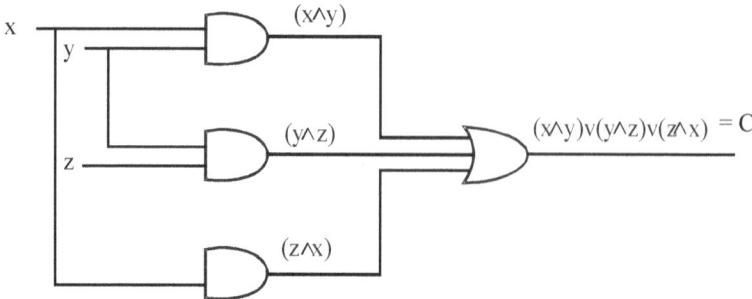

(b) Find the domain and range of the function $\sqrt{\frac{1+x}{1-x}}$, **where x takes real values.**

Let $x = 0$, $f(x) = \sqrt{\frac{1+0}{1-0}} = 1$

$x = 0.5$, $f(x) = \sqrt{\frac{1+0.5}{1-0.5}} = \sqrt{\frac{1.5}{0.5}} = \sqrt{3}$

$x = 1$, $f(x) = \sqrt{\frac{1+1}{1-1}} = \infty$ (not defined)

∴ Domain is (-1, 1)

Range is $\sqrt{n}$, $n \in [0, 20)$

(c) State whether, the following statement is true or false. Give reasons for your answer.
"For any 3 sets A, B and C, and functions.
f : A → B, g : B → C such that g o f is surjective, then f and g must be surjective.
f: A → B,
    g: B → C
  g of : A → C
  g of is surjective (onto)
It means that every element of the Set C is the f-image of at least one element of A therefore gof is onto
f = c.

It is only possible when f: A → B is surjective and
g: B → C is surjective
because if there is f-image of every element B in f of A and of g-image of B in C then A → C must be surjective. Hence given statement is true.

Q.5(a) How many boolean functions of n variables are there? Give reasons for your answer.

Let us first consider the Boolean expression

$$X(x_1, x_2) = x_1 \wedge x_2^1$$

where x_1 and x_2 can take values in
B= (0, 1) where $0 \wedge 1^1 = 0 \wedge 0 = 0 \Rightarrow x(0,1) = 0$

and we may find values of $x_1 \wedge x_2^1$ over B

∴ Let a function $B_2 \to B$,
such that

$$f(e_1, e_2) = X(e_1, e_2) = e_1 \wedge e_2^1$$

So, f is obtained by replacing x_i with e_i in the expression $X(x_1, x_2)$
So, in general way we can say that each Boolean expression $X(x_1, x_2, \ldots x_n)$ in n variables, where each variable can take values from two elements of Boolean Algebra B defines a function:

$f : B^n : f(e_1, \ldots e_n) = X(e_1 \ldots e_n)$ in other words from the counting of product rule it follows that there are 2^n different n-tuples of 0's (zero's) and 1's and Boolean function is an assignment of 0 or 1 to each of these 2^n different n tuples, therefore, there are 2^n different Boolean functions of n variables. Proved.

(b) Check whether the following argument is valid, using a truth table. "If Shalini leaves home before 9.00 AM or it she takes a taxi, she will reach office in time. She did leave after 10.00 AM and she did reach office in time. Therefore, Shalini must have taken a taxi."

For checking the given argument, we will find is there any tautology or not. So,
p = Shalini leaves home before 9:00 A.M.
q = Shalini takes a taxi
r = Shalini reaches office in time

p	q	r	~p	~p∧q	(~p∧r→q)
T	T	T	F	F	T
T	T	F	F	F	T
T	F	T	F	F	T
T	F	F	F	F	T
F	T	T	T	T	T
F	T	F	T	F	T
F	F	T	T	T	T
F	F	F	T	F	T

From the truth table we see that in the last column, there is T in every row, therefore, there is Tautology and our given argument is valid i.e. Shalini must have taken a taxi.

MCS-013: DISCRETE MATHEMATICS
June, 2007

Note : Question number 1 is **compulsory**. Attempt any **three** questions from the rest.

1. (a) A question bank has m questions of type I, n questions of type II and p questions of type III. A question paper consisting of 3 sections is created by randomly picking 15 questions of type I for Section A, 10 questions of type II for Section B and 5 questions of type III for Section C. If 2 question papers have to be created with none of the questions being repeated, find a formula in terms of m, n and p for the numbers of ways in which this can be done.

Ans. Sections in questions paper 3
No. of question of Type I (m) = 15
No. of question of Type II (n) = 10
No. of question of Type III (p) = 5
Total no. of ways of selecting 'I' paper: $^m C_{15} *{}^n C_{10} \times {}^p C_5$
Ways for selecting II paper : $^{m-15} C_{15} \times {}^{n-10} C_{10} \times {}^{p-5} C_5$

Total no. of ways = $\boxed{{}^m C_{15} \times {}^n C_{10} \times {}^p C_5 + {}^{m-15} C_{15} \times {}^{n-10} C_{10} \times {}^{p-5} C_5}$

(b) Show that $(\sim q \wedge (p \to q)) \to \sim p$ is a tautology using truth table.

Ans.

P	q	~p	~q	p→q	~q^(p→q)	(~q^(p→q~))→p
T	T	F	F	T	F	T
T	F	F	T	F	F	T
F	T	T	F	T	F	T
F	F	T	T	T	T	T

(c) Find the number of permutations of the word 'BANDANA' in which no more than 2 As are together.

Ans. Total number of characters in the word = 7
No. of permutation in which 2 As come together are treating 2A's as one (single letter) = No. of ways of selecting A = $3C_2$
$\Rightarrow$ Total no. of permutation = $6! \times 3C_2$
$720 \times 3 = 2160$ ways.

(d) In how many ways can 6 men and 6 women sit on a round table. If each woman and each man sits alternately? What will be number of ways if it is a single line of alternate man and woman?

Ans. Circular Permutation

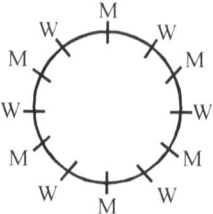

6 men can sit on a round table = (6 – 1)! = 5! = 120 ways
6 women can sit = 6! = 720
Total no. of ways men and women sit alternatively = 120 × 720 = 86400
Row
W M WM WM WM WM W M W
Total no. of ways man can be seated = 6! = 720
Total no. of ways women can be seated = 7! = 5040
Total number of ways = 6! × 7! = 5040 × 720 = 3628800 ways

(e) Let $f = \begin{pmatrix} 1 & 2 & 3 & 4 \\ 2 & 3 & 4 & 1 \end{pmatrix}$ and $g = \begin{pmatrix} 1 & 2 & 3 & 4 \\ 3 & 4 & 1 & 2 \end{pmatrix}$. Check whether f and g commute where $f = \begin{pmatrix} 1 & 2 & 3 & 4 \\ 2 & 3 & 4 & 1 \end{pmatrix}$ means f(1) = 2, f(2) = 3 and so on.

Ans. Multiplication does not hold commutative property
∴ f and g will not commute

(f) Show $A \oplus B$ using Venn diagram.
($A \oplus B$ is the symmetric difference)
Ans.

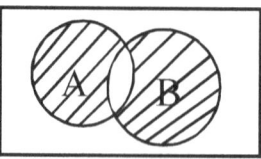

$A \oplus B = (A \cup B) \sim (A \cap B)$

(g) Draw the logic circuit for the boolean expression $((x'_1 \wedge x_2) \vee (x_2 \wedge x'_3))'$.
Ans.

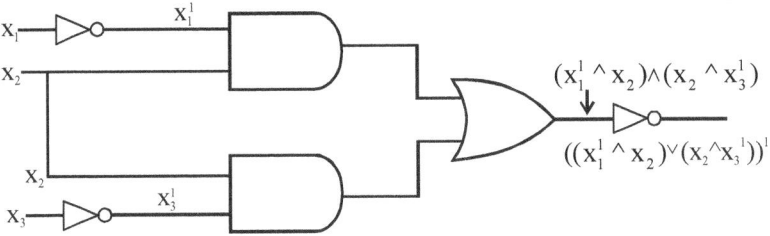

2. (a) Express the following statement using logical quantifiers and logical connectives:
'An applicant is admitted into the MBA programme if the applicant clears the entrance examination and has either a post graduate degree or has worked in a supervisory capacity for at least 3 years.'
Write also the contrapositive.
Ans. A(x): Applicant admitted to M.B.A.
B(x): Cleared entrance exam
C(x): Has a P.G. degree
D(x): Worked in supervisory capacity for allowed 3 years.

Logical statement : $\forall(x)\big((B(x) \wedge C(x) \vee D(x))\big) \to A(x)$ ... (1)

where $\forall(x)$ = universal quantifier

$\wedge$: & $\vee$: OR

Contrapositive = $\boxed{\sim q \to \sim p}$
= Negative of (i) statement
= $\exists x(\sim A(x)) \to \big((\sim B(x) \vee \sim C(x)) \wedge \sim D(x)\big)$

(b) For n $\geq$ 3, prove
$$1^2 + 2^2 + 3^2 + \ldots + b^2 = \frac{b}{6}(b+1)(2b+1)$$

Ans. Basis of induction: n = 3 $\boxed{3^2 + 4^2 + b^2 = \frac{b}{6}(b+1)(2b+1) - 5}$

n = 3 = $3^2 + 4^2 + \text{---} + b^2 = \boxed{\frac{b}{6}(b+1)(2b+1) - 5}$

L.H.S. $3^2 = 9$

R.H.S. $\frac{3(3+1)(6+1)}{6} = \frac{84}{6} = 14 - 5 = 9$ ... (1)

L.H.S. = R.H.S.
Induction Step
b = k

$(k) = 1^2 + 2^2 + 3^2 + \cdots - k^2 = \dfrac{k(k+1)(2k+1)}{6}$ is true ... (2)

for b = k + 1 adding (k + 1)² on both sides

$\Rightarrow 1^2 + 2^2 + 3^2 + \ldots + k^2 + (k+1)^2 = \dfrac{k(k+1)(2k+1)}{6} + (k+1)^2$

$\Rightarrow \dfrac{k(k+1)(2k+1) + 6(k+1)^2}{6}$

$\Rightarrow (k+1)\left[\dfrac{k(2k+1) + 6(k+1)}{6}\right]$

$\Rightarrow \dfrac{k+1}{6}\left[k(2k+1) + 6(k+1)\right] = \dfrac{k+1}{6}\left[2k^2 + 7k + 6\right]$

$\Rightarrow \boxed{\dfrac{(k+1)(k+2)(2k+3)}{6}}$ ... (3)

As P(k) is true hence P(k + 1) is true, we conclude

$1^2 + 2^2 + 3^2 + \ldots + b^2 = \dfrac{b(b+1)(2b+1)}{6}$ is true.

Hence proved

(c) Define equivalence relation. Let A be a set and R be the equivalence relation on A. Define A/R with the help of example.

Ans. A relation R on a set A is called an equivalence relation if and only if following three conditions hold.
* R is reflexive
* R is symmetric
* R is transitive

Let A = {a, b, c} be any set of numbers. The relation R on the set A is defined by equal to (=) is an equivalence relation because

(a) It is reflexive since every element in A is equal to itself.

(b) It is symmetric because $a = b \Rightarrow b = a$

(c) It is transitive as, $a = b$ & $b = c \Rightarrow a = c$

As $\boxed{a}, \boxed{b}, \boxed{c}$ holds the above relation R is equivalent on A.

3. (a) Determine the validity of the following argument using a truth table:

If the train arrives late and there are no taxis in the station, Farida is late for her meeting. Farida is not late for the meeting. The train did arrive late. Therefore, there were taxis at the station.

Ans. p: Train arrives on time

q: Taxis at station
r: Farida reaches for meeting
According to the problem logical statement.
$(\sim p \wedge r) \rightarrow q$, Validity, check if tautology exists

p	q	r	~p	~p ∧ r	(~p ∧ r)→q
T	T	T	F	F	T
T	T	F	F	F	T
T	F	T	F	F	T
T	F	F	F	F	T
F	T	T	T	T	T
F	T	F	T	F	T
F	F	T	T	T	T
F	F	F	T	F	T

→ As the logical statement hold.

This is a valid statement

(b) A die is rolled twice and the sum of the numbers that appear is observed. What is the probability that the sum is either a perfect square or a perfect cube?

Ans. Max number appearing on die = 6
Sum of max on two die = 12

Perfect square = (4, 9) = $\dfrac{2}{36}$

Perfect cube = (8) = $\dfrac{1}{36}$

Total no. of ways either square on cube = $\dfrac{1}{36} + \dfrac{2}{36} = \dfrac{3}{36} = \dfrac{1}{12}$

4. (a) Fill the missing entries in the following truth table:

p	q	p ∨ q	~(p ∧ q)
		T	F
T			T
F	T		
F		F	

Ans.

p	q	p ∨ q	~(p ∧ q)
T	T	T	F
T	F	T	T
F	T	T	T
F	F	F	T

(b) State the distributive properties for seats. Verify any one of them for A = {1, 2, 3, 4}, B = {3, 4, 5} and C = {1, 2, 5}.

Ans. Distributive Laws States

* Union is distributive over intersection

$$A \cup (B \cap C) = (A \cup B) \cap (A \cup C)$$

* Intersection is distributive over union

$$A \cap (B \cup C) = (A \cap B) \cup (A \cap C)$$

Given A = {1, 2, 3, 4, 5}
B = {3, 4, 5}
C = {1, 2, 5}

T.P.T: Intersection is distributive over union

$$A \cap (B \cup C) = (A \cap B) \cup (A \cap C)$$

R.H.S = $(B \cup C) = \{1, 2, 3, 4, 5\}$

$\boxed{A \cap (B \cup C) = \{1, 2, 3, 4, 5\}}$

L.H.S = $(A \cap B) = \{3, 4, 5\}$ $(A \cap C) = \{1, 2, 5\}$

$\boxed{(A \cap B) \cup (A \cap C) = \{1, 2, 3, 4, 5\}}$ = R.H.S

Hence proved

(c) If 50 balls are put in 11 different boxes, show that at least two boxes have the same number of balls.

Ans. Let the 11 boxes be pigeon holes and 50 balls be the pigeons.
According to pigeon hole principle, if n pigeons occupy m pigeon holes and m < n, then atleast two pigeon hole has two or more pigeons roost on it.
⇒ Assign each one ball to 11 box
There exist atleast two boxes that have same number of balls.

5. (a) For the function below, find Boolean expressions in CNF and DNF.

x_1	x_2	x_3	$f(x_1, x_2, x_3)$	
1	1	1	1	$x_1 \wedge x_2 \wedge x_3$
1	0	1	0	
0	1	1	0	
1	1	0	0	
1	0	0	1	$x_1 \wedge x_2 \wedge x_3^1$
0	1	0	1	$x_1^1 \wedge x_2 \wedge x_3^1$
0	0	1	1	$x_1^1 \wedge x_2^1 \wedge x_3$
0	0	0	0	

Ans. DNF =
$$(x_1 \wedge x_2 \wedge x_3) \vee (x_1 \wedge x_{2'} \wedge x_{3'}) \vee (x_{1'} \wedge x_2 \wedge x_{3'}) \vee (x_{1'} \wedge x_{2'} \wedge x_3)$$
CNF =
$$(x_1 \vee x_2 \vee x_3) \wedge (x_1 \vee x_{2'} \vee x_{3'}) \wedge (x_{1'} \vee x_2 \vee x_{3'}) \wedge (x_{1'} \vee x_{2'} \vee x_3)$$

(b) Check whether the boolean expressions $(x_1 \wedge x'_2) \vee x_3$ and $(x_1 \vee x_2) \wedge x'_3$ are equivalent. (Use truth table)

x_1	x_2	x_3	x_2'	x_3'	$(x_1 \wedge x_{2'})$	$(x_1 \wedge x_{2'}) \vee x_3$	$(x_1 \vee x_2)$	$(x_1 \vee x_2) \wedge x_{3'}$
T	T	T	F	F	F	T	T	T
T	T	F	F	T	F	F	T	F
T	F	T	T	F	T	T	T	T
T	F	F	T	T	T	T	T	F
F	T	T	F	F	F	T	T	T
F	T	F	F	T	F	F	T	F
F	F	T	T	F	F	T	F	F
F	F	F	T	T	F	F	F	F
						↓		↓
						1		2

Marked column 1 does not matches 2

$\Rightarrow \boxed{1} \neq \boxed{2}$

(c) 10 persons arrived at a meeting venue carrying identical brief-cases. When they left after the meeting they found on checking that 5 of them got back their own brief-case from the reception while none of the remaining 5 got back their own brief-cases. In how many ways can this happen?

Ans. Total briefcase = 10
No. of person got there briefcase right = 5
No. of person who couldn't get right briefcase = 5
Total no. of ways 5 people couldn't get the briefcase

$$10C_5 = \frac{10!}{5!5!} = \frac{10 \times 9 \times 7 \times 7 \times 6}{120}$$

Total number of ways = 756

MCS-013 : DISCRETE MATHEMATICS
December, 2007

Note : Questions number 1 is **compulsory.** Attempt any **three** questions from the rest.

1. (a) Find the Boolean expression for the following circuit.

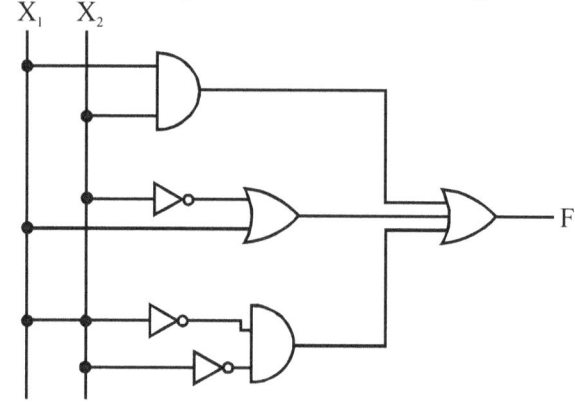

Ans.

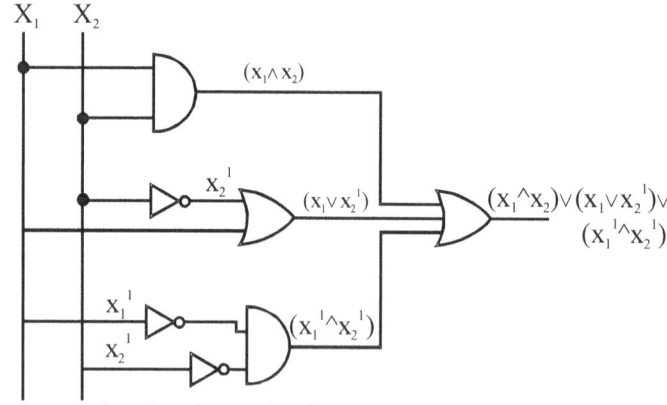

Boolean expression for above circuit
$$(x_1 \wedge x_2) \vee (x_1 \vee x_2^1) \vee (x_{1'} \vee x_2^1)$$

(b) Prove by induction
$$1 + 2 + 2^2 + 2^3 + \ldots + 2^n = 2^{n+1} - 1$$
Ans. Basic step: $n = 1$
$1 = 2^{1+1} - 1 = 1 \Rightarrow$ LHS = RHS

Induction step: Assuming P(n) is true for n = k, we get
$1 + 2 + 2^2 + 2^3 + \ldots + 2^k = 2^{k+1} - 1$
for k +1
Adding 2^{k+1} on both sides
$1 + 2 + 2^2 + 2^3 + \ldots + 2^k + 2^{k+1} = 2^{k+1} - 1 + 2^{k+1}$
$1 + 2 + 2^2 + 2^3 + \ldots + 2^k + 2^{k+1} = 2^{k+1} - 1 + 2^{k+1}$ (as $4 = 2^2$)
$\Rightarrow 2^{k+1} - 1 + 2^{k+1} \Rightarrow 2^k [2^1 + 2^1] - 1 (as\, 4 = 2^2)$
$\Rightarrow 2^k [2^2] - 1 \Rightarrow 2^{k+2} - 1$
As P(k) is true, P(k+1) is true, we conclude = $1+2+2^2+2^3+\ldots 2^k = 2^{k+1} - 1$
Hence Proved

**(c) For the sets A = {a, b, c, d, e}, B = {a, b, e, g, h}
and C = {b, d, e, g, h, k, m, n} prove
$|A \cup B \cup C| = |A| + |B| + |C| - |A \cap B| - |B \cap C| - |A \cap C| + |A \cap B \cap C|$
| X | denotes the number of elements in X.**
Ans. $\Rightarrow$ A, B, C are three finite sets
Using $|P \cup Q| = |P| + |Q|$
$\Rightarrow |P \cup (Q \cup R)| = |P| + |Q \cup R| - |P \cap (Q \cup R)|$
$\Rightarrow |P| + |Q| + |R| - |Q \cap R| - |P \cap (Q \cup R)|$ ... (1)
$\boxed{P \cap (Q \cup R) = (P \cap Q) \cup (P \cap R)}$
$\Rightarrow |(P \cap (Q \cup R))| = |P \cap Q| + |P \cap R| - |(P \cap Q) \cap (P \cap R)|$
$= |P \cap Q| + |P \cap R| - |P \cap Q \cap R|$ ... (2)
Putting (2) in (1)
$(P \cup Q \cup R) = |P| + |Q| + |R| - |P \cap Q| - |P \cap R| - |Q \cap R| + |P \cap Q \cap R|$

**(d) By using truth table show that
$(\sim q \wedge (p \to q)) \to \sim p$
is a tautology.**
Ans.

p	q	~p	~q	p → q	~q ∧ (p → q)	(~q ∧ (p → q)) → ~p
T	T	F	F	T	F	T
T	F	F	T	F	F	T
F	T	T	F	T	F	T
F	F	T	T	T	T	T

(e) In how many ways can a committee of 3 faculty members and 2 students be formed form a group of 7 faculty members and 8 students?
Ans. $7C_3 \times 8C_2 = 35 \times 25 = 980$

(f) Let A = {1, 2, 3, 4, 8} = B. R is a relation from A to B aRb iff a divides b. What are the elements of R?
Ans. A = {1, 2, 3, 4, 8}
B = {1, 2, 3, 4, 8}
R =: A/B
R = {(1, 1) (2, 2) (3, 3) (4, 4) (8, 8), (2, 4), (2, 8), (4, 2), (8, 2), (8, 4)}

2. (a) Let A = B = R (set of real numbers).
Let $f : A \to B$ and $g : B \to C$ be defined by
$f(a) = a - 1$ and $g(b) = b^2$. Find
(i) (fog) (2)
(ii) (gof) (x)
Ans. (i) fog (2) => fo (gof) (2)
gof $\Rightarrow b^2 \Rightarrow fo(2)^2 \Rightarrow fo(4)$
$\Rightarrow f(a) = a - 1 = 4 - 1 = 3$
(ii)
Ans. gof(x)
$f(a) = (x - 1)$
gof $= (x - 1)^2$

(b) Define an equivalence relation. Show that divisibility in the set of real number is not an equivalence relation.
Ans. A relation is said to be equivalent iff
* it is reflexive (i.e. $aRa \in R \forall a \in R$
* it is symmetric (i.e. $(a,b) \in R \Rightarrow (b,a) \in R$)
* it is transitive (i.e. if $aRb \& bRc \Rightarrow aRc$)
Let A = {1, 2, 3} & B = {3, 4, 5, 6}
$R(a,b) \in R$ a divides b
2 divides 4 and 2 divides 6 = (2, 4), (2, 6) $\in R$
3 divides 3 and 3 divides 6 = (3, 3) (3, 6) $\in R$
R = {(2, 4), (2, 6), (3, 3) (3, 6)}
Reflexive : In the above relation, reflexive hold when $aRa \in R$ i.e.
from {3, 3}

but, $\{(1, 1), (2, 2)\} \notin R$
$\Rightarrow$ Reflexivity does not hold ... (1)
Symmetric : $(2, 4) \notin R$ but $(4, 2) \notin R$
and $(3, 6) \in R$ but $(6, 3) \notin R$
$\Rightarrow$ Relation is non symmetric
Transitive : $(2, 4)$ and $(2, 6) \in R$ but $(4, 6) \notin R$ ... (2)
$\Rightarrow$ Relation is not transitive ... (3)
from (1), (2), (3) the equivalence conditions does not hold.
$\Rightarrow$ Relation R is not equivalence

(c) In how many ways can 6 men and 6 women be seated in a row if men and women must occupy alternate seats?
Ans. No. of ways in which 6 men are seated = 6!
No. of ways in which 6 women are seated = 7!
$\Rightarrow$ Total number of ways = 6! × 7! = 3628800

| W | M | W | M | W | M | W | M | W | M | W | M | W |

3. (a) Prove by contrapositive. "Let n be an integer. If n is odd then n^2 is odd."
Ans. $p \Rightarrow$ n be an odd integer
$q \Rightarrow n^2$ is odd
Contrapositive of this statement = "If n^2 is not odd then n is not odd" i.e.
$\sim q \Rightarrow \sim p$

p	q	~p	~q	p→q	~q→~p
T	T	F	F	T	T
T	F	F	T	F	F
F	T	T	F	T	T
F	F	T	T	T	T

As (1) & (2) are same = p→q = ~q→~p
Hence proved

(b) Show that the statements
(p ∧ q ∧ r`∨(p ∧ q`∧r`) and p ∧ r`
are logically equivalent.

p	q	r	q'	r'	p∧r'	p∧q∧r'	p∧q'∧r'	(p∧q∧r')∨(p∧q'∧r')
T	T	T	F	F	F	F	F	F
T	T	F	F	T	T	T	F	T
T	F	T	T	F	F	F	F	F
T	F	F	T	T	T	F	T	T
F	T	T	F	F	F	F	F	F
F	T	F	F	T	F	F	F	F
F	F	T	T	F	F	F	F	F
F	F	F	T	T	F	F	F	F

(c) Draw the logic diagram of
$(p \wedge q) \vee (q \wedge r`)$
Ans.

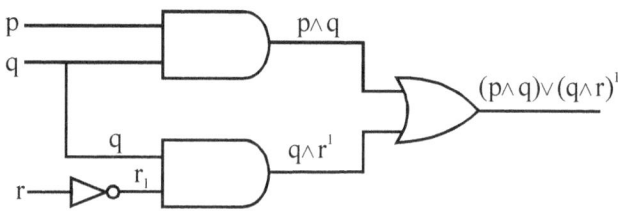

4. (a) Write the DNF and CNF for the Boolean function f(x, y, z).

x	y	z	f(x, y, z)
0	0	0	0
0	0	1	1
0	1	0	1
0	1	1	0
1	0	0	1
1	0	1	0
1	1	0	1
1	1	1	0

Ans. DNF
$f(x_1, x_2, x_3) \Rightarrow (x' \wedge y' \wedge z) \vee (x' \wedge y \wedge z') \vee (x \wedge y' \wedge z') \vee (x \wedge y \wedge z')$
CNF
$(x' \vee y' \vee z) \wedge (x' \vee y \vee z') \wedge (x \vee y' \vee z') \wedge (x \vee y \vee z')$
$\Rightarrow (x' \vee y' \vee z) \wedge (x' \vee y \vee z') \wedge (x \vee y' \vee z') \wedge (x \vee y \vee z')$

(b) Simplify the following Boolean expression.
$(a` \wedge b \wedge c) \vee (a` \wedge b` \wedge c) \vee (a \wedge b \wedge c`) \vee$
$(a` \wedge b` \wedge c`) \vee (a \wedge b` \wedge c`)$

Ans.

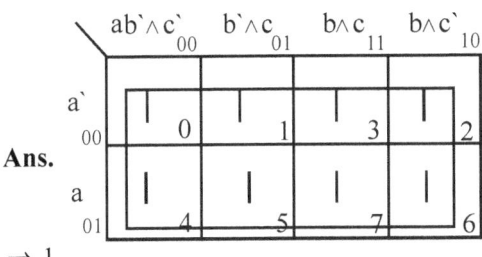

$\Rightarrow 1$

(c) Using truth table show that $p \rightarrow q \equiv p`\vee q$.
Ans.

p	q	p'	p'∨q	p→q
T	T	F	T	T
T	F	F	F	F
F	T	T	T	T
F	F	T	T	T

5. (a) Using Pigeonhole principle show
"If any 14 numbers from 1 to 25 are chosen, then one of them is a multiple of the other."
Ans. Let each number from 1 – 25 = pigeon = 25 pigeon
Assign each of selected 14 pigeon holes via odd part
$\Rightarrow$ Only 11 such pigeon holes
$\therefore$ Out of 11 numbers, two must have same odd part, one of which is a multiple of other.

(b) A basket contains 3 apples, 5 bananas, 4 oranges and 6 pears. A piece of fruit is chosen at random form the basket. Compute the probability that
(i) an apple oar pear is chosen.
(ii) the fruit chosen is not an orange.
Ans. No. of apples = 3
Bananas = 5
Oranges = 4
Pears = 6
Total fruits = 18

(i) $P(apple) = \dfrac{3}{18} = \dfrac{1}{6}$ $P(pear) = \dfrac{6}{18} = \dfrac{1}{3}$

$P(apple \text{ or } pear \text{ chosen}) = \dfrac{1}{6} \times \dfrac{1}{3} = \dfrac{1}{18}$

(ii) $P(\text{Orange}) = \dfrac{4}{18}$

$P(\text{not an orange}) = 1 - \dfrac{4}{18} = \dfrac{14}{18} = \dfrac{7}{9}$

(c) Let R = {(1, 1), (1, 3), (1, 4)} be a relation on A = {1, 2, 3, 4,} It is not reflexive. Why?

Ans. R is said to be reflexive if aRa holds $\forall aRa$ i.e., if $(a,a) \in R \, \forall a \in R$

	1	2	3	4
1	1		1	1
2		×		
3			×	
4				×

$\Rightarrow$ The diagonal elements (2, 2) (3, 3) (4, 4) doesn't exist
$\Rightarrow$ R is not reflexive.

MCS-013: DISCRETE MATHEMATICS
June, 2008

Note: Question number 1 is **compulsory**. Attempt any **three** questions from the rest.

Q1. (a) The chairs of an auditorium are to be labeled with a letter from the English alphabet {A, B, ..., Z} and a positive integer not exceeding 100. What is the largest number of chairs that can be labeled differently?
Ans. The largest no. of chairs will be 26 × 100 = 2600

(b) If R = {(1, 1), (2, 1), (3, 2), (4, 3)}, find R^2, R^4.
Ans. R = {(1, 1), (2, 1), (3, 2), (4, 3)}
R^2 = {((1, 1), (1, 1)), ((1, 1), (2, 1)), ((1, 1), (3, 2)), ((1, 1), (4, 3)), ((2, 1) (1, 1)), ((2, 1), (2, 1)), ((2, 1), (3, 2)), ((2, 1), (4, 3)), ((3, 2), (1, 1)), ((3, 2), (2, 1)), ((3, 2) (3, 2)), ((3, 2), (4, 3)), ((4, 3), (1, 1)), ((4, 3), (2, 1)), ((4, 3), (3, 2)), ((4, 3), (4, 3))}
Similarly $R^4 = R^2 \times R^2$

(c) How many bit strings of length 10 contain at least four 1's?
Ans. No. of bit strings
$$^{10}C_4 + {}^{10}C_5 + {}^{10}C_6 + {}^{10}C_7 + {}^{10}C_8 + {}^{10}C_9 + {}^{10}C_{10}$$

(d) Show that $\neg(q \to r) \land r \land (p \to q)$ is a contradiction.
Ans. $\sim(q \to r) \land r \land (p \to q)$

p	q	r	$q \to r$	$\sim(q \to r)$	$\sim(q \to r) \land r$	$\sim(q \to r) \land (p \to q)$
T	T	T	T	F	F	F
T	T	F	F	T	F	F
T	F	T	T	F	F	F
T	F	F	T	F	F	F
F	T	T	T	F	F	F
F	T	F	F	T	F	F
F	F	T	T	F	F	F
F	F	F	T	F	F	F

Hence column 7 indicate this is contradiction.

(e) Draw the logic circuit for the Boolean function

Y = AB' + (A + B)' + (A' B)'
Ans. Y = AB' + (A + B)' + (A' B)'

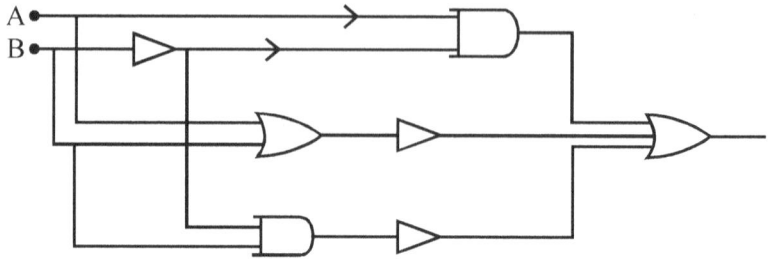

(f) Write down all the partitions of 6. Also find P_6^3 and P_6^4.

Ans. Partition of 6

No. of parts	Particulars
1	6
2	1 + 5, 2 + 4, 3 + 3
3	1 + 1 + 4, 1 + 2 + 3, 2 + 2 + 2
4	1 + 1 + 1 + 3, 1 + 1 + 2 + 2
5	1 + 1 + 1 + 1 + 2
6	1 + 1 + 1 + 1 + 1 + 1

$P_6^3 = 3$

$P_6^4 = 2$

(g) Let Q(x, y) denote "x + y = 0". What are the truth values of the quantification $\exists y \, \forall x \, Q(x,y)$?

Ans. $(\exists y \in I)(\forall x \in N) Q(x, y)$ where I = -x is true statement.

Q2. (a) Find the number of integers between 1 and 250 both inclusive that are not divisible by any of the integers 2, 3, 5 and 7.

Ans. If A, B, C and D are the integers divisible by 2, 3, 5, 7 respectively then

$\left|\overline{A} \cap \overline{B} \cap \overline{C} \cap \overline{D}\right| = 250 - \left[\frac{250}{2}\right] - \left[\frac{250}{3}\right] - \left[\frac{250}{5}\right] - \left[\frac{250}{7}\right]$

$+ \left[\frac{250}{6}\right] + \left[\frac{250}{15}\right] + \left[\frac{250}{35}\right] + \left[\frac{250}{14}\right] + \left[\frac{250}{21}\right] + \left[\frac{250}{10}\right]$

$$-\left[\frac{250}{30}\right]-\left[\frac{250}{42}\right]-\left[\frac{250}{105}\right]-\left[\frac{250}{70}\right]+\left[\frac{250}{210}\right]$$
where [x] denotes the greatest integer

(b) From a club consisting of 6 men and 7 women, in how many ways can we select a committee of 4 persons that has at most one man?

Ans. Committee of 4 persons = $^6C_0 \times ^7C_4 + ^6C_1 \times ^7C_3$

Q3. (a) Show that $p \vee (q \wedge r)$ **and** $(p \vee q) \wedge (p \vee r)$ **are logically equivalent.**

Ans.

p	q	r	$q \wedge r$	$p \vee (q \wedge r)$	$p \vee q$	$p \vee r$	$(p \vee q) \wedge (p \vee r)$
T	T	T	T	T	T	T	T
T	T	F	F	T	T	T	T
T	F	T	F	T	T	T	T
T	F	F	F	T	T	T	T
F	T	T	T	T	T	T	T
F	T	F	F	F	T	F	F
F	F	T	F	F	F	T	F
F	F	F	F	F	F	F	F

From column 5 and column 8

$p \vee (q \wedge r)$ and $(p \vee q) \wedge (p \vee r)$ are logically same.

(b) Prove, by mathematical induction, that
$$\frac{1}{1.2}+\frac{1}{2.3}+\frac{1}{3.4}+\ldots+\frac{1}{n(n+1)}=\frac{n}{n+1}$$

Ans. $p(n) = \frac{1}{1.2}+\frac{1}{2.3}+\frac{1}{3.4}+\ldots+\frac{1}{n(n+1)}=\frac{n}{n+1}$

for n = 1

$\frac{1}{1.2}=\frac{1}{2}$ true for n = 1

for n = 2

$\frac{1}{1.2}+\frac{1}{2.3}=\frac{1}{2}+\frac{1}{6}=\frac{3+1}{6}=\frac{2}{6}$ true for n = 2

it true for n = k

$$p(k) = \frac{1}{1.2} + \frac{1}{2.3} + \ldots + \frac{1}{k(k+1)} = \frac{k}{k+1}$$

for n = k + 1

$$\frac{1}{1.2} + \frac{1}{2.3} + \ldots + \frac{1}{k(k+1)} + \frac{1}{(k+1)(k+2)}$$

$$= \frac{k}{k+1} + \frac{1}{(k+1)(k+2)}$$

$$= \frac{1}{k+1}\left[k + \frac{1}{k+2}\right]$$

$$= \frac{1}{k+1}\left[\frac{k^2 + 2k + 1}{k+2}\right]$$

$$= \frac{1}{k+1}\left[\frac{(k+1)^2}{k+2}\right]$$

$$= \frac{k+1}{k+2} \text{ proved}$$

Hence, true for all k.

(c) How many permutations are there of the letters, taken all at a time, of the word ALLAHABAD?

Ans. No. of permutations are $\dfrac{\lfloor 2}{\lfloor 2 \lfloor 4}$

Q4. (a) Let A = {0, 1, 2, 3 …} and R = {(x, y) : x – y = 3k, k is an integer} i.e., x R y iff x – y is divisible by 3, then prove that R is an equivalence relations.

Ans. R = {(x, y) : x – y = 3k, k is an integer}
R = {(0, 0), (0, 3), (0, 6), (1, 4), (1, 7), (3, 0), (6, 0) …}
Matrix representation

$$\begin{bmatrix} 1 & 0 & 0 & 1 & 0 \\ 0 & 0 & 0 & 0 & 1 \\ 0 & 0 & 0 & 0 & 0 \\ 1 & 0 & 0 & 1 & 0 \end{bmatrix}$$

This relation is not reflexive.
A relation is called equivalence relation if and only if it is reflexive, symmetric and transitive.
So it is not equivalence relation.

(b) A car manufacturer has 5 service centres in a city. 10 identical cars were served in these centres for a particular mechanical defect. In how many ways could the cars have been distributed at various centres?

Ans. Number of ways the cars have been distributed at various centres =

$P_{10}^1 + P_{10}^2 + P_{10}^3 + P_{10}^4 + P_{10}^5$

$= P_{15}^5$

(c) Write the CNF of the function (xy' + xz)' + x'

Ans. $(xy' + xz)' + x'$

$= (xy' \vee xz)' \vee x'$

$= ((xy')' \wedge (x,z)') \vee x'$

$= x' \vee ((xy') \wedge (xz)')$

$= (x' \vee (xy')' \wedge (x' \vee (xz)'))$

Q5. (a) Prove that $\sqrt{7}$ is irrational.

Ans. Let $\sqrt{7}$ is rational no.

$\therefore \sqrt{7} = \dfrac{p}{q}$ where there is no common divisor in p and q and $q \neq 0$

or $7 = \dfrac{p^2}{q^2}$

or $7q = \dfrac{p^2}{q}$

integer = fraction
This is not possible. Our assumption is wrong.

$\sqrt{7}$ is not rational no.

(b) Check whether the following argument is valid:

$((p \to q) \wedge (q \to r)) \Rightarrow (p \to r)$

Ans. $((p \to q) \wedge (q \to r)) \leftrightarrow p \to r$

p	q	r	$p \to q$	$q \to r$	$(p \to q) \wedge (q \to r)$	$p \to r$	$((p \to q) \wedge (q \to r)) \leftrightarrow (p \to r)$
T	T	T	T	T	T	T	T
T	T	F	T	F	F	F	T
T	F	T	F	T	F	T	F
T	F	F	F	T	F	F	T
F	T	T	T	T	T	T	T
F	T	F	T	F	F	T	F
F	F	T	T	T	T	T	T
F	F	F	T	T	T	T	T

Hence this argument is not valid.

(c) Suppose A and B are mutually exclusive events such that P(A) = 0.3 and P(B) = 0.4. What is the probability that
(i) A does not occur?
(ii) A or B occurs?
Ans. P(A) = 0.3
P(B) = 0.4
(i) $P(A^c) = 1 - 0.3 = 0.7$
(ii) $P(A \cup B) = 0.3 + 0.4 = 0.7$

MCS-013: DISCRETE MATHEMATICS
December, 2008

Note: Question number 1 is **compulsory**. Attempt any **three** questions from the rest.

Q1. (a) Show that
$((p \vee \sim q) \wedge (\sim p \vee \sim q)) \vee q$ **is a tautology.**
Ans.

p	q	~p	~q	$p \vee \sim q$ $= R_1$	$\sim p \vee \sim q$ $= R_2$	$R_1 \wedge R_2$ $= R_3$	$R_3 \vee q$
T	T	F	F	T	F	F	T
T	F	F	T	T	T	T	T
F	T	T	F	F	T	F	T
F	F	T	T	T	T	T	T

Hence, this is tautology.

(b) Find the Boolean expression for the circuit.

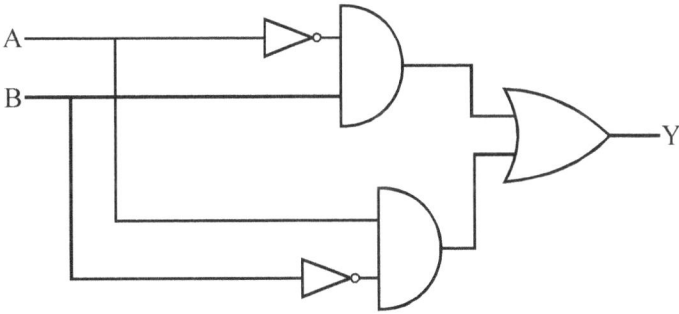

Ans. Boolean Expression
$(A' \wedge B) \vee (A \wedge B')$
or $(\sim A \wedge B) \vee (A \wedge \sim B)$

(c) Show that $n^2 > 2n + 1$ for $n \geq 3$ by Mathematical Induction.
Ans. The given statement P(n) is
$n^2 > 2n + 1$
for n = 3

(175)

$3^2 > 2 \times 3 + 1$ true for n = 3
for n = 4
$4^2 > 2 \times 4 + 1$ true for n = 4
Hence, true for n = k
$p(k) = k^2 > 2k + 1$
Now for n = k + 1
$(k + 1)^2 = k^2 + 2k + 1$
$> 2k + 1 + 2k + 1$
$= 2k + 2 + 2k$
$> 2(k + 1) + 1$
$(k + 1)^2 > 2(k + 1) + 1$

(d) In a class of 80 students, 50 students know English, 55 know French and 46 know German. 37 know English and French, 28 know French and German, 7 students know none of the languages. Find how many students know exactly 2 languages.

Ans. E is the set of students who know English
F is the set of students who know French
G is the set of students who know German

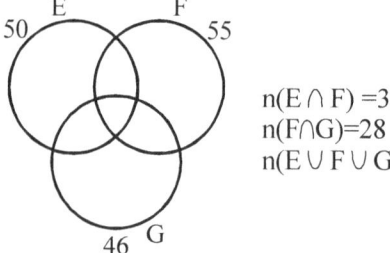

$n(E \cap F) = 37$
$n(F \cap G) = 28$
$n(E \cup F \cup G) = 80 - 7$
- Not Sufficient data.

(e) For the set A = {1, 2, 3, 4}, let R be a relation on A defined as R = {(1, 2), (1, 3), (2, 4), (3, 2)}.
Find whether (i) R is reflexive (ii) R is symmetric (iii) R is transitive.
Ans. The matrix representation of relation is

$$M_R = \begin{bmatrix} 1 & 1 & 0 \\ 0 & 0 & 1 \\ 1 & 0 & 0 \end{bmatrix}$$

(i) R is reflexive if and only if $m_{ii} = 1$
So it is not reflexive.

(ii) R is symmetric if $m_{ij} = 1$ then $m_{ji} = 1$
So it is not symmetric.

(iii) R is transitive if $m_{ij} = 1$ and $m_{jk} = 1$
Then $m_{ik} = 1$.
or, $M_R^2 = M_R$
Hence this condition is also not satisfied. So it is not transitive.

(f) Let $f : R \to R$, $g : R \to R$ be defined by f(x) = x + 1, g(x) = 2x² + 3. Then find (fog) (x) and (gof) (x).

Ans. f(x) = x + 1
g(x) = 2x² + 3
(fog) (x) = f(g(x))
= f(2x² + 3)
= 2x² + 3 + 1
= 2x² + 4
(gof) (x) = g(f(x))
= 2(x + 1)² + 3
= 2(x² + 2x + 1) + 3
= 2x² + 4x + 5

Q2. (a) Show that contrapositives are logically equivalent, i.e. $p \to q \equiv \sim p \to \sim q$.

Ans. $p \to q \equiv \sim p \to \sim q$

p	q	~p	~q	$p \to q$	$\sim q \to \sim p$
T	T	F	F	T	T
T	F	F	T	F	F
F	T	T	F	T	T
F	F	T	T	T	T

From column 3 and 4 both are equivalent.

(b) X is a family of sets and R is a relation on X, defined by "x is subset of y". Find whether the relation R is: (i) symmetric and (ii) transitive.

Ans. $R = \left[xRy \,|\, (x,y) \in x \times \& \text{ "x is subset of y"} \right]$

(i) If x is subset of y then it is not necessary to y is subset of x

So it is not symmetric.

(ii) If x is subset of y and y is subset of z then x must be subset of z
So it is transitive.

(c) If A = {a, b}, B = {p, q, r}, then find A × B and B × A.
Ans. A = {a, b}
B = {p, q, r}
A × B = {(a, p), (a, q), (a, r), (b, p), (b, q), (b, r)}
B × A = {(p, a), (p, b), (q, a), (q, b), (r, a), (r, b)}

Q3. (a) Make a truth table for the Boolean expression :
$p \wedge (p \to q)$
Further, from the table, find DNF for the expression.
Ans. $p \wedge (p \to q)$

p	q	$p \to q$	$p \wedge (p \to q)$
T	T	T	T
T	F	F	F
F	T	T	F
F	F	T	F

DNF of given expression
$p \wedge (p \to q)$
$\equiv p \wedge (\sim p \vee q)$
$\equiv (p \wedge \sim p) \vee (p \vee q)$

(b) Prove that A − B = $A \cap B'$.
Ans. A − B = $A \cap B'$
Let A − B = {x}
$\Leftrightarrow x \in A - B$
$\Leftrightarrow x \in A$ and $x \notin B$
$\Leftrightarrow x \in A$ and $x \in B'$
$\Leftrightarrow x \in A \cap B'$
Hence $A - B \subset A \cap B'$ and
$A \cap B' \subset A - B$
$\therefore A - B = A \cap B'$ proved.

(c) Convert each of the following into language of symbols:
(i) Ram and Abdul are fond of football.
(ii) If it rains then I take the umbrella with me.
Ans. (i) Let p = Ram is fond of football
q = Abdul is fond of football
∴ $p \wedge q$

(ii) p = It rains
q = I take the umbrella with me
∴ $p \to q$

Q4. (a) For $f: R \to R$,
$$f(x) = \begin{cases} 3x-4, & x > 0 \\ -3x+2, & x \leq 0 \end{cases}$$
Find $f^{-1}(0)$.
Ans. $f: R \to R$
$$f(x) = \begin{cases} 3x-4, & x > 0 \\ -3x+2, & x \leq 0 \end{cases}$$
The function is f(x) = – 3x + 2 for $x \leq 0$
f o f⁻¹(x) = – 3 f⁻¹(x) + 2 = x
or –3 f⁻¹(x) = x – 2
or $f^{-1}(x) = \dfrac{x-2}{-3}$
$f^{-1}(0) = \dfrac{0-2}{-3} = \dfrac{2}{3}$

(b) How many five digit numbers are even? How many five digit numbers are composed of only odd digits?
Ans. 5 digit even number is 9 × 10 × 10 × 10 × 5 = 45000
5 digit (odd) number is 5 × 5 × 5 × 5 × 5 = 3125

(c) Consider the set {a, b, c, d}. In how many ways can two letters be selected out of these letters when repetition is allowed?
Ans.

4	4

4 × 4 = 16 ways

Q5. (a) Show that
$(p \wedge (\sim p \vee q)) \vee (q \wedge \sim (p \wedge q)) \equiv q.$

Ans. $(p \wedge (\sim p \vee q)) \vee (q \wedge \sim (p \wedge q))$
$\equiv ((p \wedge \sim q) \vee (p \wedge q)) \vee (q \wedge (\sim p \vee \sim q))$
$\equiv (p \wedge q) \vee ((q \wedge \sim p) \vee (q \wedge \sim q))$
$\equiv (p \wedge q) \vee (q \wedge \sim p)$
$\equiv (q \wedge p) \vee (q \wedge \sim p)$
$\equiv q \wedge (p \vee \sim p)$
$\equiv q \wedge T$
$\equiv q$

(b) Find the number of ways of placing 8 similar balls in 5 numbered boxes.

Ans. The number of ways of placing 8 similar balls in 5 numbered boxes
$= 8 \times 7 \times 6 \times 5 \times 4$
$= 6720$

(c) Show that $\sqrt{7}$ is an irrational number.

Ans. Let $\sqrt{7}$ is rational number

and $\sqrt{7} = \dfrac{p}{q}$

where p and q have not common divisor and $q \neq o$

or $7 = \dfrac{p^2}{q^2}$

or $7q = \dfrac{p^2}{q}$

integer = fraction
it is not possible

Hence $\sqrt{7}$ is irrational number.

MCS-013: DISCRETE MATHEMATICS
June, 2009

Note: Question number **1** is **compulsory**. Attempt **any three** questions from the rest.

Q1. (a) A coin is tossed n times. What is the probability of getting exactly r heads?
Refer to Page No.-122, Q.No.-29

(b) Construct the logic circuit for the expression $(x'_1 \wedge x_2) \vee (x_1 \vee x_3)$

Ans. Logic circuit for the expression

x_1	x_2	x_3	$x'_1 \wedge x_2$	$x_1 \vee x_3$	$(x'_1 \wedge x_2) \vee (x_1 \vee x_3)$
T	T	T	F	T	T
T	T	F	F	T	T
T	F	T	F	T	T
T	F	F	F	T	T
F	T	T	T	T	T
F	T	F	T	F	T
F	F	T	F	T	T
F	F	F	F	F	F

(c) Let the function $f : R \to R$ be defined by

$$f(x) = \begin{cases} 3x - 12 & \text{for } x > 3 \\ 2x^2 + 3 & \text{for } -2 < x \leq 3 \\ 3x^2 - 7 & \text{for } x \leq -2 \end{cases}$$

Find out $f^{-1}(5)$.

Ans. $f(x) = \begin{cases} 3x - 12 & \text{for } x > 3 \\ 2x^2 + 3 & \text{for } -2 < x \leq 3 \\ 3x^2 - 7 & \text{for } x \leq -2 \end{cases}$

The function is $f(x) = 3x - 12$ for $x > 3$
$fof^{-1}(x) = 3f^{-1}(x) - 12 = x$ or, $3f^{-1}(x) = x + 12$

or, $f^{-1}(x) = \dfrac{x+12}{3}$ $\therefore f^{-1}(5) = \dfrac{5+12}{3} = \dfrac{17}{3}$

(d) Universal Set $U = \{1, 2, \ldots 9\}$ and given the sets $A = \{1, 2, 3, 4, 5\}$, $B = \{4, 5, 6, 7\}$. Find (i) $A \backslash B$ (ii) $A \oplus B$

Ans. $U = \{1, 2, 3, 4, \ldots, 9\}$
$A = \{1, 2, 3, 4, 5\}$
$B = \{4, 5, 6, 7\}$

(i) A \ B = {1, 2, 3}
(ii) $A \oplus B = (A - B) \cup (B - A)$
$= \{1, 2, 3\} \cup \{6, 7\}$ = {1, 2, 3, 6, 7}

(e) Consider a set A = {a, b, c} and the relation R on A defined by R = {(a, a), (a, b), (b, c), (a, c)}. Find whether R is:
(i) reflexive (ii) symmetric (iii) transitive. Justify your answers with reason.

Ans. The matrix representation of relation is MR

	a	b	c
a	1	1	1
b			1
c			

1. R is reflexive if and only if m_{ii} = 1. So, it is not reflexive
2. R is symmetric if m_{ij} = 1 then m_{ji} = 1. So, it is not symmetric
3. R is transitive if m_{ij} = 1 and m_{jk} = 1. This condition is satisfied. So, it is transitive.

(f) A survey among 1000 people, 595 are democrats, 595 wear glasses and 550 like ice-creams. 395 of them are democrats who wear glasses, 350 of them are democrats who like ice-cream. 400 of them wear glasses and like ice-cream and 250 have all the three properties.
(i) How many of them are not democrats do not wear glasses and do not like ice creams?
(ii) How many of them are democrats who do not wear glasses and do not like ice cream?

Ans. n(d) Total No. of non democrats = 1000 − 595 = 405
n(dG)' Non-democrats not wearing glass = 595 − 395 = 200
n(dI)' Non-democrats not like Ice-cream
= 405 − (595 − 395) = 205
(i) According to Formula,
No. of not democrats do not wear glasses and do not like ice-creams = −405 + 205 + 205 = 5
(ii) No. of democrats who do not wear glasses and do not like ice-cream
= −345 + (200 + 245) = −345 + 445 = 100

Q2. (a) Show that $(P \wedge (P \to Q)) \to q$ is tautology.

Ans.

P	Q	P→Q	$P \wedge (P \to Q)$	$(P \wedge (P \to Q)) \to Q$
T	T	T	T	T
T	F	F	F	T
F	T	T	F	T
F	F	T	F	T

Hence, $(P \wedge (P \to Q)) \to Q$ is tautology.

(b) Find DNF form of $\neg(P \vee Q) \leftrightarrow P \wedge Q$

Ans. $\neg(P \vee Q) \Leftrightarrow (P \wedge Q)$
$\equiv \neg P(P \vee Q) \wedge (P \wedge Q) \vee ((P \vee Q) \wedge \neg(P \wedge Q))$
$\equiv (\neg P \wedge \neg Q \wedge P \wedge Q) \vee ((P \vee Q) \wedge \neg P \wedge \neg Q)$
$\equiv (\neg P \wedge \neg Q \wedge P \wedge Q) \vee ((P \vee Q) \wedge \neg P) \vee ((P \vee \neg Q) \wedge \neg Q)$
$\equiv (\neg P \wedge \neg Q \wedge P \wedge Q) \vee (P \wedge \neg P) \vee (Q \wedge \neg P) \vee (P \wedge \neg Q) \vee (Q \wedge \neg Q)$

(c) Prove that for every positive integer n, $n^3 + n$ is even.

Ans. $P(n) : n^3 + n$ is even. Let $n = 1$
$1^3 + 1 = 1 + 1 = 2$ is even. Put $n = 2$
$2^3 + 2 = 10$ is even. $\therefore P(2)$ is true
$\therefore$ Thus given statement is true for $n = k$
$\therefore P(k) = k^3 + k$ is even
It will be true for $n = k + 1$. Let us check,
$\therefore P(k)$ is true
$\therefore P(k) = k^3 + k$
$P(k + 1) = (k + 1)^3 + (k + 1)$
$= (k + 1) \{(k + 1)^2 + 1\} = (k + 1) \{k^2 + 2k + 1 + 1\}$
$= (k + 1) \{k^2 + 2k + 2\} = k^3 + 2k^2 + 2k + k^2 + 2k + 2$
$= k^3 + k + 3k^2 + 3k + 2 = (k^3 + k) + (3k^2 + 3k + 2)$
Since, part 1 of the given statement is even and part 2 in also even.
$\therefore P(k + 1)$ is true.
$\therefore P(n)$ is true $\forall n \in N$. Hence proved.

Q3. (a) By the principal of mathematical induction, prove that: $3^{2n+1} + (-1)^n 2$ is divisible by 5.

Ans. Let $P(n) + 3^{2n+1} + (-1)^n 2$ be divisible by 5 for $n = 1$
$P(1) = 3^{2 \times 1+1} + (-1)^1 .2 = 3^3 + (-1) 2 = 27 - 2 = 25$ which is divisible by 5.
Let statement is true for $n = k$ i.e. $P(k)$ is true.
$P(k) : 3^{2k+1} + (-1)^k 2$ is divisible by 5.
Now, we have to test $P(k+1)$ is true.
$P(k + 1) = 3^{2(k+1)+1} + (-1)^{k+1} .2$
$= 3^{2k+2+1} + (-1)^k (-1)^1 .2 = 3^{2k+1+2} + (-1)^k (-1)^1 2 = 3^{2k+1} 3^2 + (-1)^k (-1)^1 2$
$= 3^{2k+1} (10 - 1) + (-1)^k (-2) = -3^{2k+1} - 2 (-1)^k + 10.3^{2k+1}$
$= -(3^{2k+1} + 2 (-1)^k) + 10.3^{2k+1} = -P(k) + 10.3^{2k+1}$
Both are divisible by 5. Hence proved.

(b) Define the De-Morgan's Laws for complementation. Further illustrate with suitable examples.

Ans. De Morgan's Law: For any two set A and B (i) $(A \cup B)^1 = A^1 \cap B^1$
(ii) $(A \cap B)^1 = A^1 \cup B^1$ It can also expressed as

$A - (B \cup C) = (A - B) \cap (A - C)$
$A - (B \cap C) = (A - B) \cup (A - C)$

(c) Find the coefficient of x^2y^4 in $(x + y)^6$.

Ans. Binomial Theorem:
$(a + b)^n = a^n + {}^nc_1 a^{n-1} b^1 + {}^nc_2 a^{n-2} b^2 + {}^nc_3 a^{n-3} b^3 + \ldots + b^n$

Coefficient of x^2y^4 in $(x + y)^6 = \dfrac{\lfloor 6}{\lfloor 2 \lfloor 4} = \dfrac{6 \times 5 \times \lfloor 4}{2 \times 1 \times \lfloor 4} = 15$

Q4. (a) Write down all the partitions of 7. Also find P_7^4 and P_7^5.

Refer to Page No.-133, Q.No.-11

(b) By contrapositive method of proof, prove that x^2 is divisible by 4, then x is even.

Ans. Suppose x is odd, then x^2 is not divisible by 4.
$x^2 \neq 4$ $\quad x = \pm 2$
Here, x is not a odd no. Hence, we can say x^2 is divisible by 4, then x is even.

(c) Establish the equivalence $(P \rightarrow Q) \rightarrow (P \wedge Q) = (7P \rightarrow Q) \wedge (Q \rightarrow P)$
Refer to Page No.-10, Q.No.-13(v)

Q5. (a) If set X has 10 members, how many members do P(X) has? How many members of P(X) are proper subset of X?

Ans. Set x has 10 members
P(x) has 2^n members i.e. $2^{10} = 1024$. 2^{11} members of P(x) are proper subset of x.

(b) Prove that $A - (A - B) = A \cap B$

Ans. Let A = {1, 2, 3, 4, 5}
B = {4, 5, 6, 7, 8}
L.H.S. = A − (A − B)
= A − {1, 2, 3} = {4, 5}
R.H.S. = $A \cap B$ = {4, 5}
Thus, L.H.S. = R.H.S. Hence proved

(c) Let $f : R \rightarrow R$ is defined by $f(x) = ax + b$ where $a, b, x \in R$ and $a \neq 0$. Show that f is invertible and find the inverse of f.

Ans. Let $f(x) = ax + b$ $\qquad$ Let $y = f(x)$

$\Rightarrow y = ax + b \Rightarrow x = \dfrac{y-b}{a} = \dfrac{1}{a}(y-b) \Rightarrow f^{-1}(y) = \dfrac{1}{a}(y-b)$

Thus, we define $f^{-1} : R \rightarrow R . f^{-1}(y) = \dfrac{1}{a}(y-b)$

MCS-013: DISCRETE MATHEMATICS
December, 2009

Note: Question number 1 is **compulsory**. Attempt **any three** questions from the rest.

Q1. (a) If a five digit number is chosen at random, what is the probability that the product of the digits is 20?
Refer to Page No.-122, Q.No.-30

(b) If the function $f : R \to R$ is defined by $f(x) = x^2$. Find $f^{-1}(4)$ and $f^{-1}(-4)$.
Ans. $f(x) = x^2 \qquad f^{-1}(x) = \sqrt{x}$
$f^{-1}(4) = \sqrt{4} = \pm 2 \qquad f^{-1}(-4) = \sqrt{-4} = \sqrt{(2i)^2} = 2i$

(c) In how many ways can a prize winner choose any 3 CDs from the 'Ten Best' list?
Refer to Page No.-118, Q.No.-16

(d) Let A = {a, b} be a given set and R = {(a, a), (b, a), (b, b)} and S = {(a, b), (b, a), (b, b)} be relations on A. Then verify $(SoR)^{-1} = R^{-1} \text{ o } S^{-1}$.
Ans. R = {(a, a), (b, a), (b, b)}
S = {(a, b), (b, a), (b, b)}
SOR = {(a, a), (b, a), (b, b)}
$(SOR)^{-1}$ = {(a, a), (a, b), (b, b)}
S^{-1} = {(b, a), (a, b), (b, b)}
R^{-1} = {(a, b), (a, b), (b, b)}
$R^{-1} \text{ O } S^{-1}$ = {(a, b), (a, b), (b, b)}
Thus, we can say $(SOR)^{-1} = R^{-1} \text{ O } S^{-1}$

(e) Find contrapositive of:
(i) If John is a poet than he is poor.
(ii) Only if Marc studies will he pass the test.
Ans. (i) If John is not poor, then he is not a poet.
(ii) If Marc does not study, then he will not pass the test.

(f) Show that $2^n > n^3$ for $n \geq 10$.
Ans. We write P(n) for the predicate $2^n > n^3$
Step 1: For n = 10

$2^{10} = 1024$ which is greater than 10^3.
Therefore, P(10) is true.
Step 2: Let P(k) is true for an arbitrary $k \geq 10$. Thus, $2^k > k^3$.
Step 3: We want to prove that $2^{k+1} > (k + 1)^3$
$2^{k+1} = 2.2^k > 2k^3$ by our assumption.

$$> \left(1+\frac{1}{10}\right)^3 .k^3, \text{ since } 2 > \left(1+\frac{1}{10}\right)^3$$

$$\geq \left(1+\frac{1}{k}\right)^3 .k^3, \text{ since } \geq 10 = (k+1)^3$$

Thus, P(k + 1) is true if P(k) is true for $k \geq 10$. Therefore, by the principal of mathematical Induction P(n) is true $\forall\ n \geq 10$.

Q2. (a) Construct the logic circuit of $x_1' \wedge (x_2 \vee x_3')$.

Ans. Logic circuit for $x_1^1 \wedge (x_2 \vee x_3^1)$

x_1	x_2	x_3	$(x_2 \vee x_3^1)$	$x_1^1 \wedge (x_2 \vee x_3^1)$
T	T	T	T	F
T	T	F	T	F
T	F	T	F	F
T	F	F	T	F
F	T	T	T	T
F	T	F	T	T
F	F	T	F	F
F	F	F	T	T

(b) What is the sum of the coefficients of all the terms in expansion of $(a + b + c)^7$?
Refer to Page No.-119, Q.No.-20

(c) Show that the relation 'equality' defined in any set A is an equivalence relation.
Ans. A relation R on a set A is called an equivalence relation if and only if
(i) R is reflexive $\left(\forall\ a \in R, (a,a) \in R\right)$
(ii) R is symmetric $(a, b) \in R \Rightarrow (b, a) \in R,\ \forall\ a,b \in A$ and
(iii) R is transitive $(a, b) \in R$ and $(b, c) \in R \Rightarrow (a, c) \in R$, for all $a, b, c \in A$.

One of the most trivial examples of an equivalence relation is equality for any element (a, b, c) in a set A.
(i) $a = a$ i.e. reflexivity
(ii) $a = b \Rightarrow b = a$ i.e. symmetric
(iii) $a = b$ and $b = c \Rightarrow a = c$ i.e. transitivity

Q3. (a) Find CNF form of $\neg(P \vee Q) \leftrightarrow P \wedge Q$.

Ans. $\neg(P \vee Q) \Leftrightarrow P \wedge Q$

$\equiv (\neg(P \vee Q) \rightarrow (P \wedge Q)) \wedge ((P \wedge Q) \Rightarrow \neg(P \vee Q))$

$\equiv ((P \vee Q) \vee (P \wedge Q)) \wedge (\neg P \wedge Q) \vee (\neg P \wedge \neg Q)$

$\equiv ((P \vee Q \vee P) \wedge (P \vee Q \vee Q)) \wedge ((\neg P \vee \neg Q) \vee (\neg P \wedge \neg Q))$

$\equiv (P \vee Q \vee P) \wedge (P \vee Q \vee Q) \wedge (\neg P \vee \neg Q \vee \neg P) \wedge (\neg P \vee \neg Q \vee \neg Q)$

(b) Establish the equivalence for $P \rightarrow (Q \rightarrow R) = (P \wedge Q) \rightarrow R$.

Ans. Taking L.H.S.

$P \rightarrow (Q \rightarrow R)$

$\equiv P \rightarrow (\neg Q \vee R) \equiv \neg P \vee (\neg Q \vee R) \equiv \neg P \vee \neg Q \vee R \equiv \neg P \vee \neg Q \vee R$

$\equiv \neg(P \wedge Q) \vee R \equiv (P \wedge Q) \rightarrow R$ = R.H.S. Proved

(c) Show that if any 20 people are selected, then we may choose a subset of 3 so that all 3 were born on the same day of the week?

Ans. 20 people can be selected to 7 days of the week. Then at least $\left\lceil \dfrac{20}{7} \right\rceil + 1 = 4$ of them must have been born on the same day.

Q4. (a) Use induction to prove that any integer $n \geq 2$ **is either a prime or a product of primes.**

Refer to Page No.-33, Q.No.-11

(b) Given the set A = {1, 2, 3}, consider a relation in A : R = {(1, 1), (2, 2), (2, 3), (3, 2)}. Find RoR.

Ans. A = {1, 2, 3}

R = {(1, 1), (2, 2), (2, 3), (3, 2)}
ROR = {(1, 1), (2, 3), (2, 2), (3, 2), (3, 3)}

(c) In how many ways can 12 balloons be distributed at a Birthday party among 10 children?

Ans. This is required number of positive solution of $x_1 + x_2 + x_3 \ldots + x_{10} = 12$. So required number is $c(12 - 1, 12 - 10) = c(11, 2) = 55$

Q5. (a) Among the integers 1 to 200 find the number of integers that are
(i) divisible by 2 or 5 or 9.
(ii) not divisible by 5.

Ans. (i) A1 = Set of integer between 1 and 200 that is divisible by 2
A2 = Set of integer between 1 and 200 that is divisible by 5
A3 = Set of integer between 1 and 200 that is divisible by 9

$A1 = \left[\dfrac{200}{2}\right] = 100 \qquad A2 = \left[\dfrac{200}{5}\right] = 40 \qquad A3 = \left[\dfrac{200}{9}\right] = 22$

$|A1 \wedge A2 \wedge A3| = \dfrac{200}{2 \times 5 \times 9} = 2$

$|A1 \cup A2 \cup A3| = |A1| + |A2| + |A3| - |A1 \cap A2| - |A1 \cap A3|$

$- |A2 \cap A3| + |A1 \cap A2 \cap A3| = 100 + 40 + 22 - 20 - 11 - 4 + 2$

$= 140 + 2 - 11 - 2 = 129$

(ii) A1 = Set of integers between 1 to 200 i.e. divisible by 5

$A1 = \left|\dfrac{200}{5}\right| = 40$. Total number of integer N = 200. Therefore, total number of integer which is not divisible by 5 is 200 – 40 = 160.

(b) Determine the number of integer solutions to the equation $x_1 + x_2 + x_3 + x_4 = 7$, where $x_i \geq 0$ for all i = 1, 2, 3, 4.
Refer to Page No.-149, Q.No.(e)

(c) Find the number of ways of placing n people in n - 1 rooms, no rooms being empty.
Refer to Page No.-131, Q.No.-5

MCS-013: DISCRETE MATHEMATICS
June, 2010

Note: *Question Number **1** is **compulsory**. Attempt any **three** questions from the rest.*

Q1. (a) Show that $\sim(A \cup B) = \sim A \cup \sim B$

Ans. $\sim(A \cap B) = \sim A \cup \sim B$

Let x be the element of $\sim(A \cap B)$

$\Rightarrow x \in \sim(A \cap B)$

$\Rightarrow x \notin A \cap B$

$= X \notin A \text{ and } X \notin B$

$= x \in A' \text{ or } x \in B'$

$= x \in A' \cup B'$

$= x \in \sim A \cup \sim B$

So, $\sim(A \cap B) \subseteq \sim A \cup \sim B$ ....(i)

again

$\sim(A) \cup \sim B$

$= x \notin A \text{ or } x \notin B$

$= x \notin A \cap B$

$= x \in (A \cap B)$

or, $\sim A \cup \sim B \subseteq \sim(A \cap B)$ ....(ii)

So, $\sim(A \cap B) = \sim A \cup \sim B$

(b) In how many ways can three examinations be scheduled within a five-day period so that no two examinations are scheduled on the same day.

Ans. $5p_3 = \dfrac{\lfloor 5}{\lfloor 5-3} = \dfrac{5 \times 4 \times 3 \times \lfloor 2}{\lfloor 2} = 60 \text{ ways}$

(c) Using principle of Mathematical Induction or otherwise, prove that

$$1^2 + 3^2 + 5^2 + \ldots + (2n-1)^2 = \frac{n(2n-1)(2n+1)}{3}$$

Ans. Let statement S(n)

$$S(n): 1^1 + 3^2 + 5^2 + \ldots + (2n-1)^2 = \frac{n(2n-1)(2n+1)}{3}$$

Basic step :
S(1) is true

LHS $= S(1) = (2 \times 1 - 1)^2 = 1$

RHS $= \dfrac{1(2 \times 1 - 1)(2 \times 1 + 1)}{8} = 1$

LHS = RHS
So, S(1) is true
Induction step: Let S(n) is true for all n = K

$$S(K): 1^1 + 3^2 + 5^2 + \ldots + (2K-1)^2 = \frac{K(2K-1)(2K+1)}{3}$$

Now we have to prove that S(n) is true for n = K + 1

$$S(K+1): 1^1 + 3^2 + 5^2 + \ldots + (2K-1)^2 + (2K+1)^2 = \frac{(K+1)(2K+1)(2K+3)}{3}$$

LHS: $\underbrace{1^2 + 3^2 + 5^2 + \ldots + (2K-1)^2}_{} + (2K+1)^2$

$= \dfrac{K(2K-1)(2K+1)}{3} + (2K+1)^2$

$= \dfrac{(2K+1)\{2K^2 - K + 6K + 3\}}{3}$

$= \dfrac{(2K+1)(2K^2 + 5K + 3)}{3} = \dfrac{(2K+1)(K+1)(2K+3)}{3}$

$= \dfrac{(K+1)(2K+1)(2K+3)}{3}$

So, by principle of mathematical induction S(n) is true $\forall$ natural number.

(d) Construct the truth table for following: $(p \to q) \leftrightarrow (\overline{p} \vee q)$

Ans.

p	q	$\overline{p}$	$p \to q$	$\overline{p} \vee q$	$(p \to q) \leftrightarrow \overline{p} \vee q$
T	T	F	T	T	T
T	F	F	F	F	T
F	T	T	T	T	T
F	F	T	T	T	T

(e) Consider a set X = [2, 3, 4] and the Relation defined on X by.
R = {(2, 2) (2, 3) (3, 3) (3, 4) (2, 4) (4, 4)}.
Find whether R is :
(i) Reflexive, (ii) Symmetric, (iii) Transitive, Justify your answer
Ans. (i) Reflexive
This relation is reflexive because (2,2) (3,3), and (4,4) is in relation.

(ii) Symmetric

R is not symmetric because (2,3) is in relation but (3,2) is not $(2,3) \notin R$
$(3,2) \notin R$

(iii) Transitive
R is transitive $(2,3) \in R$

$(3,4) \in R$

$\Rightarrow (2,4) \in R$

(f) Construct the logic circuit for expression
$(y_1 \vee y_2) \wedge (y_3 \wedge y_4)'$.
Ans.

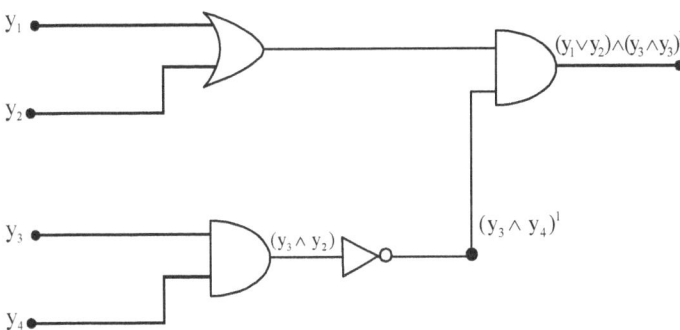

Q2. (a) (i) Calculate $S_3^2 + S_4^2$ where 'S' Denotes Stirling Number of the second kind.
Refer to Page No.-133, Q.No.-12

(ii) Verify that $[(p \wedge q) \vee \sim p]$ **is contradiction.**
Ans.

p	q	~p	p∧q	(p∧q)∨~p
T	T	F	T	F
T	F	F	F	F
F	T	T	F	F
F	F	T	F	F

from col. S the expression has all False Values so it is contradiction.

(b) If A = {1, 2, 3, 4, 5} B = {3, 5, 6, 7} Then find $A \triangle B$

Ans. A = {1, 2, 3, 4, 5}
B = {3, 5, 6, 7}

$A \triangle B = (A \cup B) - (A \cap B)$
$A \cup B = \{1, 2, 3, 4, 5, 6, 7\}$

$A \cap B = \{3, 5\}$

$A \triangle B = (A \cup B) - (A \cap B)$
$= \{1, 2, 4, 6, 7\}$

Q3. (a) A survey among the students of college. 65 Study Hindi, 45 study Spanish, and 42 study Japanese, Further 20 study Hindi and Spanish, 25 study Hindi and Japanese, 15 study Spanish and Japanese and 8 study all the languages.
(i) How many students are studying at least, one language?
(ii) How many students are studying only Hindi.
Ans. Let the sets of student who read Hindi – H
" " " " " " " " " Spanish – S
" " " " " " " " " Japanese – J

n(H) = 65   n(H∩S) = 20
h(J) = 42   n(H∩J) = 25
n(S) = 45   n(S∩J) = 15
n(H∩S∩J) = 8

(i) h(H∪S∪J) = n(H) + n(S) + n(J) – n(H∩S) – n(S∩J) – n(H∩J) + h(H∩S∩J)
= 65+45+42-20-15-25+8
=100

(ii) = h(H) – n(H∩S) – n(H∩J) + n(H∩S∩J)

no. of student studying only Hindi
= 65-20-25+8
= 28

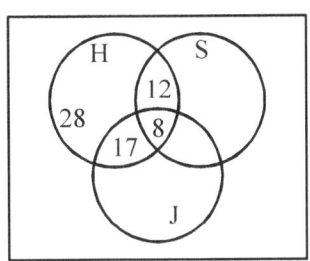

(b) If $f = \begin{bmatrix} 1 & 2 & 3 & 4 \\ 1 & 3 & 4 & 2 \end{bmatrix} g = \begin{bmatrix} 1 & 2 & 3 & 4 \\ 2 & 3 & 4 & 1 \end{bmatrix} h = \begin{bmatrix} 1 & 2 & 3 & 4 \\ 4 & 2 & 1 & 3 \end{bmatrix}$

be permutation on A = {1, 2, 3, 4, 5}. Then find (f o g) o h.

Ans. $\text{fog} \Rightarrow \begin{bmatrix} g = \begin{pmatrix} 1 & 2 & 3 & 4 \\ 2 & 3 & 4 & 1 \end{pmatrix} \\ f = \begin{pmatrix} 1 & 2 & 3 & 4 \\ 1 & 3 & 4 & 2 \end{pmatrix} \end{bmatrix}$

$\Rightarrow \begin{bmatrix} g = \begin{pmatrix} 1 & 2 & 3 & 4 \\ 2 & 3 & 4 & 1 \end{pmatrix} \\ \downarrow \downarrow \downarrow \downarrow \\ f = \begin{pmatrix} 2 & 3 & 4 & 1 \\ 3 & 4 & 2 & 1 \end{pmatrix} \text{ruffled} \end{bmatrix}$

$\text{fog} \Rightarrow \begin{pmatrix} 1 & 2 & 3 & 4 \\ 3 & 4 & 2 & 1 \end{pmatrix}$

Now $(\text{fog}) \circ h \Rightarrow \begin{bmatrix} h = \begin{pmatrix} 1 & 2 & 3 & 4 \\ 4 & 2 & 1 & 3 \end{pmatrix} \\ (\text{fog}) = \begin{pmatrix} 1 & 2 & 3 & 4 \\ 3 & 4 & 2 & 1 \end{pmatrix} \end{bmatrix}$

$$h = \begin{pmatrix} 1 & 2 & 3 & 4 \\ 4 & 2 & 1 & 3 \end{pmatrix}$$

$$\downarrow \downarrow \downarrow \downarrow$$

$$(fog) = \begin{pmatrix} 4 & 2 & 1 & 3 \\ 1 & 4 & 3 & 2 \end{pmatrix} \text{ruffled}$$

$$(fog) \circ h \Rightarrow \begin{pmatrix} 1 & 2 & 3 & 4 \\ 1 & 4 & 3 & 2 \end{pmatrix}$$

Q4. (a) Show that $n^3 + 2n$ is divisible by 3 for all $n \geq 1$ by induction.

Ans. Set $S(n) : n^3 + 2n$ is divisible by by 3 for all $n \geq 1$
Basic step:
Let $S(1)$ is true then
$S(1): (1)^3 + 2 = 3$ is divisible by 3
So, $S(1)$ is true
Induction step: Let $S(n)$ is true for all $n = K$.
$S(K): K^3 + 2K$ is divisible by 3
LHS $= (K+1)^3 + 2K+1$
   $= K^3+1+3K^2+3K+2K+2$
   $= (K^3+2K)+3(K^2+K+1)$
   $= 3d+3(K^2+k+1)$
   $= 3(d+R^2+K+1)$
Since $S(K+1)$ is multiple of 3 so, it is divisible by 3. So by induction $S(n)$ is true for all $n = K+1$

(b) If $A = R - \{3\}$ and $B = R - \{1\}$ and function $f: A \to B$ is defined by $f(x) = \dfrac{x-2}{x-3}$. Show that 'f' is Invertible and find its Inverse.

Ans. $f(x) = \dfrac{x-2}{x-3}$

Any function is invertible if it in <u>one-one onto</u> so, first we check it is one-one or not

let $f(a) = \dfrac{a-2}{a-3}$, $f(b) = \dfrac{b-2}{b-3}$

Now $f(a) = f(b)$

$$\frac{a-2}{a-3} = \frac{b-2}{b-3}$$

$\Rightarrow ab - 3a - 2b + 6 = ab - 3b - 2a + 6$

$= -3a+2a = -3a+2b = -a = -a$

So it is one to one, now check it is onto or not

$y = f(x) = \dfrac{x-a}{x-3}$

$\Rightarrow xy - 3y = x - 2$

$x(y-1) = -2 + 3y$

$x = \dfrac{-2+3y}{y-1}$

For all value of y there is an image in x so it is onto. Therefore f(x) is invertible

$f^{-1}(x) = \dfrac{3x-2}{x-1}$

(c) Look at following figure. Is it a function? Why/why not?

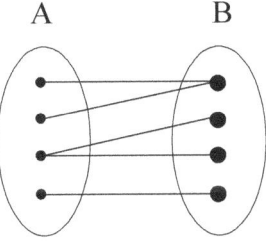

Ans. A function is a special kind of 'Relation'. It can be 'one to one' or 'many to one', but it can not be 'one to many'. But in the given figure, it shows a 'one to many' mapping from A to B. so, it is not a function.

Q5. (a) In the Binomial Expansion $\left(3x - \dfrac{1}{3x}\right)^8$. Find the Term Independent of 'x'.

Ans. Given Term is $= \left(3x - \dfrac{1}{3x}\right)^8$

So, General Term

$T_{r+1} 8_{C_r} (3x)^{8-r} \left(-\dfrac{1}{3x}\right)^r$

$= (-1)^r \, 8_{C_r} \, (3)^{8-r} \cdot x^{16-2r} \left(\dfrac{1}{3^r \cdot x^r} \right)$

$= (-1) \cdot 8c_r \cdot 3^{8-r} \cdot x^{16-2-r}$

putting $16 - 2^r = 0 \Rightarrow r = 8$

So $\Rightarrow r = 8$, 9th terms is independent of x and its value is

$T_9 = (-1)^8 \cdot 8c_8 \cdot 3^{8-0} \cdot x^0 = 1 \cdot \dfrac{\lfloor 8}{\lfloor 8 \, \lfloor 8-8} \cdot 6561.1 = 6561$

(b) Suppose we have seven rooms and want to assign four of them to four programmers as offices and use the remaining three rooms for computer terminals. In how many ways this can be done.
Ans.

$7c_4 + 4c_3 = \dfrac{\lfloor 7}{\lfloor 4 \cdot \lfloor 4-3} + \dfrac{\lfloor 4}{\lfloor 4 \cdot \lfloor 4-3} = \dfrac{7 \times 6 \times 5 \times \lfloor 4}{\lfloor 4 \times 3 \times 2 \times 1} + 1 = 35 + 1 = 36$ ways

(c) Define relation mathematically.
Ans. Let A and B be sets, A binary relation from A to B is a subset of A x B. In other words, a binary relation from A to B is a set R of ordered pairs where the first element of each ordered pair comes from A and the second element comes from B. we use notation a Rb to denote that (a, b) $\in$ R and a $\cancel{R}$ b to denote (a, b) $\notin$ R. When (a, b) belongs to R, a is laid to be related to b by R.

MCS-013: DISCRETE MATHEMATICS
December, 2010

Note: *Question Number 1 is **compulsory**. Attempt any **three** questions from the rest.*

Q1. (a) Use the principal of Mathematical Induction to show that

$$a + ar + ar^2 + \ldots\ldots\ldots + ar^{n-1} = \frac{a(r^n - 1)}{(r - 1)}$$

Ans. Let statement $S(n) = a + ar + ar^2 + ----- + ar^{n-1} = \dfrac{a(r^n - 1)}{r - 1}$

$S(n) = a + ar + ar^2 + ----- + ar^{n-1} = \dfrac{a(r^n - 1)}{r - 1}$

Basis step:-
Let $S(1)$ is true
LHS
$S(1) = a \cdot r^{1-1} = ar^0 = a$
RHS
$\dfrac{a(r^1 - 1)}{(r - 1)} = a$
LHS=RHS

Induction step:-
Now assume that $S(K)$ is true for all natural number

$S(K) = a + ar + ar^2 + ---ar^{K-1} = \dfrac{a(r^K - 1)}{(r - 1)}$

Now we have to verify that $S(K+1)$ is true for all natural number.

$S(K+1) = \underbrace{a + ar + ar^2 + ----- ar^{K-1}}_{S(K)} + ar^K = \dfrac{a(a^{K+1} - 1)}{r - 1}$

$\text{LHS} = \underbrace{a + ar + ar^2 + ----- ar^{K-1} + ar^K}$

$= \dfrac{a(r^K - 1)}{r - 1} + ar^K = \dfrac{a(r^K - 1) + ar^K(r - 1)}{r - 1}$

$= \dfrac{\cancel{ar^K} - a + ar^{K+1} - \cancel{ar^K}}{(r - 1)} = \dfrac{ar^{K+1} - a}{r - 1}$

$= \dfrac{a(r^{K+1} - 1)}{r - 1} =$ **RHS verified.**

(b) How many permutations are there of the letters taken all at time of the word "PATTIVEERANPATI".
Refer to Page No.-115, Q.No.-7

(c) In how many ways can two integers 1, 2, ……., 100. So that their difference is exactly seven?
Ans. We have to select two integer having their differences is exactly seven

a	b

So we take 1st digit from 1 to 93 by 93 ways and 2nd digit by 8 to 100 by next 93 ways. So total number of ways = 93×93

(d) Draw a Venn Diagram to represent $A \cup (B \cap C)$
Refer to Page No.-86, Q.No.-3

(e) Show that $\{[p \rightarrow q] \wedge \sim q\} \rightarrow \sim p$ is tautology.
Ans.

p	q	~p	~q	$(p \rightarrow q)$	$(p \rightarrow q) \wedge \sim q$	$\{[p \rightarrow q] \wedge \sim q\} \rightarrow \sim p$
F	F	T	T	T	T	T
F	T	T	F	T	F	T
T	F	F	T	F	F	T
T	T	F	F	T	F	T

Since from the above table the all the truth value of given Boolean Expression is true. So this expression is a tautology.

(f) If $f(x) = \log x$ and $g(x) = e^x$ show that $(fog)(x) = (gof)(x)$.
Ans. $f(x) = \log x$
$g(x) = e^x$
Show that $fog(x) = gof(x)$
$fog(x) = f(g(x)) = f(e^x) = \log e^x = x$
$gof(x) = g(f(x)) = g(\log x) = e^{\log x} = x$
So $gof(x) = fog(x)$ proved.

(g) Let A be the set of all people on earth. A relation R is defined on the set A by $_aR_b$ if and only if' a loves b' for a, b A. Example if R is (i) Reflexive (ii) Symmetric. Justify Answer.
Ans. i) R is reflexive iff mii = 1, So it is not reflexive
ii) R is symmetric, if mij = 1 then mji = 1, So it is not symmetric

Q2. (a) Among 100 students, 32 study mathematics, 20 study physics, 45 study biology, 15 study mathematics and biology, 7 study mathematics and physics, 10 study physics and biology and 30 do not study any of three subjects

(i) Find the number of students studying all three subjects.

Ans. Let the set of student who study mathematics = M
The set of student who study physics = P
The sets of student who study biology = B
Total group of students = 100

$n(U) = 100$ $\quad\quad n(M) = 32$

$n(P) = 20$ $\quad\quad n(B) = 45$

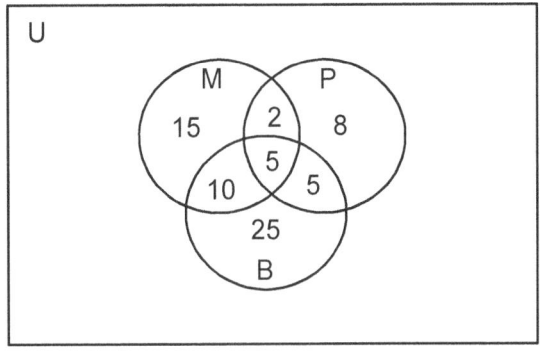

$n(M \cap B) = 15$ $\quad\quad n(P \cap B) = 10$

$n(M \cap P) = 7$ $\quad\quad n(M \cup P \cup B)' = 30$

$\therefore n(M \cup P \cup B) = n(U) - n(M \cup P \cup B)'$

$= 100 - 30 = 70$

$n(M \cup P \cup B) = n(M) + n(P) + n(B) - n(M \cap B) - n(P \cap B) - n(M \cap P)$
$+ n(M \cap P \cap B)$

$= n(M \cap P \cap B) = 70 - 65 = 5$

The number of students who study all three subjects = 5

(ii) find the number of students studying exactly one of three subjects.

Ans. Number of student who study only math

$= n(M) - n(M \cap P) - n(M \cap B) + n(M \cap P \cap B)$

$= 32 - 7 - 15 + 5 = 15$

Similarly No. of students who study only biology = 25
Similarly No. of students who study only physics = 8
Total students who study only one subject
= 15 + 25 + 8 = 48

(b) Let P be the set of all people. Let R be a binary relation on P such that (a,b) is in R if 'a is brother of b'. (Disregard step-brothers and fraternity brothers). Is R
(i) Antisymmetric
(ii) Equivalence relation
Ans. R is binary relation that
a R b where R: a is brother of b
(i) Antsymmetric Relation:-
R is said to be an anti symmetric relation is $(a,b) \in R$ and $(b,a) \in R \Rightarrow a = b$
here a R b (because a is brother of b)
b R a
$\Rightarrow a \neq b$
So it is not anti symmetric
(ii) Equivalence relation

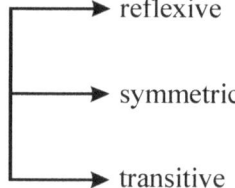

Reflexive :
a R a (a is brother of a)
Symmetric:
a R b (a is brother of b)
= b R a (b is brother of a)
Transitive relation:
a R b (a is brother of b)
b R c (b is brother of c)
= a R c (then a is brother of c)
So this relation is equivalence relation

Q3. (a) Use Truth Table to show $\sim(\sim p \wedge q) \wedge (p \vee q) \equiv p$
Ans.

p	q	~p	~p∧q	p∨q	~(~p∧q)	~(~p∧q)∧(p∨q)
T	T	F	F	T	T	T
T	F	F	F	T	T	T
F	T	T	T	T	F	F
F	F	T	F	F	T	F

From column 1 and 7 we show that the expression is logically equivalent.

(b) Five boys and five girls are to be seated in a row. In how many ways can they be seated if all boys must be seated in five left most seats?
Ans. Let B_1, B_2, B_3, B_4, B_5 are the Boys and
G_1, G_2, G_3, G_4, G_5, are the girls

All boys seated five left most seat by 5! ways.
Girls also seat rest five seats by %! Ways
So total ways = 5!× 5!

(c) Construct the logic circuit for the expression $(x_1{}' \wedge x_2) \vee (x_1 \vee x_3)$
Ans.

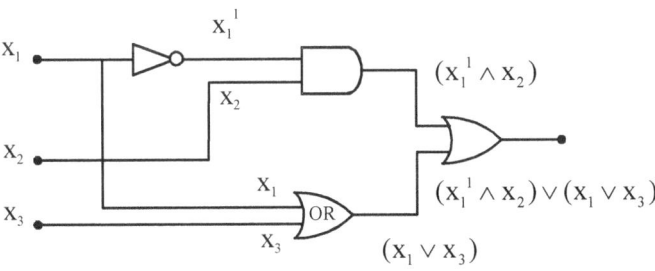

Q4. (a) How many "words" can be formed using letters of 'IGNOU' (each at most once).
(i) If all the letters must be used.
Ans. If all the letters must be used
Then total number of ways:-

= $^5p_5 = 5! = 120$

(ii) If some (or all) of the letters may be omitted.

Ans. (ii) When one letter omitted = $^4p_4 = 24$
When two letter omitted = $^3p_3 = 6$
When three letter omitted = $^2p_2 = 2$
When four letters omitted = $^1p_1 = 1$
When all letter omitted = $^0p_0$
Total words:- $24+6+2+1+1 = 34$

(b) An island has two tribes of natives. Any native from the first tribe always tells the truth, while any native from the other tribe tells lies always. You arrive at the island and ask a native if there is a gold on the island. He answers, "There is gold on island if only if I always tell the truth". Is there gold on island. Prove / Disprove.

Ans. There is no gold on island

Refer to GullyBaba.com download section

Q5. (a) Show that
$$\frac{1}{1.2} + \frac{1}{2.3} + \frac{1}{3.4} + \ldots\ldots + \frac{1}{n(n+1)} = \frac{n}{n+1}$$

Ans. $S(n) = \frac{1}{1.2} + \frac{1}{2.3} + \frac{1}{3.4} + ---- \frac{1}{n(n+1)} = \frac{n}{n+1}$

Let S(1) is true

LHSs $\qquad S(1) = \frac{1}{1.2}$

RHS $\qquad \frac{1}{1+1} = \frac{1}{1.2}$

LHS=RHS

So S(1) is true

Now assume that S(K) is true for all $K \in N$

$$S(K) = \frac{1}{1.2} + \frac{1}{2.3} + \frac{1}{3.4} + ---- + \frac{1}{K(K+1)} = \frac{K}{K+1}$$

Now we have to proved that S(K+1) is true * natural number.

$$S(K+1) = \frac{1}{1.2} + \frac{1}{2.3} + \frac{1}{3.4} + ---- + \frac{1}{K(K+1)} + \frac{1}{(K+1)(K+2)} = \frac{K+1}{K+2}$$

LHS

$$\underbrace{\frac{1}{1.2} + \frac{1}{2.3} + \frac{1}{3.4} + ---- + \frac{1}{K(K+1)}}_{S(K)} + \frac{1}{(K+1)(K+2)}$$

$$= \frac{K}{K+1} + \frac{1}{(K+1)(K+2)}$$

$$= \frac{1}{K+1}\left\{K + \frac{1}{(K+2)}\right\} = \left(\frac{1}{K+1}\right)\left\{\frac{K^2+2K+1}{(K+2)}\right\}$$

$$= \frac{(K+1)^2}{(K+1)(K+2)} = \frac{K+1}{K+2} = \text{RHS proved.}$$

So by induction is true for all natural number.

(b) Suppose n different games are to be distributed among n children. In how many ways can this be done so that exactly one child gets no game.

Ans. $nc_{n-1} = \dfrac{\lfloor n}{\lfloor n-1 \times \lfloor n-n+1} + \dfrac{\lfloor n}{\lfloor n-1 \times 1}$

$= \dfrac{n \times \lfloor n-1}{\lfloor n-1} = n$ ways

(c) If $f = \begin{bmatrix} 1 & 2 & 3 \\ 2 & 3 & 1 \end{bmatrix}$ $g = \begin{bmatrix} 1 & 2 & 3 \\ 2 & 1 & 3 \end{bmatrix}$. **Check either (fog) is equal to (gof) or not.**

Ans. $f = \begin{pmatrix} 1 & 2 & 3 \\ 2 & 3 & 1 \end{pmatrix}, g = \begin{pmatrix} 1 & 2 & 3 \\ 2 & 1 & 3 \end{pmatrix}$

fog= f(g(x))
fog(1)= f(g(1))= f(2)=2
fog (2)= f(g(2))= f(1)=2
fog(3)=f(g(3))= f(g)=1

$\text{fog} = \begin{pmatrix} 1 & 2 & 3 \\ 3 & 2 & 1 \end{pmatrix}$

$\text{gof} = \begin{pmatrix} 1 & 2 & 3 \\ 1 & 3 & 2 \end{pmatrix}$

So, gof ≠ fog

MCS-013: DISCRETE MATHEMATICS
June, 2011

Note: *Question Number 1 is* **compulsory.** *Attempt any* **three** *questions from the rest.*

Q1. (a) It is required to sit 5 men and 4 women in a row so that the women occupy the even places. How many such arrangements are possible?

Ans. This is a case of restricted combination. Total Person=5 men + 4 women =9 person. Thus, no. of ways are

$$= {}^9C_5 + {}^9C_4 = \frac{\lfloor 9}{\lfloor 5 \lfloor 4} + \frac{\lfloor 9}{\lfloor 4 \lfloor 5} = \frac{9\times 8\times 7\times 6\times \lfloor 5}{\lfloor 5\times 4\times 3\times 2} + \frac{9\times 8\times 7\times 6\times \lfloor 5}{4\times 3\times 2\times \lfloor 5} = 126 + 126 = 252$$

(b) A question paper of discrete mathematics has two sections of five questions each. In how many ways can an examinee answer six questions taking at least two questions from each group?

Ans. Total questions in both sections are 10. The possible is
$\lfloor 2 \times \lfloor 3 \times \lfloor 4 = 2\times 3\times 2\times 4\times 3\times 2 = 288$

(c) If A and B are sets, prove that. $A \cup B = (A - B) \cup B$

Ans. L.H.S= $A \cup B$

$x \in A$ and $x \in B$ = $(x \in A$ and $x \in B)$ and $x \in B$

= $(A - B)$ and $x \in B$ = $(A - B) \cup B$

(d) Find $f^{-1}(x)$ **where** $f(x) = \dfrac{x+4}{x-3}$

Ans. Given $f(x) = \dfrac{x+4}{x-3}$

Steps for finding $f^{-1}(x)$

Step 1: Replace $f(x)$ by y in the equation describing the function. Such that
$y = \dfrac{x+4}{x-3}$

Step 2: $x = \dfrac{y+4}{y-3}$ (replace x by y and y by x)

Step 3: $x(y - 3) = y + 4$, $xy - 3x = y + 4$ $\Rightarrow$ $y = \dfrac{3x+4}{x-1}$

Step 4: Therefore $f^{-1}(x) = \dfrac{3x+4}{x-1}$

(e) Show that; $\sim (PV(\sim P \wedge Q)) \equiv \sim P \wedge \sim Q$ using logical equivalent formulas.

Ans. Given, $\sim (PV(\sim P \wedge Q)) \equiv \sim P \wedge \sim Q$, by truth table

P	Q	~P	~Q	~P∧Q	PV(~P∧Q)	~PV(~P∧Q))	~P∧~Q
F	F	T	T	F	F	T	T
F	T	T	F	T	T	F	F
T	F	F	T	F	T	F	F
T	T	F	F	F	T	F	F

By the above table, the given formula is logically equivalent.

(f) What is pigeon hole principle? Using this principle show that in any group of 36 people, we can always find 6 people who were born on the same day of week.

Ans. Pigeon hole principle: If x pigeons are assigned to m pigeon holes and m<n, then there is at least one pigeonhole that contains two or more pigeon. For the given problem, we assigned each person the one number and so on, since there are 30 days in a month. So, according to pigeon hole principle, there must be atleast 6 people, who were born on the same day of week.

Q2. (a) Express the Boolean expression in three variables $(x + y + z)(xy + x'z)$ in DNF.

Ans. $(x + y + z)(xy + x'z)$

The truth table will be

x	y	z	f(x, y, z)
1	1	1	0
1	0	1	1 (x + y'+ z)
0	1	1	1 (x' + y + z)
1	1	0	0
1	0	0	1 (x + y' + z')
0	1	0	1 (x' + y + z')
0	0	1	0
0	0	0	1 (x + y + z)

$\therefore \text{DNF} = xy'z + x'yz + xy'z' + x'yz' + xyz$

(b) Use mathematical induction method, prove that:

$$1+2+3+\underline{\quad\quad\quad}+n = \frac{n(n+1)}{2}$$

Ans. The proposition holds for n=1 since $P(1): 1 = \frac{1}{2}(1)(1+1)$

Assuming P(n) is true, we add n+1 to both sides of P(n), obtaining

$$1+2+3+\ldots\ldots+n+(n+1) = \frac{1}{2}n(n+1)+(n+1) = \frac{1}{2}\left[n(n+1)+2(n+1)\right]$$

$$= \frac{1}{2}[(n+1)(n+2)]$$

which is P(n+1). That is P(n+1) is true whenever P(n) is true. By the principle of induction, P is true for all n.

(c) Prove that a relation R in the set Z of integers defined by 'aRb ⇔ a - b is even' is an equivalence relation.

Ans. Given, 'aRb ⇔ a – b' is also written as 'aRb ⇔ a = b'

∴ let a = b ⇒ R(a) = R(b). Since R is reflective, we have b ∈ R(b)

Now b ∈ R(b) ⇒ b ∈ R(a) [Since R(a)=R(b)]
⇒ aRb

Therefore aRb if R(a)=R(b) ....(i)

Since R is an equivalence relation, both a and b belong to the same equivalence class which is either R(a) or R(b)

∴ if aRb then R(a)=R(b) .....………..(ii)

Combining eq. (i) and (ii) we have

aRb if R(a)=R(b) or aRb ⇔ a-b

Q3. (a) Prove that $(P \Rightarrow q) \vee r \equiv (P \vee r) \Rightarrow (q \vee r)$.

Ans. L.H.S $= (P \Rightarrow q) \vee r = (\sim P \vee q) \vee r =\sim (P \vee r) \vee (q \vee r)$

$= (P \vee r) \Rightarrow (q \vee r)$ $(\because \sim P \vee q = P \Rightarrow q)$

(b) If $f: R \to R$ is a function such that $f(x) = 3x+5$ prove that f is one - one onto. Also find the inverse of f.

Ans. Given $f: R \to R$ is defined by $f(x)=3x+5$

(i) Is f one to me?

A function $f: A \to B$ is said to be one to one in different elements in domain A has distinct images. This means f is one to one if $f(a)=f(a')$ implies a= a'. The graph of $f(x)=3x+2$ tells us that f is one to one. There are no two distinct pairs (a_1, b) and (a_2, b) in the graph of $f(x)$.

(ii) Is $f(x)$ is on to function?

The function $f(x)=3x+5$ also onto function because each horizontal line must intersect its graph at least once.

(c) Determine the number of integer solutions to the equation $x_1 + x_2 + x_3 + x_4 = 7$ where $xi \geq 0 \,\forall i=1,2,3,4$

Refer to Page No.-118, Q.No.-19

Q4. (a) Two dice, one red and one white are rolled. What is the probability that the white die turns up a smaller number than the red die?

Ans. Max, number appearing on dice=6

Here, Let E_1=Event of getting smaller no. of getting white die than the red die.

S_1= sample space.

$\Rightarrow E_1=\{(1,2), (2,3), (3,4), (4,5), (5,6), (1,3), (1,4), (1,5), (1,6), (2,4), (2,5), (2,6), (3,5), (3,6), (4,6)\}$
$n(S_1)=36; n(E_1)=15$
$P(E_1)=n(E_1)/n(S_1)= 15/36= 5/12$.

(b) What is duality principle? Find dual of $(A \cup B) \wedge C$)
Ans. Duality principle: To compounded statements S_1 and S_2 are said to be duals of each other if one can be obtained from other by replacing $\wedge$ by $\vee$ and $\vee$ by $\wedge$. The connection $\wedge$ and $\vee$ are also called dual of each other.
The dual of given expression $(A \cup B) \wedge C$ is $(A \cap B) \vee C$.

(c) Verify that $p \wedge q \wedge \sim p$ is a contradiction and $p \rightarrow q \Leftrightarrow \sim p \vee q$ is a tautology
Ans. First we make truth table for the given expression $p \wedge q \wedge \sim p$ and $p \rightarrow q \Leftrightarrow \sim p \vee q$.

p	q	~p	~q	p∧q∧~p	~p∨q	p→q	(p→q)⇔(~p∨q)
T	T	F	F	F	T	T	T
T	F	F	T	F	F	F	T
F	T	T	F	F	T	T	T
F	F	T	T	F	T	T	T

From the above table $p \wedge q \wedge \sim p$, all values are f (false). Therefore it is a contradiction and $(p \rightarrow q) \Leftrightarrow (\sim p \vee q)$, all values are T(True), it is a tautology.

Q5. (a) Show that $\sqrt{3}$ is irrational.

Ans. Let $\sqrt{3}$ is rational number and $\sqrt{3} = \dfrac{p}{q}$.
Where p and q have not common divisor and $q \neq 0$
Or $3 = \dfrac{p^2}{q^2}$, Or $3q = \dfrac{p^2}{q}$

integer=fraction, it is not possible, Hence $\sqrt{3}$ is irrational number

(b) Construct the logic circuit and obtain the logic table for the expression $x_1 \vee (x_2' \wedge x_3')$
Refer to Page No.-58, Q.No.-16

(c) How many numbers are there between 100 and 1000 such that 7 is in the unit's place?
Ans. From 100 to 200 unit's place of 7 are 107, 117, 127, 137, 147, 157, 167, 170,171,172,173,174,175,176,177,178,187,197. So that total unit places are 20 between 100 to 200. Similarly, the same value will occurs in 200 to 300, 300 to 400 and so on. Therefore total value is 20×9=180.

MCS-013: DISCRETE MATHEMATICS
December, 2011

Note: *Question Number 1 is* ***compulsory.*** *Attempt any* ***three*** *questions from the rest.*

Q1. (a) If there are 12 persons in a party, and if each two of them shake hands with each other how many handshakes happen in the party?

Ans. In a normal case, a handshakes involves two persons. This case is of counting 2-elements subset of a set containing 12 elements. And the count is

$$^{12}C_2 = \frac{\lfloor 12}{\lfloor 12 \times \lfloor 10} = \frac{12 \times 11 \times \lfloor 10}{2 \times \lfloor 10} = 66$$

(b) Prove that $A - B = A \Leftrightarrow A \cap B = Q$

Ans. L.H.S = $A - B$

$= x \in A$ and $x \in B$

$= (x \in A, x \notin B$ and $x \in B, x \notin A)$ and $x \in A$ and $x \in B$

$= (x \in A, x \notin B)$ and $(x \in B, x \notin A$ and $x \in A$ and $x \in B) = A \Leftrightarrow A \cap B$

(c) Let R be the binary relation defined as $R = \{(a,b) \in R^2 \mid a - b \leq 3\}$. Determine whether R is reflexive, symmetric antisymmetric or transitive.

Ans. Given, R is a binary relation, s.t. $R = \{(a,b) \in R^2 / a - b \leq 3\}$. Let $a, b \leftarrow R$ and $(a,b) \leftarrow R^2$, where $(a - b) \leq 3$, it is true. Therefore given relation is reflexive. Now suppose aRb, then $(a,b) \leftarrow R^2$ so that $(b,a) \leftarrow R^2$, Hence bRa. It follows that R is symmetric. If aRb and bRc, than $(a,b),(b,c)$ are integers. Therefore $(a,b) \leftarrow R^2, (b,c) \leftarrow R^2$, then $(a,c) \leftarrow R^2$. Hence aRc. Thus R is transitive. Consequently, R is an equivalence relation.

(d) What is a propositional function? Write propositional function for following statement. Always there are some students in a class who are hardworking.

Ans. Propositional function: It is a statement expressed in a way that would assume the value of true or false, except that within the statement is a variable (x), that is not defined or specified, which leaves the statement undetermined. The given statement "Always there are some students in a class who are hardworking". This statement is a existential qualification namely $\exists x P(x)$ and "who are hardworking" is expressed by the original propositional function. So the propositional function of the given statement can be written as $\exists x P(x) \equiv \forall x P(x)$.

(e) Represent the following argument symbolically and determine whether the argument is valid?

"If today is Children's day then today is Pt. Jawaharlal Nehru's birthday". "If today is Pr. Jawaharlal Nehru's birthday then today is 14th Nov". Hence "If today is Children's day then today is 14th Nov."
Ans. Let F(x) be the statement "if today is children's day".
Let P(x) be the statement "today is Pt. Jawaharlal Nehru's birthday".
Let M(x) be the statement "today is 14th Nov."
Consequently we can translate the sentence as $\forall(x)((F(x) \wedge P(x))) \rightarrow \exists y M(x, y)$.

(f) Simplify the Boolean function
$B(x_1, x_2, x_3) = [(x_1 \wedge x_2) \vee ((x_1 \wedge x_2) \wedge x_3)] \vee (x_2 \wedge x_3)$
Ans. Given expression is $B(x_1, x_2, x_3) = [(x_1 \wedge x_2) \vee ((x_1 \wedge x_2) \wedge x_3)] \vee (x_2 \wedge x_3)$
$= [(x_1 \wedge x_2) \vee ((x_1 \wedge x_3) \wedge (x_2 \wedge x_3))] \vee (x_2 \wedge x_3)$
$= [((x_1 \wedge x_2) \vee (x_1 \wedge x_3)) \wedge ((x_1 \wedge x_2) \vee (x_2 \wedge x_3)] \vee (x_2 \wedge x_3)$
$= (x_1 \vee x_1) \wedge (x_1 \vee x_3) \wedge (x_2 \wedge x_3) \wedge (x_1 \vee x_2) \wedge (x_1 \vee x_3) \wedge (x_2 \wedge x_3) \wedge (x_2 \vee x_1) \vee (x_2 \wedge x_3)$
$= (x_1 \wedge x_2 \wedge x_3) \vee (x_2 \wedge x_3)$

Q2. (a) Using mathematical induction method, show that:
$1^3 + 2^3 + 3^3 + \ldots + n^3 = \left[\dfrac{n(n+1)}{2}\right]^2$
Refer to Page No-159, Q.No.-3(a)

(b) Find the number of different messages that can be represented by sequences of 4 dashes and 3 dots.
Ans. Total possible message are $^4C_3 = \dfrac{\lfloor 4}{\lfloor 3.\lfloor 1} = 4$

(c) If I be the set of integers, find whether $f : I \rightarrow I$ defined by $f(x) = x^3$ is one-one onto or both.
Ans. Given $f : I \rightarrow I$ is defined by $f(x) = x^3$
(i) Is it one to one?
A function $f : A \rightarrow B$ is said to be one to one in different elements in domain A has distinct images. This means f is one to one if $f(a) = f(a')$. For $f(x) = x^3$, there are no two distinct pairs (a_1, b) and (a_2, b) in the graph $f(x)$. Therefore $f(x)$ is one to one.
(ii) Is $f(x)$ is onto?
Given function is not onto because each horizontal line intersect its graph.

Q3. (a) Construct a logic circuit represented by the Boolean expression $(x_1' \wedge x_2) \vee (x_1 \wedge x_3') \wedge (x_2 \vee x_3)$ where $x_i (1 \leq i \leq 3)$ are assumed to be inputs to that circuitry.
Ans. We know that $\wedge \rightarrow$ and ⟶⊐—, $\vee \rightarrow$ or ⟶⊐—, $' \rightarrow$ not ⟶⊳∘—

Given expression is $(x_1' \wedge x_2) \vee (x_1 \wedge x_3') \wedge (x_2 \vee x_3)$

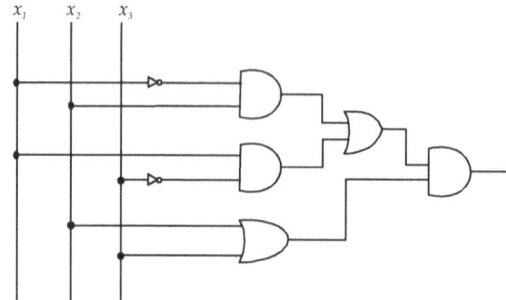

(b) Verify that the proposition p∨ ~ (P ∧ Q) is a tautology.

Ans. Given proposition pv ~ (P ∧ Q). We construct truth table for the given proposition.

p	q	p∧q	~(p∧q)	p∨ ~(p∧q)
T	T	T	F	T
T	F	F	T	T
F	T	F	T	T
F	F	F	T	T

From the above truth table, given proposition have all value T(True). So, it is a tautology.

(c) A valid Computer password consists of nine characters, the first of which is the digit 1, 5 or 7 the third character is either a # or A$ and the remaining a english alphabet or a digit. Find how many different passwords are possible?

Ans. Total characters are nine, such that

	I	II	III	IV	V	VI	VII	VIII	IX	
	1 or 5 or 7	a or A	# or $	Remain are a English alphabet of digit						∴ 26+9=35
Total possibility	3	2	2	35	35	35	35	35	35	

∴ Total different password possibility are = 3×2×2×35×35×35×35×35×35=22059187500 by basic counting principle.

Q4. (a) Let I be the set of all integers. Let R be a relation on I, defined by R = {(x,y) : x-y is divisible by 6 ∀x, y ∈ I}. Show that R is an equivalence relation.

Ans. Let R be a relation on I, s.t. R= {(x, y) : x − y is divisible by 6 ∀x, y ∈ I}

To show R is an equivalence Relation. A relation should be:

(i) Reflective: Since I is a set of integers, and R is a relation such that (x-y) is divisible. It is a reflective relation

(ii) Symmetric: If aRb then bRa. If is also true for the given relation. It is a symmetric relation.

(iii) Transitive: If aRb and bRc then aRc. For the given relation R such that (x-y) divisible by 6 for all integer, it is also true. Therefore given relation is a equivalence relation.

(b) Give the geometric representation of {3}×R.
Ans. A relation between finite sets can be represented using a zero-one matrix. Let R is a relation from A{a_1, a_2 ....} to B={}. The relation R can be represented by the matrix $M_R = \{m_{ij}\}$, where

$$m_{ij} = \begin{cases} 1 & \text{if}(a_i, b_j) \in R \\ 0 & \text{if}(a_i, b_j) \notin R \end{cases}$$

Given expression is {3}×R. The matrix representation for this expression will be

$$\begin{bmatrix} 1 & 0 & 0 \\ 0 & 1 & 0 \\ 0 & 0 & 1 \end{bmatrix} \begin{bmatrix} R_1 \\ R_2 \\ R_3 \end{bmatrix}$$

(c) There are 15 points in a plane, no three of which are collinear. Find the number of straight lines formed by joining them.
Ans. Total points in the plane are 15. No. 3 of which are collinear. The no. of straight line formed by joining them will be the combination of total points and number of collinear point. Therefore

$$^{15}C_3 = \frac{\lfloor 15}{\lfloor 3 \lfloor 12} = \frac{15 \times 14 \times 13 \times \lfloor 12}{3 \times 2 \times \lfloor 12} = 455.$$

Q5. (a) If 100 bulbs are placed in 15 boxes. Show that two of the boxes must have the same number of bulbs.
Ans. By generalized pigeonhole principle, we knowing n objects are placed into K boxes, then there is at least one box containing at least $\lceil N/K \rceil$ objects.

∴ $\lceil 100/15 \rceil = 7$

Thus at least 2 of the boxes must here the same number of bulbs.

(b) If $f(x) = x^2$ and $g(x) = x + 1$, then find $(fog)x$ and $(gof)x$
Ans. $f(x) = x^2$
$g(x) = x+1$
$fog(x) = g(f(x)) = g(x^2) = (x+1)^2 + 1 = x^2 + 1 + 2x + 1 = x^2 + 2x + 2$
$gof(x) = f(g(x)) = f(x+1) = (x+1)^2 = x^2 + 2x + 1$

(c) Explain with reason, whether or not
(i) the collection of all good teachers is a set.
Ans. Given statement is 'the collection of all good teacher is a set' is not true, because collection of teachers is a set, and selecting then good teacher is a subset.
(ii) the set of points on a line is finite.
Ans. Given statement 'the set of points on a line is finite' is true, because if a line is finite then the pixel required for the line should also be finite.

MCS-013: DISCRETE MATHEMATICS
June, 2012

Note: *Question Number 1 is **compulsory**. Attempt any **three** from the rest.*

Q1. (a) Show that $pV \sim (p \wedge q)$ is a tautology.
Refer to Page No.-226, Q.No.-3(b)

(b) Prove the following equivalence $\sim \forall x P(x) \equiv \exists x \sim P(x)$.
Refer to June-2006, Q.No.-1(b)

(c) Use principle of mathematical induction to prove that $n^3 - n$ is divisible by 3.
Refer to Page No.-33, Q.No.-12

(d) Write the output of following circuit.

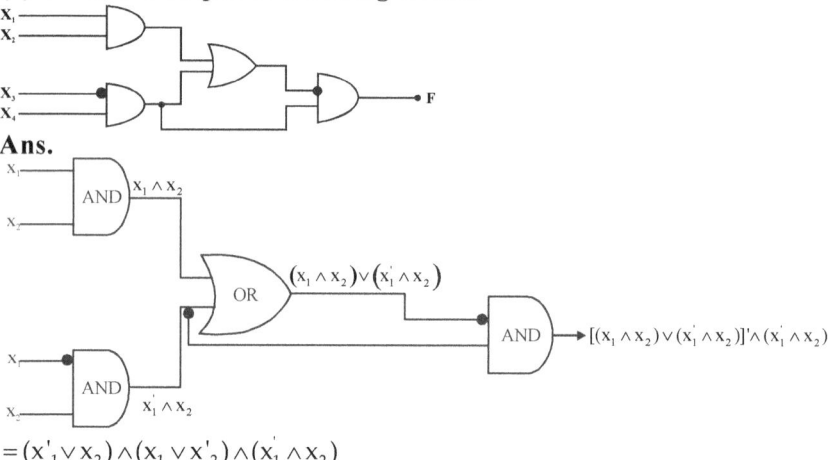

Ans.

$= (x'_1 \vee x_2) \wedge (x_1 \vee x'_2) \wedge (x'_1 \wedge x_2)$

(e) Let R be a relation on the set A = {1, 2, 3, 4} such that aRb if and only if a + b > 5. Check if R is reflexive, symmetric, transitive.
Ans. We have R be a relation defined by aRb if $a + b > 5$
(i) Let $a = 2 \in A$, then
$aRa \Rightarrow 2 + 2 > 5$ which is not possible.
Hence, $a \in A$, is not reflexive.
(ii) We observe that $1R2 \notin A, 2R1 \notin A$.
Therefore, R is not symmetric.
(iii) Let $(a, b) \in A$ and $(b, c) \in A$.
$\Rightarrow a + b > 5$ and $b + c > 5 \Rightarrow a + c > 5$

Hence, R is transitive
Therefore, this relation is transitive but not reflexive nor symmetric.

(f) How many permutations are there for the word ASSOCIATION?
Ans. Here,
A — 2
S — 2
O — 2
C — 1
I — 2
T — 1
N — 1

$\therefore$ No. of permutations = $\dfrac{11!}{2! \times 2! \times 2! \times 1! \times 2! \times 1! \times 1!}$

$= \dfrac{11 \times 10 \times 9 \times 8 \times 7 \times 6 \times 5 \times 4 \times 3 \times 2!}{2! \times 2 \times 1 \times 2 \times 1 \times 2 \times 1}$ = $11 \times 10 \times 9 \times 7 \times 6 \times 5 \times 4 \times 3 = 2494800$.

(g) Three coins are tossed and number of heads are observed. Find the probability that
(i) at least one head appears
Ans. Possible Outcomes: HHH, TTT, HHT, HTT, THH, TTH, THT, HTH
Total probability = 1
P (At least one head appear) = $1 - \dfrac{1}{8} = \dfrac{7}{8}$

(ii) all heads or all tails appear.
Ans. P(All Heads or Tails) = $\dfrac{1}{8}$

Q2. (a) Prove De Morgan's laws using truth table.
Ans. De Morgan's laws states that:
P or Q = not (not P and not Q)
P and Q = not (not P or not Q)
So, let's build a truth table. It's hard to make a decent grid on Y!A, so we'll just use comma-separated values:
P,Q,P or Q,not P,not Q,not P and not Q,not (not P and not Q),P and Q,not P or not Q,not (not P or not Q)
F, F, F, T, T, T, F, F, T, F
T, F, T, F, T, F, T, F, T, F
F, T, T, T, F, F, T, F, T, F
T, T, T, F, F, F, T, T, F, T
To prove De Morgan's laws, columns 3 and 7 must be equal, and columns 8 and 10 must be equal for all combinations of P and Q's truth values, and they are.

(b) Present a Direct proof of the statement, "Square of an odd integer is odd".

Ans. *The square of an odd integer is odd*
Proof: Let n be an odd integer then 1 more than n is an even integer. Therefore n can be rewritten as: $2k + 1$ for some integer k.
Therefore $n^2 = (2k+1)^2 \Rightarrow n^2 = 4k^2 + 4k + 1 = 4(k^2 + k) + 1$
This is 1 more than $4(k^2 + k)$ which is an even number.
Therefore n^2 is odd.

(c) Explain:
(i) Proof by contrapositive
(ii) Proof by contradiction
with the help of suitable examples.
Refer to Page No.-27 [Proof by contrapositive, Proof by contradiction]

Q3. (a) Write Boolean equation for the following circuit.

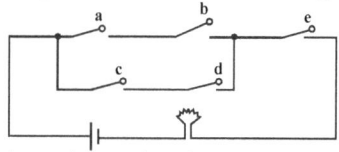

Ans. Switch a & b are in series and switch c & d are also in series but their combination are in parallel with each other.
The resultant is in series with e.
∴ Boolean equation is $((a \wedge b) \vee (c \wedge d)) \wedge e$

(b) Reduce the following Boolean equation to simplest form.
$(a \wedge b' \wedge c) \vee (a \wedge b' \wedge c') \vee (a' \wedge b \wedge c') \vee (a' \wedge b' \wedge c')$
Ans. $(a \wedge b' \wedge c) \vee (a \wedge b' \wedge c') \vee (a' \wedge b \wedge c') \vee (a' \wedge b' \wedge c')$
$(a \wedge b') \wedge (c \vee c') \vee (a' \wedge b \wedge c') \vee (a' \wedge b' \wedge c')$
$(a \wedge b') \wedge 1 \vee ((a' \wedge b \wedge c') \vee (a' \wedge b' \wedge c'))$
$(a \wedge b') \vee ((a' \wedge c') \wedge (b \vee b'))$
$(a \wedge b') \vee (a' \wedge c')$
$(a \wedge b' \vee a') \wedge (a \wedge b' \vee c')$
$(a \wedge a' \vee b') \wedge (a \wedge b' \vee c')$
$(b') \wedge (a \wedge b' \vee c')$
$(a \wedge b' \vee c')$

(c) Write a short note on "Principal of Duality".
Refer to Page No.-40 [Principal of Duality]

Q4. (a) Let A, B and C be three sets such that $A \cup B = A \cup C$. Does it imply B = C? Support your answer by suitable example.

Ans. Let b be an arbitrary element of B.
Then, $(a,b) \in A \cup B \, \forall a \in A$ [$\because A \cup B = A \cup C$]
$\Rightarrow (a,b) \in A \cup C \, \forall a \in A \Rightarrow b \in c$
Thus, $b \in B \Rightarrow b \in C$
$\therefore B \subset C$ ... (i)
Now, let C be an arbitrary element of C. Then,
$(a,c) \in A \cup C \, \forall \, a \in A \Rightarrow (a,c) \in A \cup B \, \forall \, a \in A \Rightarrow C \in B$
Thus, $C \in C \Rightarrow C \in B$
$\therefore C \subset B$ ... (ii)
Form (i) and (ii), we get
B = C

(b) Prove $AX(B \cup C) = (AXB) \cup (AXC)$

Ans. Let (a,b) be an arbitrary element of $A \times (B \cup C)$. Then,
$(a,b) \in A \times (B \cup C) \Rightarrow a \in A$ and $b \in B \cup C$ [by def. of union]
$\Rightarrow a \in A$ and $(b \in B \text{ or } b \in C)$ [by def. of union]
$\Rightarrow (a \in A \text{ and } b \in B)$ or $(a \in A \text{ and } b \in C)$
$\Rightarrow (a,b) \in A \times B$ or $(a,b) \in A \times C \Rightarrow (a,b) \in (A \times B) \cup (A \times C)$
$\therefore A \times (B \cup C) \subseteq (A \times B) \cup (A \times C)$ ... (i)
Again, let (x,y) be an arbitrary element of $(A \times B) \cup (A \times C)$. Then,
$(x,y) \in (A \times B) \cup (A \times C) \Rightarrow (x,y) \in A \times B$ or $(x,y) \in A \times C$
$\Rightarrow (x \in A \text{ and } y \in B)$ or $(x \in A \text{ and } y \in C) \Rightarrow x \in A$ and $(y \in B \text{ or } y \in C)$
$\Rightarrow x \in A$ and $y \in (B \cup C) \Rightarrow (x,y) \in A \times (B \cup C)$
$\therefore (A \times B) \cup (A \times C) \subseteq A \times (B \cup C)$ ... (ii)
Hence, from (i) and (ii), we have $A \times (B \cup C) = (A \times B) \cup (A \times C)$.

(c) Let $f(x) = x^2$ and g(x) = x + 7. Find fog (x) and gof (x).
Same as Page No.-227, Q.No.-5(b)

(d) Let A be the set of natural nos. 1, 2, 3, 4...., Let R be a relation on A such that aRb if and only if a mod 5 = b mod 5. Prove that R is equivalence relation.

Ans. Here, a mod 5 = b mod 5 $\Leftrightarrow$ a–b is divisible by 5
Reflexivity: let a be an arbitrary natural number

Then, $a - a = 0 = 0 \times 5 \Rightarrow a - a$ is divisible by $5 \Rightarrow a \bmod 5 = a \bmod 5$
Therefore, R is reflexive

Symmetry: let $a, b \in A$ such that $a \bmod 5 = b \bmod 5$
Then $a - b$ divisible by 5
$\Rightarrow a - b = 5\lambda$ for $\lambda \in A \Rightarrow$ for $\lambda \in A$
$\Rightarrow b - a$ is divisible by $5 \Rightarrow b \bmod 5 = a \bmod 5$
Thus, R is symmetrix.

Transitivity: let $a, b, c \in A$ such that $a \bmod 5 = b \bmod 5$ and $b \bmod 5 = c \bmod 5$
Then, $a - b$ is divisible by $b - a = 5(-\lambda)$ for some $\lambda_1 \in A$
$b - c$ is divisible by $5 \Rightarrow b - c = \lambda_2 5$ for some $\lambda_2 \in A$
$\therefore (a - b) + (b - c) = \lambda_1 5 + \lambda_2 5 = (\lambda_1 + \lambda_2) 5$
$\Rightarrow a - c = \lambda_3 5$ where $\lambda_3 = \lambda_1 + \lambda_2 \in A$
Thus, $a \bmod 5 = c \bmod 5$
Therefore, R is transitive
Hence, we conclude that R is an equivalence relation.

Q5. (a) In how many ways can a party of 9 people arrange themselves around a circular table?
Same as Page No.-114, Q.No.-3

(b) What is the sum of coefficients of all the terms in the expansion of $(a + b + c)^5$?
Same as Page No.-119, Q.No.-20

(c) In how many ways r distinct objects can be distributed into 5 different boxes with at least one box empty?
Ans. Let A_i be the set of distribution that leave box i empty for $i = 1, 2, 3, 4, 5$.
we want $|A_1 \cup A_2 \cup A_3 \cup A_4 \cup A_5|$

Therefore, $|A_1 \cup A_2 \cup ... \cup A_5| = \sum_{i=1}^{5} N(i) - \sum_{1 \le i \le j \le 5} N(i, j) + \sum_{1 \le i \le j \le k \le 5} N(i, j, k)$
$- ..... + (-1)^6 N(1, 2, 3, 4, 5)$.

By Product rule, $N(i) = 4^r, N(i, j) = 3^r, N(i, j, k) = 2^r$,
$N(i, j, k, l) = 1, N(1, 2, 3, 4, 5) = 0$.
Hence,
$|A_1 \cup A_2 \cup .... \cup A_5| = (5) 4^r - C(5, 2) 3^r + C(5, 3) 2^r - C(5, 4) 1 + C(5, 5) 0$.

MCS-013: DISCRETE MATHEMATICS
December, 2012

Note: *Question Number 1 is **compulsory**. Attempt any **three** from the rest.*

Q1. (a) Prove the following equivalence $\sim(\exists_x \sim P(x)) \equiv \forall_x P(x)$

Ans. $\sim(\exists_x \sim P(x)) \equiv \forall_x P(x)$

P	~P	$\sim(\exists_n \sim P)$
T	F	T
F	T	F

By truth table, it is clear that $\forall_x P(x) \equiv \sim(\exists_x \sim P(x))$

(b) Use proof by contradiction to prove that $\sqrt{2}$ is irrational.

Refer to Page No.-31, Q.No.-6

(c) Simplify the following Boolean expression
$(a' \wedge b' \wedge c') \vee (a' \wedge b' \wedge c) \vee (a \wedge b' \wedge c') \vee (a' \wedge b \wedge c')$

Ans. $(a' \wedge b' \wedge c') \vee (a' \wedge b' \wedge c) \vee (a \wedge b' \wedge c') \vee (a' \wedge b \wedge c')$

Using K-Map

bc	b'c'	b'c	bc	bc'
a'	1	1	0	1
a	1	0	0	0

By making pairs, the simplified boolean expression is $(b'c') \vee (a'b') \vee (a'c')$

(d) Use Venn diagram to show the following set operation.

(i) $\overline{A}$

Ans. (i) The Venn diagram showing the complement of A is the set of those elements of the universal set U which are outside A (see Fig.)

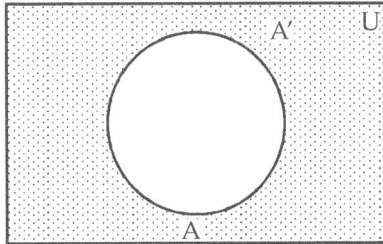

Fig: Venn diagram for.

(ii) $A \cup (B \cap C)$
Refer to Page No.-86, Q.No.-3

(iii) $A \cap (B \cup C)$
Ans.

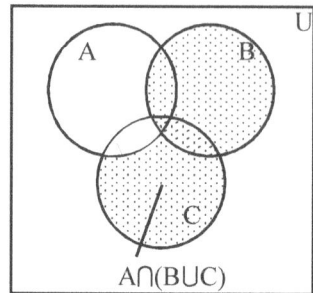

The Lined Portion represents $A \cap (B \cup C)$

(e) Why is $y^2 = x$ not a function?
Ans. A function by definition can have only one possible y value for any given x value.
So take $x = (5)^2$
Substituting into the equation we get $y^2 = (5)^2 \Rightarrow y \pm 5$
It could be either 5 or –5. So there are two y-values that match one x value and the equation is not a function.

(f) An urn contains 15 balls, 8 of which are red and 7 are black. In how many ways 5 balls can be drawn such that
(i) all 5 are red.
Ans. There are 15 balls in the bag out of which 5 balls can be drawn in $15C_5$ ways.
So, total number of elementary events $= 15C_5 = 3003$.
(i) There are 8 red balls out of which 5 balls can be drawn in $8C_5$ ways
∴ favourable number of elementary events $= 8C_5 = 56$
So, required probability $= \dfrac{56}{3003} = \dfrac{8}{429}$

(ii) 3 are red and 2 are black.
Ans. There are 8 red balls out of which 3 balls can be drawn in $8C_3$ ways and there are 7 black balls out of which 2 balls can be drawn in $7C_2$ ways.
Therefore, three red and two black balls can be drawn in $8C_3 \times 7C_2$ ways.

∴ favourable number of elementary events $= 8C_3 \times 7C_2 = 1176$

So, required probability $= \dfrac{1176}{3003} = \dfrac{56}{143}$

**(g) In a survey of 260 college students following data was obtained.
64 had taken mathematics course
94 had taken computer science.
58 had taken business studies.
28 had taken both mathematics and business studies
26 had taken both mathematics and computer science
22 had taken both computer science and business studies
14 had taken all three types of courses.
What is the probability that a student chosen at random had not taken any course?**

Ans. Let M represent the set of student who had taken mathematics course. Further let C and B represent the set of students who had taken computer science and business courses, respectively. It is given that

$|M| = 64$ $|M \cap B| = 28$
$|C| = 64$ $|M \cap C| = 26$
$|B| = 58$ $|C \cap B| = 22$
$|M \cap B \cap C| = 14$ and $|U| = 260$

Let us draw the Venn diagram of the situation displaying all the above results.

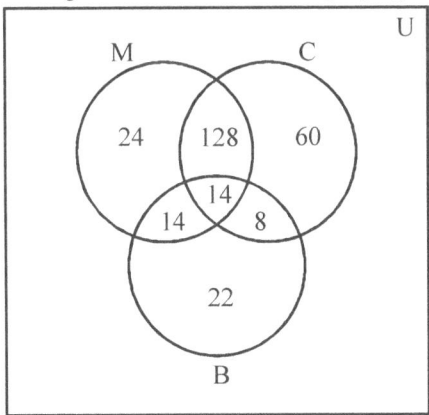

So,
The number of students who had taken at least one course
= (Total number of students who took only one course) + (Total number of students who took two courses) + (Total number of students who took all the three courses).

= Sum of all the figures inside the circular boundary of Venn diagram
= (24 + 60 + 22) + (12 + 14 + 8) + (14) = 154
Therefore, total number of students who had taken none of the three types of courses = (Total number of student surveyed) − (Total number of students who opted for at least one course) = 260 − 154 = 106

Q2. (a) Construct truth table to check whether the following is a tautology, contingency or absurdity.
(i) $p \wedge \sim p$
Ans.

p	$\sim p$	$p \wedge \sim p$
T	F	F
F	T	F

It is a contingency

(ii) $q \rightarrow (q \rightarrow p)$
Ans.

p	q	$q \rightarrow p$	$q \rightarrow (q \rightarrow p)$
T	T	T	T
T	F	F	T
F	T	T	T
F	F	T	T

It is a tautology

(b) If $p \rightarrow q$ is false, what is the truth value of $(\sim (p \wedge q)) \rightarrow q$? Explain.
Ans.

p	q	$p \wedge q$	$\sim (p \wedge q)$	$(\sim (p \wedge q)) \rightarrow q$
T	T	T	F	T
T	F	F	T	F
F	T	F	T	T
F	F	F	T	F

The truth table is neither tautology nor fallacy.

(c) Write the contrapositive & converse of the statement: If it rains then I will get wet.
Ans. Let p: It is raining
q: I get wet
then the contrapositive is
$\sim q \rightarrow \sim p$: If I do not get wet, then it is not raining.

(d) Prove by mathematical induction $1^3 + 2^3 + 3^3 + --- + n^3 = \dfrac{n^2(n+1)^2}{4}$

Ans. Let the given statement be P(n), i.e.
$$1^3 + 2^3 + 3^3 + --- + n^3 = \dfrac{n^2(n+1)^2}{4}$$
P(n): For n = 1, we have
$$P(1): 1^3 = 1 = \dfrac{1^2(1+1)^2}{4} = \dfrac{4}{4} = 1, \text{ which is true.}$$
Let P(k) be true for some positive integer k, i.e.
$$1^3 + 2^3 + 3^3 + --- + k^3 = \dfrac{k^2(k+1)^2}{4} \qquad \ldots (i)$$
We shall now prove that P(k + 1) is true.

Consider $1^3 + 2^3 + 3^3 + --- + k^3 + (k+1)^3 = \dfrac{k^2(k+1)^2}{4} + (k+1)^3$ [Using (i)]

$= \dfrac{k^2(k+1)^2 + 4(k+1)^3}{4} = \dfrac{(k+1)^2\{k^2 + 4(k+1)\}}{4} = \dfrac{(k+1)^2(k^2 + 4k + 4)}{4}$

$= \dfrac{(k+1)^2(k+2)^2}{4} = \dfrac{(k+1)^2(k+1+1)^2}{4}$

$\therefore (1^3 + 2^3 + 3^3 + --- + k^3) + (k+1)^3 = \dfrac{(k+1)^2(k+1+1)^2}{4}$

Thus, P(k + 1) is true whenever P(k) is true. Hence, by the principle of mathematical induction, statement P(n) is true for all natural numbers, i.e. n.

Q3. (a) For the following circuit write the boolean expression

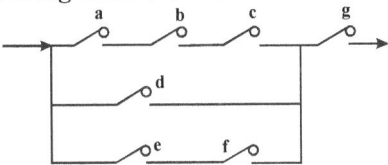

Ans. According to circuit diagram
Series combination are = (i) a, b, c, g
(ii) e, f
Parallel Combination are = abc, d, ef
Then Boolean Expression is
$$\big(((a \wedge b \wedge c) \vee d \vee (e \wedge f)) \wedge g\big)$$

(b) Make the circuit for the following boolean expression using logic gates $\big((x_1 \wedge x_2)' \vee (x_3 \vee x_4)\big) \wedge (x_1 \wedge x_3)' \wedge (x_2 \wedge x'_4)$

Ans. $\big((x_1 \wedge x_2)' \vee (x_3 \vee x_4)\big) \wedge (x_1 \wedge x_3)' \wedge (x_2 \wedge x'_4)$

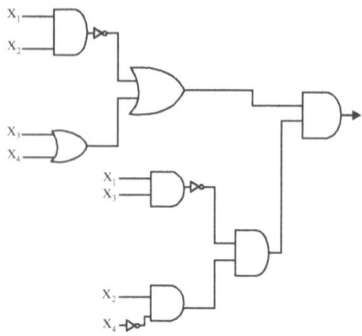

(c) For the following truth table write DNF and CNF.

x_1	x_2	x_3	$f(x_1,x_2,x_3)$
0	0	0	0
0	0	1	1
0	1	0	1
0	1	1	0
1	0	0	1
1	0	1	0
1	1	0	1
1	1	1	1

Same as Page No.-182, Q.No.-4(a)

Q4. (a) Explain the following types of relations with the help of suitable examples.
(i) Reflexive   (ii) Anti-symmetric
(iii) Transitive   (iv) Equivalence
Refer to Page No.-81 [Relations], Page No.-83 [Examples]

(b) Let:
$$f = \begin{pmatrix} 1 & 2 & 3 & 4 \\ 2 & 4 & 1 & 3 \end{pmatrix} \text{ and } g = \begin{pmatrix} 1 & 2 & 3 & 4 \\ 3 & 2 & 1 & 4 \end{pmatrix}$$
Find fog and gof.
Same as Chapter-4, Q.No.-42

(c) In how many ways 6 men and 6 women can sit alternately in a row.
Refer to Page No.-171, Q.No.-1(d)

(d) "If a function is not one to one then it is not invertible." Explain.
Ans. The given statement can be proved by proving the equivalent statement given below:
f^{-1} is a not function, if and only if f is not one-to-one. Let f^{-1} is not a function. Then, for some $b \in B, f^{-1}(b)$ must contain at least two distinct elements,

a_1 and a_2. Then $f(a_1) = b = f(a_2)$, so f is not one-to-one. Hence, we have, if f^{-1} is not a function then f is not one-to-one.

Now, let f is not one-to-one. Then, $f(a_1) = f(a_2) = b$, for two distinct elements $a_1, a_2 \in A$. Thus, $f^{-1}(b)$ contains both a_1 and a_2. So, f^{-1} cannot be a function. Hence, if f is not one-to-one, then f^{-1} is not a function, So f^{-1} is not a function if f is not one-to-one. That is, f^{-1} is a function if and only if f is one to one.

Q5. (a) Prove that $^{n+1}C_r = {}^nC_r + {}^nC_{r-1}$.

Ans. We have,

$$\text{R.H.S.} = {}^nC_{r-1} + {}^nC_r = \frac{n!}{(r-1)!(n-r+1)!} + \frac{n!}{r!(n-r)!}$$

$$= \frac{r \cdot n!}{r(r-1)!(n-r+1)(n-r)!} + \frac{n!(n-r+1)}{r!(n-r+1)(n+r)}$$

$$= \frac{r \cdot n!}{r!(n+1-r)} + \frac{(n-r+1)n!}{r!(n+1-r)!} = \frac{(r+n-r+1)n!}{r!(n+1-r)} = \frac{(n+1)}{r!(n+1-r)!} = {}^{n+1}C_r = \text{L.H.S.}$$

(b) A and B are two mutually exclusive events such that P(A) = 0.3 and P(B) = 0.6. What is the probability that
(i) B does not occur?
(ii) A or B occurs.

Ans. (i) By the Complement rule, P (not B) = $P(B^c) = 1 - P(B) = 1 - 0.6 = 0.4$
(ii) For mutually exclusive events, by the addition rule,
$P(A \text{ or } B) = P(A) + P(B) = 0.3 + 0.6 = 0.9$

(c) If there be a set A partitioned into n number of subsets. Show that the largest subset contains at least $\frac{|A|}{n}$ number of elements.

Refer to Page No.-112 [Theorem]

(d) How many 7 digits numbers are composed of only odd digits?
Same as Page No.-132, Q.No.-8

MCS-013: DISCRETE MATHEMATICS
June, 2013

Note: *Question Number 1 is* **compulsory.** *Attempt any* **three** *questions from the rest.*

Q1. (a) A carpenter has twelve patterns of chairs and five patterns of tables. In how many ways can he make a pair of chair and table?

(b) If 30 books in a school contain a total of 61,327 pages, then show that one of the books must have at least 2045 pages.

(c) Prove that $A - B = A \Rightarrow A \cap B = Q$

(d) Find the domain for which the functions $f(x) = 2x^2 - 1$ and $g(x) = 1 - 3x$ are equal. Also find a domain for which the functions are not equal.

(e) Construct the truth table of $(7p \vee q) \wedge (7r \vee p)$.

(f) Show that $a.b + a'.b' = (a' + b).(a + b')$

Q2. (a) Use mathematical induction method to prove that
$1 + 3 + 5 + \ldots + (2n-1) = n^2$.

(b) Prove that $n! (n + 2) = n! + (n + 1)!$

(c) Consider the set of ordered pair of natural numbers $N \times N$ defined by:
$(a, b) R (c, d) \Leftrightarrow a + d = b + c$. Prove that R is an equivalence relation.

Q3. (a) Show that $(p \wedge q) \Rightarrow (p \vee q)$ is a tautology.

(b) Prove that the inverse of one-one onto mapping is unique.

(c) How many solutions does the equation $x_1 + x_2 + x_3 = 11$ have, where $x_1, x_2,$ and x_3 are non negative integers?

Q4. (a) Express the Boolean expression $xyz' + y'z + xz'$ in a sum of product form.

(b) Find the output of the given circuit.

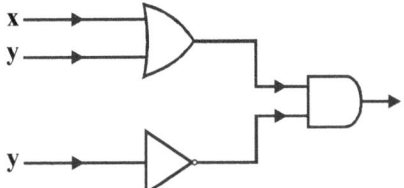

(c) Show that:

$(p \rightarrow q) \rightarrow q \Rightarrow p \vee q$

Q5. (a) In how many ways a person can invite eight of his friends to a party by inviting at least one of them be a female. Considering that the person is having 15 male and 8 female friends.

(b) Let A be the set { 1, 2, 3, 4 }. Which ordered pairs are in the relation R = {(a, b) | a divides b}?

(c) Explain duality principle with the help of example.

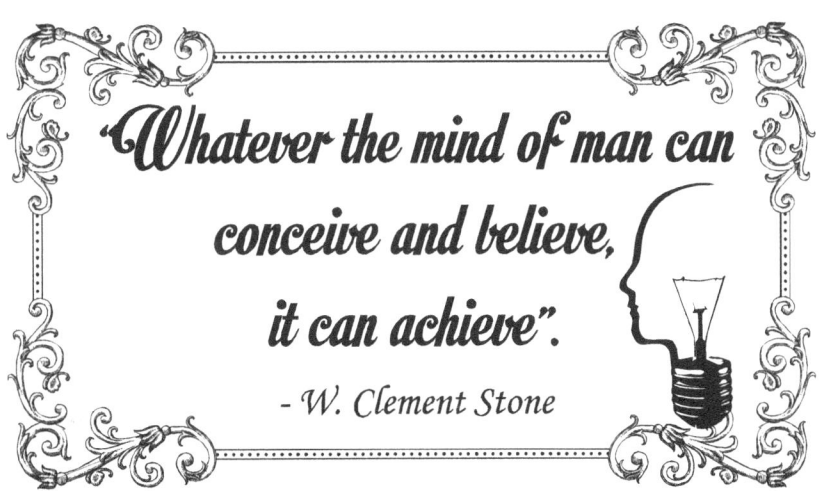

MCS-013: DISCRETE MATHEMATICS
December, 2013

Note: *Question Number 1 is* **compulsory**. *Attempt any* **three** *questions from the rest.*

Q1.(a) In how many ways 100 voters can vote for three candidates standing for the election of the post of president of their association?

(b) How many five different letter words can be formed out of the word "LOGARITHMS"?

(c) Prove that $(A \cup B)' = A' \cap B'$.

(d) Let A = {1, 2, 3, 4, 5} and define R on A by xRy if x + 1 = y. Find:
(i) R   (ii) R^2 (iii) R^3

(e) Construct a truth table for the given proposition $(7p \Leftrightarrow 7q) \Leftrightarrow (q \Leftrightarrow r)$

(f) Find the dual of $(x . \perp) + (x . y) + (y . z) + (z . 0)$

Q2. (a) Show that $((p \rightarrow q) \rightarrow q) \rightarrow (p \vee q)$ is a tautology.

(b) Use mathematical induction method to prove that $n^3 + 2n$ is divisible by 3 for $n \geq 1$.

(c) If $f : A \rightarrow B$ such that $f(x) = x - 1$ and $g : B \rightarrow C$ such that $g(y) = y^2$ find fog (y).

Q3. (a) Let R be a relation in the set of all lines in a plane defined by aRb if line 'a is parallel to line b'. Then prove that R is an equivalence relation.

(b) Find n if p(n, 4) = 42 p(n, 2).

(c) Express the Boolean expression in three variables $(x + y + z)(xy + x'z)'$ in DNF.

Q4. (a) Construct a logic circuit by minimising the Boolean function $f(x,y,z) = (xyz) + x\overline{y}z + \overline{x}\overline{y}z + \overline{x}y$.

(b) If there are 12 persons in a party and if each two of them shake hands with each other, how many hand shakes happen in the party?

Q5. (a) What is the minimum number of students required in a particular class to be sure that atleast six students will receive the same division if there are five possible divisions.
(b) Find the dual of $(A \cap B)' \cap C$.
(c) Show that $p \to q = 7q \to 7p$.

"It doesn't matter who you are, where you come from. The ability to triumph begins with you – always".
-Oprah Winfrey

MCS-013: DISCRETE MATHEMATICS
June, 2014

Note: *Question Number 1 is compulsory. Attempt any three questions from the rest.*

Q1. (a) Let $f(x) = \dfrac{1}{x}$ and $g(x) = x^3 + 2$ where $x \in R$. Find $(f+g)(x)$ and $(fg)(x)$?

(b) Draw Venn diagram to represent $A \triangle B$ where A and B are two sets.

(c) If A and B are two mutually exclusive events such that P (A) = 0.3 and P (B) = 0.4 What is the probability that either A or B does not occur?

(d) Prove that $\dfrac{1}{1.2} + \dfrac{1}{2.3} + \ldots + \dfrac{1}{n(n+1)} = \dfrac{n}{n+1}$ using Mathematical Induction.

(e) Show that $p \vee (q \wedge r)$ and $(p \vee q) \wedge (p \vee r)$ are logically equivalent.

(f) Prove that product of two odd integers is an odd integer?

(g) How many different strings can be made from the letters of the word "SUCCESS" using all the letters?

Q2. (a) Let $A = R - \{3\}$ and $B = R - \{1\}$. $f : A \to B$ defined by $f(x) = \dfrac{x-2}{x-3}$ find f^{-1}?

(b) Let R is the relation on the set of strings of Hindi letters such that a Rb iff l (a) = l (b) where l (x) is length of string x. Show that R is an equivalence relation.

Q3. (a) Write contrapositive, converse and the inverse of the implication "The home team does not win whenever it is raining."

(b) Draw the logic circuit for the expression Y = ABC + A' C' + B' C'

(c) Determine the number of integer solutions to the equation $x_1 + x_2 + x_3 + x_4 = 7$, where $x_i \geq 0 \, \forall i = 1, 2, 3, 4$.

Q4. (a) Five balls are to be placed in three boxes. Each box can hold all the five balls. In how many ways can we place the balls so that no box is empty if balls and boxes are different?

(b) Show that $r \to s$ can be derived from $p \to (q \to s), \sim r \vee p$ and q.

Q5. (a) Show that a map $f : R \to R$ defined by $f(x) = 2x + 1$ for $x \in R$ is a objective map from R to R.

(b) If $f = \begin{pmatrix} 1 & 2 & 3 \\ 2 & 3 & 1 \end{pmatrix}$ and $g = \begin{pmatrix} 1 & 2 & 3 \\ 3 & 2 & 1 \end{pmatrix}$. Find *fog* and *gof*?

(c) List all the permutations of {a, b, c}.

MCS-013: DISCRETE MATHEMATICS
December, 2014

Note: *Question Number 1 is* **compulsory**. *Attempt any* **three** *questions from the rest.*

Q1. (a) Let A = {a, b, c, d}, B = {1, 2, 3} and R = {(a, 2), (b, 1), (c, 2), (d, 1)}. Is R a function? Why?
(b) Under what conditions on sets A and B, A × B = B × A? Explain.
(c) How many bit strings of length 8 contain at least four 1s?
(d) Show that the proposition $p \to q$ and $\sim p \vee q$ are logically equivalent?
(e) Use mathematical induction to show that $n! \geq 2^{n-1}$ for $n \geq 1$.
(f) A coin is tossed n times. What is the probability of getting exactly r heads?
(g) Prove that if x and y are rational numbers, then x + y is rational.

Q2. (a) Find f^{-1}, where f is defined by $f(x) = x^3 - 3$ where $x \in R$.
(b) Let the set A = {1, 2, 3, 4, 5, 6} and R is defined $R = \{(i, j) \mid |i - j| = 2\}$. Is 'R' transitive? Is 'R' reflexive? Is 'R' symmetric?

Q3. (a) What are the inverse, converse and contrapositive of the implication "If today is holiday then I will go for a movie."?
(b) Draw the logic circuit for $Y = AB'C + ABC' + AB'C'$
(c) In how many ways can a prize winner choose three books from a list of 10 bestsellers, if repeats are allowed?

Q4. (a) What is understood by the logical quantifiers? How would you represent the following propositions and their negations using logical quantifiers:
(i) There is a lawyer who never tells lies.
(ii) All politicians are not honest.
(b) Show that
$(\sim p \wedge (\sim q \wedge r)) \vee (q \wedge r) \vee (p \wedge r) \Leftrightarrow r$
(c) Define Modus Tollens.

Q5. (a) If R is the set of all real numbers, then show that a map $g : R \to R$ defined by $g(x) = x$ for $x \in R$ is a bijective map.

(b) Let $A = \{1, 2, 3, 4\}$ and

$$f = \begin{pmatrix} 1 & 2 & 3 & 4 \\ 2 & 4 & 1 & 3 \end{pmatrix} \quad g = \begin{pmatrix} 1 & 2 & 3 & 4 \\ 4 & 1 & 2 & 3 \end{pmatrix}.$$

Find fog and gof.

(c) A club has 25 members. How many ways are there to choose four members of the club to serve on an executive committee?

MCS-013: DISCRETE MATHEMATICS
June, 2015

Note: *Question Number 1 is* **compulsory**. *Attempt any* **three** *questions from the rest.*

Q1. (a) Write down the truth table of $p \to q \wedge \sim r \leftrightarrow r \oplus q$. Also explain whether it is a tautology or not.
(b) Show that $\sqrt{5}$ is irrational.
(c) Give the geometric representation of $R \times \{2\}$.
(d) Find the f inverse of the function $f : f(x) = x^3 - 3$.
(e) Present a *direct proof* of the statement: "Square of an odd integer is odd."
(f) How many permutations are there for the word "UNIVERSITY"?

Q2. (a) (i) Check whether $(A \cup B) \cap C = A \cup (B \cap C)$ or not, using Venn Diagram.
(ii) Find the dual of $A \cup (B \cup C)$.
(b) Prove that C (n, r) = C (n, n – r), for $0 \leq r \leq n, n \in N$.

Q3. (a) State and prove Addition Theorem of Probability.
(b) Show that in any group of 30 people, we can always find 5 people who were born on the same day of the week.
(c) State Pigeonhold principle. Also give an example of its application.

Q4. (a) What is the probability that a number between 1 and 200 is divisible by neither 2, 3, 5 nor 7?
(b) In how many ways can 20 students be grouped into 3 groups?
(c) In how many ways can r distinct objects be distributed into 6 different boxes with at least two boxes empty?

Q5. (a) Give an example of a compound proposition that is neither a tautology nor a contradiction.
(b) Show that $2^n > n^3$ for $n \geq 10$.
(c) Draw the logic circuit for the following boolean expression:
$x \cdot y + x \cdot y' + x' \cdot y$.

MCS-013: DISCRETE MATHEMATICS
December, 2015

Note: *Question Number 1 is **compulsory**. Attempt any **three** questions from the rest.*

Q1. (a) Write the truth value of the disjunction of "The earth is flat" and "3 + 5 = 2".

(b) If p and q are two propositions, then show that $\sim(p \vee q) \equiv \sim p \wedge \sim q$.

(c) Use Mathematical induction to prove that
$$1 + \frac{1}{4} + \frac{1}{9} + \ldots + \frac{1}{n^2} \leq 2 - \frac{1}{n} \ \forall \ n \in \mathbb{N}.$$

(d) If $f : R \to R$ is a function such that $f(x) = 3x + 2$, prove that f is one-one onto. Also, find the inverse of f.

(e) How many integers between 100 and 999 consist of distinct even digits?

(f) Show that the number of words of length n on an alphabet of m letters is m^n.

Q2. (a) Prove that:
$$\frac{(n+1)}{(r+1)} C(n,r) = C(n+1, r+1).$$

(b) Express the Boolean expression in three variables (x + y' + z') (xy + x'z) in DNF.

Q3. (a) Two dice, one red and one white, are rolled. What is the probability that the white die turns up a smaller number than the red die?

(b) State and explain De Morgan's law for Boolean algebra. Also, explain duality principle with the help of an example.

(c) In how many distinct ways is it possible to seat eight persons at a round table?

Q4. (a) Use Mathematical induction to prove that
$$1^2 + 2^2 + 3^2 + \ldots + n^2 = \frac{n(n+1)(2n+1)}{6} \ \forall \ n \in \mathbb{N}.$$

(b) Find the Boolean expression C for the following logic circuit:

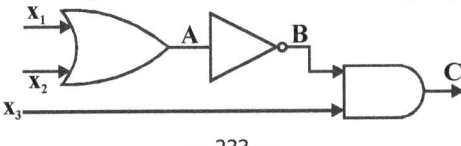

(c) Prove the following equivalence:

$\sim \forall x\, P(x) \equiv \exists x \sim P(x)$

Q5. (a) Verify that $p \wedge q \wedge \sim p$ **is a contradiction and** $p \rightarrow q \leftrightarrow \sim p \vee q$ **is a tautology.**

(b) Show that $\sqrt{2}$ **is irrational.**

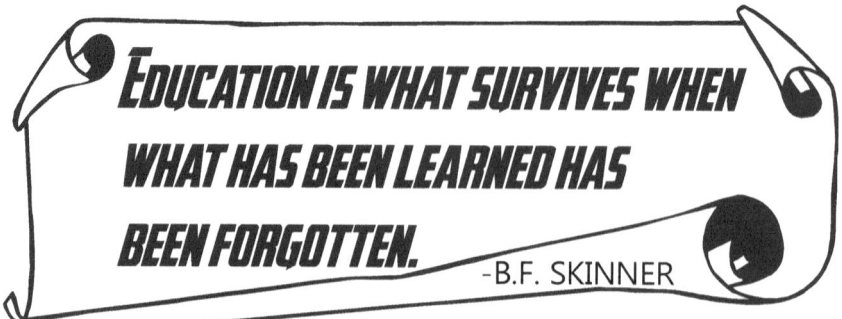

MCS-013: DISCRETE MATHEMATICS
June, 2016

Note: *Question number 1 is **compulsory**. Attempt any **three** questions from the rest.*

Q1. (a) Using the principle of mathematical induction prove that
$$5+10+15+\ldots+5n = \frac{5n(n+1)}{2}.$$
Same as June-2011, Q.No.-2(b)

(b) Let A and B be the n × n matrices and I be the identity matrix of order n × n.
Check the validity of the following statements and give justification:
(i) $\exists B \forall A \quad A + B = I$
(ii) $\exists B \forall A \quad A + B = A$

Ans. Let $A = \begin{bmatrix} 2 & 0 \\ -1 & 1 \end{bmatrix}$ and $B = \begin{bmatrix} -1 & 0 \\ 1 & 0 \end{bmatrix}$

These are 2 × 2 matrices.

Identity matrix of 2 × 2 order is $I = \begin{bmatrix} 1 & 0 \\ 0 & 1 \end{bmatrix}$

(i) $A + B = \begin{bmatrix} 2 & 0 \\ -1 & 1 \end{bmatrix} + \begin{bmatrix} -1 & 0 \\ 1 & 0 \end{bmatrix} = \begin{bmatrix} 1 & 0 \\ 0 & 1 \end{bmatrix} = I$

$\Rightarrow A + B = I$

Hence, it is valid.

(ii) $A + B = A$ is not valid for assuming values of A and B.
$A + B = A$ is valid only when B is zero matrix.

(c) Let f: $\beta^2 \to \beta$ be a function as f(0, 0) = 1, f(0, 1) = 0, f(1, 0) = 0 and f(1, 1) = 1. Find the Boolean expression specifying the function f.

Ans. Solution: f can be represented by the following table.

Input		Output
x_1	x_2	$f(x_1, x_2)$
0	0	1
1	0	0
0	1	1
1	1	1

We find the Boolean expression according to the following algorithm:

Step 1: Identify all rows of the table where the output is 1: these are the 1st, 3rd and 4th rows.

Step 2: Combine the variables in each of the rows identified in Step 1 with 'and'. Simultaneously, apply 'not' to the variables with value zero in these rows. So, for the

1st row: $x_1' \wedge x_2'$,

3rd row: $x_1' \wedge x_2$,

4th row: $x_1 \wedge x_2$.

Step 3: Combine the Boolean expressions obtained in Step 2 with 'or' get the compound expression representing f:

So, $f(x_1, x_2) = (x_1' \wedge x_2') \vee (x_1' \wedge x_2) \vee (x_1 \wedge x_2)$.

(d) Let f be a permutation function defined as follows:
f(1) = 2, f(2) = 4, f(3) = 1, f(4) = 3
Find the inverse of f i.e., f^{-1}.

Ans. $f\begin{pmatrix} 1 & 2 & 3 & 4 \\ 2 & 4 & 1 & 3 \end{pmatrix}$

Inverse of $f(f^{-1}) = \begin{pmatrix} 2 & 4 & 1 & 3 \\ 1 & 2 & 3 & 4 \end{pmatrix}$

(e) Make a table to recursively calculate P_n^k, where n is the total number, k is the number of partitions, using the following conditions:
$7 \geq n \geq 1$ and $1 \leq k < 7$.

Ans.

n \ k	1	2	3	4	5	6	7
1	1	0	0	0	0	0	0
2	1	1	0	0	0	0	0
3	1	1	1	0	0	0	0
4	1	2	1	1	0	0	0
5	1	2	2	1	1	0	0
6	1	3	3	2	1	1	0
7	1	3	4	3	2	1	1

We know that

$P_{n+k}^k = P_n^1 + P_n^2 + \cdots + P_n^k$

and $P_n^1 = P_n^n = 1$
Hence, we have
$P_1^1 = 1$, $P_2^1 = P_1^1 = 1$, $P_2^2 = P_1^1 + P_1^2 = 1 + 0 = 1$
Similarly, $P_3^1 = 1$, $P_3^2 = 1$, $P_3^3 = 1$
$P_4^1 = 1$, $P_4^2 = 2$, $P_4^3 = 1$, $P_4^4 = 1$
....
....
$P_7^1 = 1$, $P_7^2 = 3$, $P_7^3 = 4$, $P_7^4 = 3$, $P_7^5 = 2$, $P_7^6 = 1$, $P_7^7 = 1$

(f) An urn contains 15 balls, of which eight are red and seven are black. In how many ways can 5 balls be chosen such that two are red and three are black?
Same as December-2006, Q.No.-4(b)

(g) In how many ways can 7 people be seated around a circular table?
Ans. Fixing the position of our person, the remaining 6 persons can sit around a table in 6 ways
= 6 × 5 × 4 × 3 × 2 × 1= 720
7 people can sit around a circular table in 720 ways.

Q2. (a) Show that $\sim(p \rightarrow q) \rightarrow p$ is a tautology.
Same as December-2007, Q.No.-1(d)

(b) Prove:
$\sim(\forall x\ P(x)) \equiv \exists x\ P(x)$
Refer to December-2012, Q.No.-1(a)

(c) Give the direct proof of the statement "The sum of two odd integers is always even".
Ans. Let a and b be odd integers. By definition of odd we have that a = 2n + 1 and b = 2m +1. Consider the sum a + b = (2n+1) + (2m + 1) = 2n + 2m + 2 = 2k, where k = n + m + 1 is an integer. Therefore by definition of even we have shown that a + b is even and my hypothesis is true.

(d) Explain the Identity Laws of Boolean algebra.
Refer to Chapter-3, Page No.-35

Q3. (a) Reduce the following Boolean expressions to simpler form:

(i) $X(x_1, x_2, x_3) = (x_1 \wedge x_2 \wedge x_3) \vee (x_1 \wedge x_2) \vee (x_2 \wedge x_3)$

(ii) $X(x_1, x_2, x_3) = (x_1 \wedge x_3) \vee x_3 \vee x_2$

Same as December-2006, Q.No.-5(b)

(b) Find the Boolean expression for the following circuit:

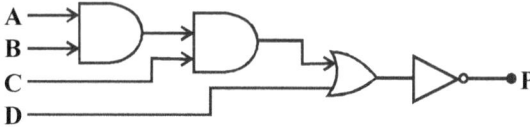

Same as December-2006, Q.No.-5(c)

(c) Make the circuit corresponding to the following Boolean expression:

$x_1' \vee (x_2 \wedge x_3)' \vee (x_2 \wedge x_3 \wedge x_1)$

Same as June-2007 Q.No.-1(g)

Q4. (a) Write the set expressions for the following Venn diagrams:

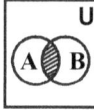

Ans. $A \cap B$

Ans. $(B \cap C) - (A \cap B \cap C)$

Ans. $B - (A \cap B)$

(b) What is an equivalence relation? Let A = {1, 2, 3, 4} be a set and R be an equivalence relation on A such that A/R = {{1, 2}, {3, 4}}. Write R.

Same as June-2007, Q.No.-2(c)

(c) **Let f and g be the two functions such that $f(x) = x^2$ and $g(x) = 2x$. Define fof, fog, gof and gog.**

Ans. $fof = f(f(x))$
$= f(x^2)$
$= (x^2)^2 = x^4$
$fog = f(g(x))$
$= f(2x)$
$= (2x)^2$
$= 4x^2$
$gof = g(f(x))$
$= g(x^2)$
$= 2(x^2)$
$= 2x^2$
$gog = g(g(x))$
$= g(2x)$
$= 2(2x)$

(d) **Find the number of distinguishable words that can be framed from the letters of 'MISSISSIPPI'.**
Refer to December-2006, Q.No.-1(e)

Q5. (a) Prove:
$^{n+1}Cr = {}^n C_{r-1} + {}^n Cr$
Refer to December-2012, Q.No.-5(a)

(b) **Use pigeonhole principle to show that if 7 colours are used to paint 50 bicycles, then at least 8 bicycles will have the same colour.**

Ans. Solution: By extended pigeon hole principle at least $\left\lceil \left\lfloor \frac{n-1}{m} \right\rfloor \right\rceil + 1$ pigeons will occupy one pigeon hole.

Hence n = 50, m = 7
Then 7 < 50

$$\left[\left|\frac{50-1}{7}\right|\right] + 1 = 7 + 1$$

= 8 bicycles will be of same colour.

(c) In how many ways can 10 students be grouped into 2 groups?
Ans. $^{10}C_2$

$$= \frac{10!}{2!(10-2)!}$$

$$= \frac{10 \times 9 \times 8!}{2 \times 8!}$$

= 45

(d) Obtain the truth value of the disjunction of Sun moves around the Earth' and '2 > 3'.
Ans. 'Sum moves around the Earth'. This statement is false. Therefore, the truth values of this is F. '2 > 3'. This is false statement. Therefore, truth value is F.

MCS-013: DISCRETE MATHEMATICS
December, 2016

Note: *Question number 1 is **compulsory**. Attempt any **three** questions from the rest.*

Q1. (a) Using the truth table, show that:
(i) $P \leftrightarrow q \equiv (p \rightarrow q) \wedge (q \rightarrow p)$
(ii) $\sim (P \rightarrow q) \equiv p \wedge \sim q$
(b) prove that $\sqrt{2}$ is irrational.
(c) Find the Boolean expression for the output of the following circuit:

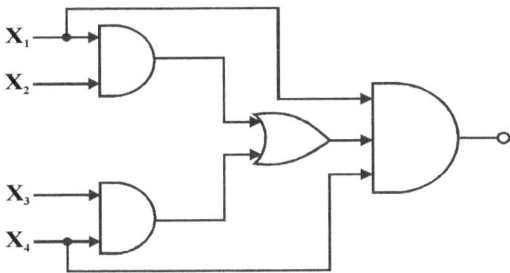

(d) Make Venn diagram for the following set of expressions:
(i) $\overline{A}$
(ii) A D B (Symmetric differences)
(iii) $A \cap B \cap C$
(iv) $A \cup B - C$
(e) Let there be a relation F defined as $F = \{(a, 1), (a, 2) (d, 3) (c, 4)\}$. Is f a function? If not, why?
(f) How many distinct three- letter words can be formed from the letters of the word MAST?
(g) In how many ways can a student choose 8 questions out of 10 in an exam?
(h) A coin is tossed n times. What is the probability of getting exactly r heads?

Q2. (a) Prove the following:
$\sim (\exists x \, P(x)) \equiv \forall x \, (\sim P(x))$
(b) Use mathematical induction to prove that

$1^2 + 2^2 + 3^2 + \dots + n^2 = \dfrac{n(n+1)(2n+1)}{6}$

(c) Write the contrapositive and converse of the following sentence: "If 2+2 = 5, then I am Prime Minister of India."

(d) Explain proof by contradiction, with the help of an example.

Q3. (a) Reduce the following equations to simpler form:

(i) $F(a, b, c) = (a' \wedge b' \wedge c') \vee (a' \wedge b' \wedge c) \vee (a \wedge b \wedge c')$

(ii) $F(a, b) = (a' \wedge b') \vee (a' \wedge b) \vee (a \wedge b')$

(b) Construct logic circuits for the following Boolean expressions:

(i) $(a \wedge b \wedge c) \vee (b \wedge c)' \vee (a \wedge b')$

(ii) $(a' \wedge b') \vee (b' \wedge c) \vee d$

(c) What is dual of a Boolean expression? Explain the principle of duality with the help of an example.

Q4. (a) Describe the following region using intersection and union:

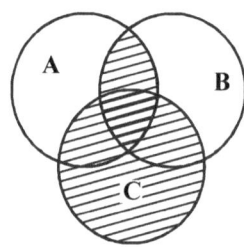

(b) Let A = {1, 2, 3, 4} be a set and a relation R is defined on A such that a Rb if a ≥ b. Check if R is (i) reflexive, (ii) symmetric, (iii) transitive and (iv) asymmetric.

(c) Let there be a function f: AB, Where A and B are sets defined as follows:
A = { a, b, c, d}, B = { p, d, r, s}
F = {(a, p), (b, q), (c, r), (d, p)}
Explain if f is
(i) one to one,
(ii) onto,
(iii) bijective.

(d) Prove that A- (A -B) = A ∩ B using Venn Diagram.

Q5. (a) Make Pascal's triangle up to n= 6.
(b) Let A and b be two mutually exclusive events such that p(A) = 0.6 and p (B) = 0.3. What is the probability that
(i) A does not occur?
(ii) A and B both occur simultaneously?
(c) How many ways are there to distribute r distinct objects into 5 distinct boxes with no empty box?
(d) Disprove the following statement:
$(\forall a \in R)(\forall b \in R) [(a^2 = b^2) \Rightarrow (a = b)]$

MCS-013: DISCRETE MATHEMATICS
June, 2017

Note: *Question number 1 is compulsory. Attempt any three questions from the rest.*

Q1. (a) Negate the following:

(i) $(\forall x \exists y)(P(x) \vee Q(Y))$

Ans.
- $\neg(\forall x \exists y)(P(x) \vee Q(y))$
- $\neg(\forall x \exists y) P(x) \wedge \neg(\forall x \exists y) Q(y)$
- $\exists x \neg \exists y P(x) \wedge \exists x \neg \exists y Q(y)$
- $\exists x \forall y \neg P(x) \wedge \exists x \forall y \neg Q(y)$

(ii) $(\forall x \forall y)(P(x) \wedge Q(y))$

Ans.
- $\neg(\forall x \forall y)(P(x) \wedge Q(y))$
- $\neg(\forall x \forall y) P(x) \vee \neg(\forall x \forall y) Q(y)$
- $\neg \exists x \neg \exists y P(x) \vee (\exists x \neg \exists y Q(y))$
- $\exists x \exists y \neg P(x) \vee \exists x \exists y \neg Q(y)$

(b) Write the contrapositive, converse and inverse of the conditional statement "The home team wins whenever it is raining."

Ans. Because "q whenever p" is one of the ways to express the conditional statement $p \to q$, the original can be rewritten as
"If it is raining, then the home team wins."
contrapositive $\neg q \to \neg p$ "If the home team does not win, then it is not raining."
converse $q \to p$ "If the home team wins, then it is raining."
inverse $\neg p \to \neg q$ "If it is not raining, then the home team does not win."
Note: Only the contrapositive is equivalent to the original statement.

(c) Prove that if $x^2 - 4 = 0$, if then $x \neq 0$ by contradiction method.

Ans. P: if x is real number such that
$x \neq 0$, Then $x^2 - 4 = 0$

Let us assume $x^2 - 4 = 0$, but $x \neq 0$

$x^2 = 4$

$x = \sqrt{4}$

$x = \pm 2$ it is a contradiction.

$x = \pm 2$ is not possible because it is given that x is a real number. Hence only solution is x = 2, but we take $x \neq 0$.
Hence we get a contradiction.
Hence our assumption is true.
Hence x is real number such that $x^2 - 4 = 0$ then $x \neq 0$.

(d) Draw Venn Diagram to show the following set operations:
(i) $\overline{A \cup B}$
Ans.

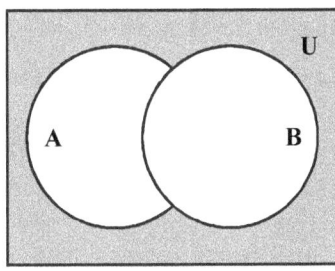

(ii) $A \subset B$
Ans.

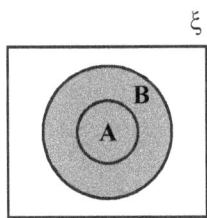

(iii) $(A \cup B) \cap C$
Ans.

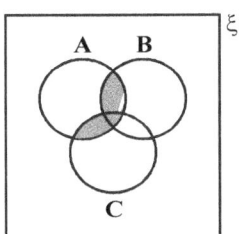

(e) A box contains 10 chocolates. Find the number of n ordered samples of (i) size 3 with replacement, and

Ans. There are 10 chocolates, and each chocolates in the ordered sample of can be chosen ways, $n = 10^r \Rightarrow 10^3$

Hence, there are $10 \times 10 \times 10 = 1000$, samples with replacement

(ii) size 3 without replacement.

Ans. The first chocolate in the ordered sample can be chosen in 10 ways and the next chocolates in the ordered sample can be chosen in 9 ways (when the first drawn chocolate is not replaced). There are $10 \times 9 \times 8 = 720$ samples without replacement.

(f) How many solutions does $x_1 + x_2 + x_3 = 11$ have where x_1, x_2 and x_3 are non-negative integers with $x_1 \leq 3, x_2 \leq 4, x_3 \leq 6$?

Ans. A way to select 11 items from a set with 3 elements, so that x_1 number of type 1, etc. The solution is equal to the number of 11 - combinations with repetitions allowed from a set with 3 elements. C (3 + 11 −1, 11) $X_1 \leq 3$ if x_1 is fixed then the number of solutions for the other variables is

$\dfrac{(11 - x_1 + 2)}{2}$ since as in 5), the solution are in 1 - 1 correspondence with recordings of 11 - x, ones and zeros. The possible values of x_1 are 0, 1, 2, 3, and hence the answer is

$\Rightarrow \dfrac{13}{2!} + \dfrac{12}{2!} + \dfrac{11}{2!} + \dfrac{10}{2!}$

$\Rightarrow \dfrac{13}{2 \times 1} + \dfrac{12}{2 \times 1} + \dfrac{11}{2 \times 1} + \dfrac{10}{2 \times 1}$

$\Rightarrow 6.5 + 6 + 5.5 + 5$

$\Rightarrow 22$

if $x_2 < 4$ is fixed then the number of solutions for the other variables is

$\dfrac{(11 - x_2 + 3)}{3}$

Since as in 4.5), the solution are in 2-2 correspondence with recordings of $11 - x_2$ two and 3 zeros. The possible values of x_2 are 0, 1, 2, 3, 4 and hence the answer is

$\Rightarrow \dfrac{14}{3!} + \dfrac{13}{3!} + \dfrac{12}{3!} + \dfrac{11}{3!} + \dfrac{10}{3!}$

$\Rightarrow \dfrac{14}{3 \times 2 \times 1} + \dfrac{13}{3 \times 2 \times 1} + \dfrac{12}{3 \times 2 \times 1} + \dfrac{11}{3 \times 2 \times 1} + \dfrac{10}{3 \times 2 \times 1}$

$\Rightarrow 2.5 + 2.17 + 2 + 1.83 + 1.67 = 10.17$

$x_3 < 6$ is fixed then the number of solutions for the other variables is

$$\dfrac{(11 - x_3 + 5)}{5}$$

Since as in 4), the solution are in 3-3 correspondence with recordings of $11 - x_3$ three and 5 zeros. The possible values of x_3 are 0, 1, 2, 3, 4, 5, 6 and hence the solution is

$\Rightarrow \dfrac{16}{5!} + \dfrac{15}{5!} + \dfrac{14}{5!} + \dfrac{13}{5!} + \dfrac{12}{5!} + \dfrac{11}{5!} + \dfrac{10}{5!}$

$\Rightarrow \dfrac{16}{5 \times 4 \times 3 \times 2 \times 1} + \dfrac{15}{5 \times 4 \times 3 \times 2 \times 1} + \dfrac{14}{5 \times 4 \times 3 \times 2 \times 1} +$

$\dfrac{13}{5 \times 4 \times 3 \times 2 \times 1} + \dfrac{12}{5 \times 4 \times 3 \times 2 \times 1} + \dfrac{11}{5 \times 4 \times 3 \times 2 \times 1} + \dfrac{10}{5 \times 4 \times 3 \times 2 \times 1}$

$\Rightarrow 0.133 + 0.125 + 0.117 + 0.108 + 0.1 + 0.09 + 0.08$

$\Rightarrow 0.753$

Q2. (a) Two dice, one red and one white are rolled. What is the probability that the white dice turns up a smaller number than the red dice?
Ans. June-2011, Q.No.-4(a)

(b) Four boys picked up 30 mangoes. In how many ways can they divide them if all the mangoes be identical?
Ans. Clearly, 30 mangoes can be distributed among 4 boys such that each boy can receive any number of mangoes.
Hence the total number of ways

$= {}^{30+4-1}C_{4-1} = {}^{33}C_3 = 5456.$

(c) Find the Boolean expression for the following circuit:

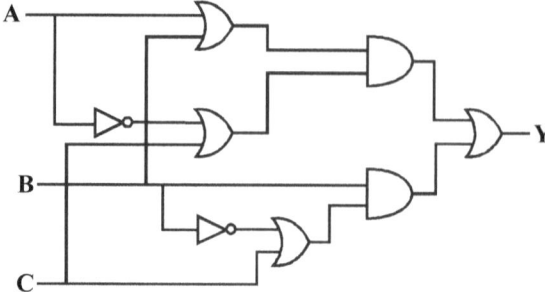

Ans. Same as to Dec-2006, Q.No.-5(c)

(d) How many words of three distinct letters can be formed from the letters of the word LAND?

Ans. The number of three distinct letter words that can be formed from the 4 letters of the word Land is $P(4,3) = \dfrac{4!}{(4-3)!} = \dfrac{4!}{1!} = 4! = 24$

Q3. (a) Find the composition of the following two permutations and show that it is not commutative:

$$f = \begin{pmatrix} 1 & 2 & 3 & 4 \\ 2 & 1 & 4 & 3 \end{pmatrix} \quad g = \begin{pmatrix} 1 & 2 & 3 & 4 \\ 3 & 2 & 1 & 4 \end{pmatrix}$$

Ans. $f = \begin{pmatrix} 1 & 2 & 3 & 4 \\ 2 & 1 & 4 & 3 \end{pmatrix} \quad g = \begin{pmatrix} 1 & 2 & 3 & 4 \\ 3 & 2 & 1 & 4 \end{pmatrix}$

$fg = \begin{pmatrix} 1 & 2 & 3 & 4 \\ 2 & 4 & 1 & 3 \end{pmatrix} \quad gf = \begin{pmatrix} 1 & 2 & 3 & 4 \\ 3 & 4 & 2 & 1 \end{pmatrix}$

Hence, we can see the multiplication of permutation is not commutative in gernal.

(b) Given S = {1, 2, ..., 10} and a relation R on S where

$R = \{(x, y) \mid x + y = 10\}$.

Find whether R has the following properties or not?
(i) Reflexive
(ii) Transitive
(iii) Symmetric

Ans. Same as to Chapter-4, Q.No.-27

(c) Show that the functions $f(x) = x^3$ and $g(x) = x^{1/3}$ for all $x \in R$ are inverse of each other.

Ans. The map $g : \mathbb{R} \to \mathbb{R}$ is a diffeomorphism, whereas $f : \mathbb{R} \to \mathbb{R}$ is a homeomorphism, but not a diffeomorphism. In fact, the inverse map $f^{-1}(x) : x^{1/3}$ is not smooth at the point $x = 0$.

To show that these functions are inverses of each other we use the property on inverse functions. Note that the domain and range of both f and g is $\mathbb{R}$. We have

$$g(f(x)) = g(x^3) = (x^3)^{1/3} = x$$

$$f(g(x)) = f(x^{1/3}) = (x^{1/3})^3 = x$$

So, by property of inverse functions, f and g are inverses of each other.

(d) Under what conditions on sets A and B is $A \times B = B \times A$?

Ans. A × B does not equal B × A unless A = B or A or B is the empty set. This is usually easy to explain to students because in the definition of a cartesian product, we define it as an ordered pair, meaning order would matter. However, once we move on from this idea to explain what the product set represents, things get a bit fuzzy. For example, If we think of the 52 cards in a standard check as a product set, we can define set A as the ranks and set B as the suits. How can we explain to students that while A × B and B × A both represents the 52 cards in a standard deck, the sets A × B and B × A are distinct and disjoint sets?

Q4. (a) Find DNF of $\sim (p \vee q) \leftrightarrow (p \vee q)$.

Ans. Same as to June-2009, Q.No.-2(b)

(b) How many five-digit numbers are even? How many five-digit numbers are composed of only odd digits?

Ans. Refer to Chapter-6, Q.No.-8

(c) Draw the circuit for the following Boolean expression: Y = AB'C + AC' + B'C, using logic gates.

Ans. Same as, June-2008, Q.No.-1(e)

Q5. (a) Construct truth table to check whether the following is a tautology or a contingency or a contradiction:
(i) $(p \wedge q) \to (p \vee q)$

(ii) $((\sim q \wedge p) \wedge q)$

Ans. Same as Dec-2012, Q.No.-2

(b) If the temperature is – 6°, then it is cold. Write the
(i) converse, and
(ii) contrapositive.

Ans. (i) If something is at low temperature, then it is cold.
(ii) If something does not have low temperature, then it is not cold.

(c) Show that
$$\frac{1}{1\cdot 2} + \frac{1}{2\cdot 3} + ... + \frac{1}{n(n+1)} = \frac{n}{n+1}$$
by mathematical induction.

Ans. June-2008, Q.No.-3(b)

MCS-013: DISCRETE MATHEMATICS
December, 2017

Note: Question number 1 is compulsory. Attempt any three questions from the rest.

Q1. (a) Translate the statement
   "The sum of two positive integers is positive" into a logical expression.

(b) Writer the negation of
   "If x is an integer then x is a rational number."

(c) Prove that if x^2 is an even integer, then x is an even integer by contraposition method.

(d) Draw a Venn Diagram to show the following set operations:

(i) A – B

(ii) (A ∩ B) ∪ C

(iii) (A ∩ B) ∩ C

(e) A box contains 5 balls. Find the number of ordered samples of size 2

(i) with replacement, and

(ii) without replacement.

(f) Check whether the function f (x)= x + 1 is one-one or not.

(g) How many numbers from 0 to 999 are not divisible by either 5 or 7?

Q2. (a) A and B are mutually exclusive events such that P (A) = 0.3 and P (B) = 0.4. What is the probability that either A or B does not occur?

(b) How many six-digit numbers contain exactly three different digits?

(c) In how many ways can an employer distribute 100 one-rupee notes among 6 employees so that each gets at least one note?

(d) How many words can be formed from A, B, C, using the letter A thrice, the letter B twice and the letter C once?

Q3. (a) Explain Pascal's Triangle.

(b) Given A = {1, 2, 3, 4} and Relation R as {(1, 1), (1, 2), (2, 1), (3, 3), (4, 4)}. Examine whether R is

(i) Symmetric

(ii) Reflexive

(iii) Transitive

(c) Let $f: R \to R$ defined by $f(x) = 3x - 4$. Find f^{-1}.

(d) Let A = {a, b, c, d}, B = {1, 2, 3},

R = {(a, 2), (b, 1), (c, 2), (d, 1)}.

Is R a function? Why?

Q4. (a) Find CNF of $\sim (p \vee q) \leftrightarrow (p \wedge q)$.

(b) What is a proper subset? Write the number of proper subsets of the set {a, b, c, d}.

(c) Draw the circuit for the following Boolean expression using logic gates

Y = A'BC + A'BC' + ABC'.

Q5. (a) Construct a truth table to check whether the following is a tautology or a contingency or a contradiction:

(i) $p \to (q \to p)$

(ii) $p \wedge (q \wedge \sim p)$

(b) 'If today is a holiday then I will go for a movie'. Write

(i) Inverse

(ii) Contrapositive

(c) Show that $n^2 > 2n + 1$ for $n \geq 3$ by Mathematical Induction.

MCS-013: DISCRETE MATHEMATICS
June, 2018

Note: Question number 1 is compulsory. Attempt any three questions from the rest.

Q1. (a) How many three digit numbers are there with no digit repeated?

Ans. The required number of three-digit numbers

= The permutations of the 10 objects 0, 1, 2, 3, 4, 5, 6, 7, 8, 9, taken 3 at a time, with the condition that 0 is not in the hundred's place.

$$= P(10, 3) - P(9, 2) = \frac{10!}{7!} - \frac{9!}{7!} = \frac{10.9.8.7!}{7!} - \frac{9.8.7!}{7!}$$

$$= 10 \cdot 9 \cdot 8 - 9 \cdot 8 = 720 - 72 = 648$$

(b) Show that

$$\sim (p \vee q) = \sim p \wedge \sim q$$

Ans. Refer to June-2005, Q.No.-3(a)

(c) Prove that

$$ab + [c(a' + b')] = ab + c$$

Ans. L.H.S = $ab + c(a' + b')$

$= ab + ca' + cb'$

$= ab + c(1-a) + c(1-b)$

$\qquad\qquad\qquad (\because a' = 1-a \text{ and } b' = 1-b)$

$= ab + c - ca + c - cb$

$= ab + 2c - c(a+b)$

$\left[\because \text{We know that } a(a+b) = a \text{ (by Absorption Low)}\right.$

Multiplying both side by c:

$ca(a+b) = ca$

$$c(a+b) = \frac{ca}{a}$$

$$c(a+b) = c\,]$$
$= ab + 2c - c = ab + c = $ R.H.S   Hence Proved

(d) **Find the domain for which the function $f(x) = 3x^2 - 1$ and $g(x) = 1 - 5x$ are equal. Also find a domain for which the functions are not equal.**

Ans. Given:

$f(x) = 3x^2 - 1$

$g(x) = 1 - 5x$

For, $f(x) = g(x)$

$\Rightarrow 3x^2 - 1 = 1 - 5x$

$\Rightarrow 3x^2 + 5x = 2$

$\Rightarrow 3x^2 + 5x - 2 = 0$

$x = \dfrac{1}{5}(2 - 3x^2)$

Integer solution:

$f(x) = x = 2 - 5n$, $x = -15n^2 + 12n - 2$, $n \in z$

$f(g) = 3 - 5n$, $x = -15n^2 + 18n - 5$, $n \in z$

$f(x) = \dfrac{-\sqrt{2} - 5x}{\sqrt{3}} = g(x) = \dfrac{x - \sqrt{2} - 5x}{\sqrt{3}}$

Hence, for integer solution, domain for the function $f(x)$ and $g(x)$ are equal.

for, $f(x) \ne g(x)$

Implicit derivatives:

$f(x) = \dfrac{\partial x(x)}{\partial x} = -\dfrac{5}{6x}$

$g(x) = \dfrac{\partial x(x)}{\partial x} = -\dfrac{6x}{5}$

Hence, for implicit derivatives, domain for the function $f(x) \ne g(x)$.

(e) **Prove that**

$(A - B) \cup B = A \cup B$

Ans. To show $(A-B) \cup B = A \cup B$ we need to show two things:

(a) $(A-B) \cup B$ is a subset of $A \cup B$ and

(b) $A \cup B$ is a subset of $(A-B) \cup B$.

To show a), let $x \varepsilon (A-B) \cup B$.

Then $x \varepsilon A - B$ or $x \varepsilon B$

If $x \varepsilon A - B$ then $x \varepsilon A$ and $x \varepsilon B'$, from which is follows that $x \varepsilon A \cup B$

If $x \varepsilon B$ then $x \varepsilon A \cup B$, from which it follows that $x \varepsilon A \cup B$

Therefore $(A-B) \cup B$ is a subset of $A \cup B$

To show b), let $x \varepsilon A \cup B$

Then, $x \varepsilon A$ or $x \varepsilon B$.

If $x \varepsilon A$ then $x \varepsilon A - B$, from which it follows that $x \varepsilon (A-B) \cup B$

If $x \varepsilon B$ then $x \varepsilon A \cup B$

Therefore, $A \cup B$ is a subset of $(A-B) \cup B$

This proves that $(A-B) \cup B = A \cup B$.

(f) **If there are 12 persons in a party, and if each two of them shake hands with each other, how many handshakes happen in the party?**

Ans. Total no. of handshakes

= The number of many selecting 2 persons from 12 person

$$= {}^{12}C_2 = \frac{12!}{2! \times (12-2)!} = \frac{12 \times 11 \times 10!}{2! 10!}$$

$$= \frac{12 \times 11}{2} = 66$$

(g) **Show that for integers greater than zero:**

$2^n >= n+1$

Ans. We can use method of induction to prove that

$2^n \geq 1 + n$ for $n \geq 1$

First we will show that n = 1

$\Rightarrow 2^1 \geq 1 + 1$

$2 \geq 2$

Hence proved.

Further, we assume that $n = k$ is T

Assume that $2^k \geq 1+k$ is true for some k in N

Here, we can show that

$n = k$ is T $\Rightarrow n = k+1$ is also T

$2^{k+1} \geq 2^k \times 2$

$\geq (1+k) \times 2$

$\geq 2 + 2k$

Since $2k \geq k$ for $k \geq 1$

$\geq 2 + k$

$2^{k+1} \geq 1 + (1+k)$

$2^{k+1} \geq 1 + (k+1)$

Since statement is true for n = 1 and truth for n = k follows that n = k + 1 is also true that n = k + 1 is also true, the statement is true for all $n \geq 1$.

Q2. **(a) Use mathematical induction method to prove that**

$$1^2 + 2^2 + 3^2 + ... + n^2 = \frac{n(n+1)(2n+1)}{6}$$

Ans. We call p(n) the predicate

$$1^2 + 2^2 + 3^2 + ... + n^2 = \frac{n}{6}(n+1)(2n+1).$$

Since we want to prove it for every $n \in N$, we take m = 1.

Step 1: p(1) is $1^2 = \frac{1}{6}(1+1)(2+1)$, which is true

Step 2: Suppose for an arbitrary $k \in N$, p(k) is true, i.e.,

$1^2 + 2^2 + ... + k^2 = \frac{k}{6}(k+1)(2k+1)$ is true.

Step 3: To check if the assumption in step 2 implies that $p(k+1)$ is true. Let's see.

$P(k+1)$ is $1^2 + 2^2 + ... + k^2 + (k+1)^2 = \frac{k+1}{6}(k+2)(2k+3)$

$\Leftrightarrow (1^2 + 2^2 + ... + k^2) + (k+1)^2 \dfrac{k+1}{6}(k+2)(2k+3)$

$\Leftrightarrow \dfrac{k}{6}(k+1)(2k+1) + (k+1)^2 = \dfrac{k+1}{6}(k+2)(2k+3),$

since p(k) is true.

$\Leftrightarrow \dfrac{k+1}{6}[k(2k+1) + 6(k+1)] = \dfrac{k+1}{6}(k+2)(2k+3)$

$\Leftrightarrow 2k^2 + 7k + 6 = (k+2)(2k+3),$ dividing throughout by $\dfrac{k+1}{6}$,

which is true.

So, p (k) is true implies that p (k+1) is true.

So, both the conditions of the principle of mathematical induction hold. Therefore, its conclusion must hold, i.e., p (n) is true for every n ε N.

(b) Draw Venn diagrams to represent the following for sets A, B and C.

(i) A Δ B

Ans.

A Δ B

(ii) A ∩ B ∪ C

Ans.

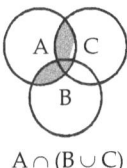

A ∩ (B ∪ C)

(c) Find n if $2P(n, 2) + 50 = P(2n, 2)$.

Ans. $nPr = \dfrac{n!}{(n-r)!}$

$2\dfrac{n!}{(n-2)!} + 50 = \dfrac{(2n)!}{(2n-2)!}$

$(n-2)! = \dfrac{n!}{n(n-1)}$

$\dfrac{2n!n(n-1)}{n!} + 50 = \dfrac{(2n)!(2n)(2n-1)}{(2n)!}$

$2n(n-1) + 50 = (2n)(2n-1)$

$2n^2 - 2n + 50 = 4n^2 - 2n,\ 2n^2 = 50,\ n^2 = 25$

$n = 5$

Q3. (a) If $f: R \to R$ is a function such that $f(x) = 3x + 5$, prove that f is one- one onto.

Ans. Checking one - one

$f(x_1) = 3x_1 + 5$

$f(x_2) = 3x_2 + 5$

Putting

$f(x_1) = f(x_2)$

$3x_1 + 5 = 3x_2 + 5$

$3x_1 = 3x_2$

$x_1 = x_2$

Hence, if $f(x_1) = f(x_2)$, $x_1 = x_2$

∴ function f is one- one.

Onto

Let $f(x) = y$, such that $y \in R$

$3x + 5 = y$

$3x = y - 5$

$x = \dfrac{y-5}{3}$

Since y is a real number.

Hence $\dfrac{y-5}{3}$ will also be a real number.

So, x will also be a real number, i.e., $x \in R$

Hence, f is onto

(b) Show that $p \vee (q \wedge r) \Leftrightarrow (p \vee q) \wedge (p \vee r)$ is a tautology.

Ans. $p \vee (q \wedge r) \Leftrightarrow (p \vee q) \wedge (p \vee r)$

p	q	r	q∧r	p∨q	p∨r	p∨(q∧r)	(p∨q)∧(q∨r)	p∨(q∧r)⇔(p∨q)∧(p∨r)
T	T	T	T	T	T	T	T	T
T	T	F	F	T	T	T	T	T
T	F	T	F	T	T	T	T	T
T	F	F	F	T	T	T	T	T
F	T	T	T	T	T	T	T	T
F	T	F	F	T	F	F	F	T
F	F	T	F	F	T	F	F	T
F	F	F	F	F	F	F	F	T

As we can see from the last column of the table $p \vee (q \wedge r) \Leftrightarrow (p \vee q) \wedge (p \vee r)$ is true. hence, the given expression is tautology.

(c) Find in how many ways can 25 identical books be placed in 5 identical boxes.

Ans. The answer is:

$$p_{25}^1 + p_{25}^2 + p_{25}^3 + p_{25}^4 + p_{25}^5 = p_{30}^5$$

Q4. (a) Find the Boolean Expression for the given circuit.

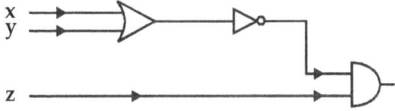

Ans.

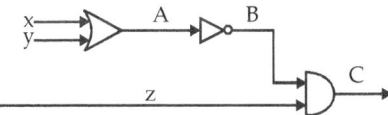

Here the first output is from an **OR**-gate which is $x \vee y$. This, in turn, serves as the input to a **NOT**-gate attached to it from the right. The resulting bit is $(x \vee y)'$. This, and z, serve as inputs to the extreme right **AND**-gate in the circuit given above. This yields an output expression $(x \vee y)' \wedge z$, the required expression for the circuit.

(b) Show whether $\sqrt{17}$ is rational or irrational.

Ans. We have to prove that $\sqrt{17}$ is irrational but we suppose that $\sqrt{17}$ is a rational no. and equal to p/q where $q \neq 0$, and there is no factor common to it.

$$\therefore \sqrt{17} = \frac{p}{q} \Rightarrow p = \sqrt{17}q$$

$$\Rightarrow p^2 = 17q^2 \qquad \qquad ...(1)$$

We see in RHS of (1) 17 is a factor of $17q^2$ and which is an odd integer, therefore, p^2 is also odd. we see p^2 will be odd only when p is odd, and so let $p = 17k$ where k is only integer.

Put this p in ...(1)

$(17k)^2 = 17q^2$

$289k^2 = 17q^2$

$\therefore q^2 = 17k^2$ which is also an odd number.

$\therefore q$ is an odd number.

Now, we see that p and q are both odd integer i.e., there is a common factor 17 $\therefore$ p and q are not indivisible but we have supposed that p and q are indivisible, so there is contradiction, therefore $\sqrt{17}$ be never rational i.e., $\sqrt{17}$ is an irrational number. Hence proved.

(c) Prove that

$p \Leftrightarrow q \equiv (p \Rightarrow q) \wedge (q \Rightarrow p)$.

Ans. $p \Leftrightarrow q \equiv (p \Rightarrow q) \wedge (q \Rightarrow p)$

p	q	$p \Leftrightarrow q$	$p \Rightarrow q$	$q \Rightarrow p$	$(p \Rightarrow q) \wedge (q \Rightarrow p)$
T	T	T	T	T	T
T	F	F	F	T	F
F	T	F	T	F	F
F	F	T	F	T	T

So, as we can see from the three and the last column, the values are same hence the given expression.

$p \Leftrightarrow q \equiv (p \Rightarrow q) \wedge (q \Rightarrow p)$ are equivalent.

Hence proved.

Q5. (a) Let $A = \{a, b, c, d\}$, $B = \{1, 2, 3\}$ and $R = \{(a, 2), (b, 1), (c, 2), (d, 1)\}$. **Is R a function? Why?**

Ans. R is a function because each element of A is assigned to a unique element of B.

(b) How many permutations are there of the letters, taken all at a time, of the word DISTINCT?

Ans. D – 1
I – 2
S – 1
T – 2
N – 1
C – 1

$\therefore$ No. of permutations $= \dfrac{8!}{1! \times 2! \times 1! \times 2! \times 1! \times 1!}$

$= \dfrac{8 \times 7 \times 6 \times 5 \times 4 \times 3 \times 2 \times 1}{4} = \dfrac{40320}{4} = 10080$

(c) Show that in any group of 30 people, we can always find 5 people who were born on the same day of the week.

Ans. 30 people can be assigned to 7 days of the week. Then at least $\left\lfloor \dfrac{30}{7} \right\rfloor + 1 = 5$ of them must have been born on the same day.

(d) Find how many 4 digit numbers are odd.

Ans. Since it can not be equal 0, there are 9 possibilities for the 1st digit. The 2nd and 3rd digits can be any numbers from 0–9, so there are 10 possibilities for them.

For the numbers to be odd, there are 5 possibilities for the 4th digit: 1, 3, 5, 7, 9

So the total probability is $9 \times 10 \times 10 \times 5 = 4500$

Hence, 4500 numbers can be odd with 4 digit.

MCS-013: DISCRETE MATHEMATICS
December, 2018

Note: Question number 1 is compulsory. Attempt any three questions from the rest.

Q1. (a) Find the dual of

(i) $A \cap (B \cap C) = (A \cap B) \cap C$ and

(ii) $(A \cup B) \cap (A \cup C)$.

(b) Give the geometric representation of $R \times \{2\}$. R is the set of Real Numbers.

(c) Find the number of distinct sets of 5 cards that can be dealt from a deck of 52 cards.

(d) Find the number of ways of placing n people in (n − 1) rooms, no room being empty.

(e) Verify that $p \wedge q \wedge (\sim p)$ is a contradiction and $p \to q \leftrightarrow \sim p \vee q$ is a tautology.

Q2. (a) Prove that if $x, y \in I$ such that xy is odd, then both x and y are odd, by proving its contrapositive. I is the set of Integers.

(b) Design a logic circuit to operate a light bulb by two switches x_1 and x_2.

Q3. (a) A box contains 3 red, 3 blue and 4 white socks. In how many ways can 8 socks be pulled out of the box, one at a time, if order is important ?

(b) Suppose 5 points are chosen at random within or on the boundary of an equilateral triangle of side 1 metre.

Show how we can find two points at a distance of at most $\frac{1}{2}$ metre.

Q4. (a) Find the boolean expression for the following circuit:

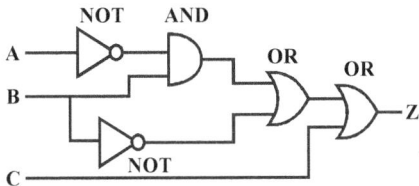

(b) Find the inverse of the following function:

$f(x) = x^3 - 3$

(c) State and explain Pigenhole principle.

Q5. (a) A car manufacture has 5 service centres in a city. 10 identical cars were served in these centres for a particular mechanical defect. In how many ways could the cars have been distributed at the various centres?

(b) Show that $\sqrt{5}$ is irrational.

MCS-013: DISCRETE MATHEMATICS
June, 2019

Note: Question number 1 is compulsory. Attempt any three questions from the rest.

Q1. **(a) Obtain the truth value of the disjunction of "The earth is flat" and "3 + 5 = 2."**

Ans. Let p denote 'The earth is flat,' and q denote '3 + 5 = 2'. Then we know that the truth values of both p and q are F. Therefore, the truth value of p ∨ q is F.

(b) **Write down the truth table of $(p \to q \wedge \sim r) \leftrightarrow (r \oplus q)$.**

Ans. We want to find the required truth value when we are given the truth values of p, q and r. Accordingly, we need to first find the truth value of ~ r, then that of (q ∧ ~ r), then that of (r ⊕ q), and then that of p → (q ∧ ~ r), and finally the truth value of [p → (q ∧ ~ r)] ↔ r ⊕ q.

So, for instance, suppose p and q are true, and r is false. Then ~ r will have value T, q ∧ ~ r will be T, r ⊕ q will be T, p → (q ∧ ~ r) will be T, and hence, p → q ∧ ~ r ↔ r ⊕ q will be T.

We can check that the rest of the values in below table. We have 8 possibilities (=2^3) because there are 3 simple propositions involved here.

Table: Truth table for $p \to q \wedge \sim r \leftrightarrow r \oplus q$

p	q	r	~ r	q ∧ ~ r	r ⊕ q	p → q ∧ ~ r	p → q ∧ ~ r ↔ r ⊕ q
T	T	T	F	F	F	F	T
T	T	F	T	T	T	T	T
T	F	T	F	F	T	F	F
T	F	F	T	F	F	F	T
F	T	T	F	F	F	T	F
F	T	F	T	T	T	T	T
F	F	T	F	F	T	T	T
F	F	F	T	F	F	T	F

(c) Show that $2^n > n^3$ for $n \geq 10$.

Ans. Refer to Dec-2009, Q.No.-1(f) (Pg. No.-201)

(d) Design a logic circuit capable of operating a central light bulb in a hall by three switches x_1, x_2, x_3 (say) placed at the three entrances to that hall.

Ans. Refer to Chapter-3, Q.No.-35 (Pg. No.-72)

(e) If $X = \{a, b, c\}$ and $Y = \{1, 2, 3\}$, find $X \times X$ and $X \times Y$.

Ans. $X = \{a, b, c\}$

$Y = (1, 2, 3)$

$X \times X = \{a^2, ab, ac, ab, b^2, bc, ac, bc, c^2\}$

$X \times Y = \{(a,1) (b,1) (c,1), (a,2) (b,2) (c,2), (a,3) (b,3), (c,3)\}$

The Cartesian product $X \times X$ is written as X^2 and we see from the above example that in general $X \times Y \neq X \times X$

Generalising the definition of the cartesian Product of two sets, we define the cartesian Product of n sets $X_1, X_2, \ldots, X_n$ as follows:

$X_1, X_2, \ldots, X_n = [(a_1, a_2, \ldots, a_n) : a_1 \in x_1, a_2 \in x_2, \ldots, a_n \in x_n]$

Q2. (a) Suppose 10 people have exactly the same briefcase, which they leave at a counter. The briefcases are handed back to the people randomly. What is the probability that no one gets the right briefcase?

Ans. Example: Suppose 10 people have exactly the same briefcases, which they leave at a counter. The cases are handed back to the people randomly. What is the probability that no one gets the right case?

Solution: The number of possibilities favourable to the event is D_{10}. The total number of possibilities is 10!. Thus, the probability that none will get the right briefcase is $D_{10}/10! = 0.36788$.

(b) What is a function? Explain the following types of functions with examples:
(i) Bijective
(ii) Surjective

Ans. Refer to Chapter-4, Pg. No.-84

Q3. (a) Show that;
$(p \to \sim q) \wedge (p \to -r) \equiv \sim [p \wedge (q \vee r)]$.

Ans. Same as Dec-2008, Q.No.-5(a) (Pg. No.-196)

(b) Prove that $(x \vee y)' = x' \wedge y'$ and $(x \wedge y)' = x' \vee y'$.

Ans. Let $a = (x \wedge y)$ and $b = (x' \vee y')$

Now

$(a \vee b) = (x \wedge y) \vee b$

$= (x \vee b) \wedge (y \vee b)$, distributive law

$= (x \vee (x' \vee y')) \wedge (y \vee (x' \vee y'))$

$= ((x \vee x') \vee y') \wedge (y \vee (x' \vee y'))$, associative law

$= (I \vee y') \wedge (y \vee (x' \vee y'))$, complement law

$= (I \vee y') \wedge (y \vee (y' \vee x'))$, commutative law

$= (I \vee y') \wedge ((y \vee y') \vee x')$, associative law

$= (I \vee y') \wedge (I \vee x')$, complement law

$= I \wedge I$, bound law

$= I.$, idempotent law

Again,

$(a \wedge b) = (x \wedge y) \vee (x' \vee y')$

$= ((x \wedge y) \wedge x') \vee ((x \wedge y) \wedge y')$, distributive law

$= ((y \wedge x) \wedge x') \vee ((x \wedge y) \wedge y')$, commutative law

$= (y \wedge (x \wedge x')) \vee (x \wedge (y \wedge y'))$, associative law

$= (y \wedge O) \vee (x \wedge O)$, complement law

$= O \vee O$, bound law

$= O$, idempotent law

Therefore, $(a \vee b) = I$ and $(a \wedge b) = O$

This implies that $b = a'$ i.e. $a' = b$

i.e. $(x \wedge y)' = (x' \vee y')$.

Similarly the other De Morgan's law
$(x \vee y)' = (x' \wedge y')$ can be proved.

Remark: Bound Laws: For all $x \in S$
$(x \vee I) = I$ and $(x \wedge O) = O$

Now $x \vee I = (x \vee I) \wedge I$, identity law
$= (x \vee I) \wedge (x \vee x')$, complement law
$= ((x \vee I) \wedge x) \vee ((x \vee I) \wedge x')$, distributive law
$= ((x \wedge x) \vee (I \wedge x)) \vee ((x \wedge x') \vee (I \wedge x'))$
$= (x \vee (I \wedge x)) \vee ((x \wedge x') \vee (I \wedge x'))$, idempotent law
$= (x \vee x) \vee ((x \wedge x') \vee x')$, identity law
$= (x \vee x) \vee (O \vee x')$, complement law
$= x \vee (O \vee x')$, idempotent law
$= (x \vee x')$, identity law
$= I$, complement law

Therefore, $(x \vee I) = I$

Similarly, the other bound law $(x \wedge O) = O$ can be proved.

Q4. **(a) Let $f: B^2 \to B$ be a function which is defined by:**

$f(0, 0) = 1$, $f(1, 0) = 0$,

$f(0, 1) = 1$, $f(1, 1) = 1$

Find the Boolean expression specifying the function f.

Ans. Refer to June-2016, Q.No.-1(c) (Pg. No.-251)

(b) Give the expression.

$(x_1' \vee (x_2 \wedge x_3')) \wedge (x_2 \vee x_4')$,

find the corresponding circuit, where $x_i (1 \le i \le 4)$ are assumed to be inputs to the circuitary.

Ans. Refer to Chapter-3, Q.No.-34 (Pg. No.-71)

Q5. **(a) There is a village that consists of two types of people-those who always tell the truth and those who always lie. Suppose that you visit the village and two villagers A and B come up to you. Further suppose:**

A says, "B always tells the truth" and B says, "A and I are of opposite types." What types are A and B?

Ans. **Solution:** Let us start by assuming A is a truth-teller.

∴ What A says is true.

∴ B is a truth-teller.

∴ What B says is true.

∴ A and B are of opposite types.

This is a contradiction, because our premises say that A and B are both truth-tellers.

∴ The assumption we started with is false.

∴ A always tells lies.

∴ What A has told you is lie.

∴ B always tells lies.

∴ A and B are of the same type, i.e., both of them always lies.

(b) Draw a Venn diagram to represent the following:

(i) $(A \cup B) \cap (A \sim C)$

Ans.

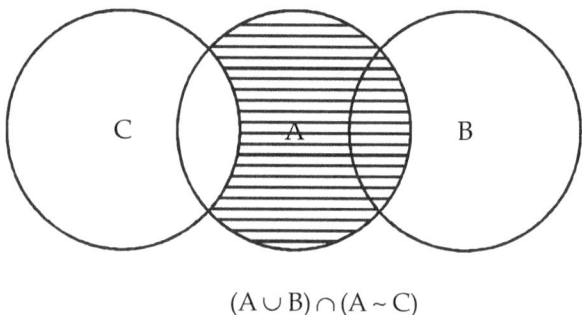

$(A \cup B) \cap (A \sim C)$

(ii) $(A \cup B) \cap C$

Ans. Refer to June-2017, Q.No.-1(d)(iii) (Pg. No.-261)

MCS-013: DISCRETE MATHEMATICS
December, 2019

Note: Question number 1 is compulsory. Attempt any three questions from the rest.

Q1. (a) Construct the truth table for the formula:

$\alpha = (P \rightarrow (Q \rightarrow R)) \rightarrow ((P \rightarrow Q) \rightarrow (P \rightarrow R))$

Check whether it is a tautology or not.

Ans.

p	q	r	$Q \rightarrow R$	A $P \rightarrow (Q \rightarrow R)$	B $r \rightarrow q$	C $(P \rightarrow R)$	$(B \rightarrow C)$	$A \rightarrow (B \rightarrow C)$
T	T	T	T	T	T	T	T	T
T	T	F	F	F	T	F	F	T
T	F	T	T	T	F	T	T	T
T	F	F	T	T	F	T	T	T
F	T	T	T	T	T	T	T	T
F	T	F	F	T	T	T	T	T
F	F	T	T	T	T	T	T	T
F	F	F	T	T	T	T	T	T

Since, the last column $(A \rightarrow (B \rightarrow C))$ all the values are true, hence the given repression,

$\alpha = (P \rightarrow (Q \rightarrow R)) \rightarrow ((P \rightarrow Q) \rightarrow (P \rightarrow R))$ is tautology.

(b) Show that $\sqrt{2}$ is irrational.

Ans. Refer to Chapter-2, Q.No.-6 (Pg. No.-31)

(c) Given $A = \{1, 3, 5, 7\}$, $B = \{2, 3, 5, 8\}$.

List all the elements of $(A \cap B) \times (B - A)$.

Ans. Given $A = \{1, 3, 5, 7\}$, $B = \{2, 3, 5 8\}$.

List all the elements of $(A \cap B) \times (B - A)$.

$A = \{1, 3, 5, 7\} \quad B = \{2, 3, 5, 8\}$

$A \cap B = \{3, 5\}$

$(B - A) = \{2, 8\}$

$(A \cap B) \times (B - A) = \{(3, 2), (3, 8), (5, 2)(5, 8)\}$

(d) Show that the function $f(x) = x^3$ and $g(x) = x^{1/3}$ for all $x \in R$ are inverse of one another.

Ans. Refer to June-2017, Q.No.-3(c) (Pg. No.-265)

(e) Give the direct proof of the statement:

"The product of two odd integers is odd."

Ans. Refer to Chapter-2, Q.No.-8 (Pg. No.-32)

(f) How many license plate containing two letter followed by three digit can be formed? If the letters as well as digits can be repeated.

Ans. Given,

Number of letters in license plates = 2

We know that there are 26 alphabets

so, without repetition letter can be arranged

= 26 × 25

= 650

Number of digits in license plates = 3

We know that there 10 digits

0	1	2	3	4	5	6	7	8	9

Hence the no. of digits with no repetitions

=10 × 9 × 8 = 720

Total number of way license plates

=720 × 650

= 468000

Q2. (a) Find the power set of:

$A = \{a, b, c, d\}$.

Ans. Same as Chapter-4, Q.No.-1 (Pg. No.-86)

(b) In a group of students, 70 have a personal computer, 120 have a personal stereo and 41 have both. How many own at least one of these device? Draw an appropriate Venn diagram.

Ans.

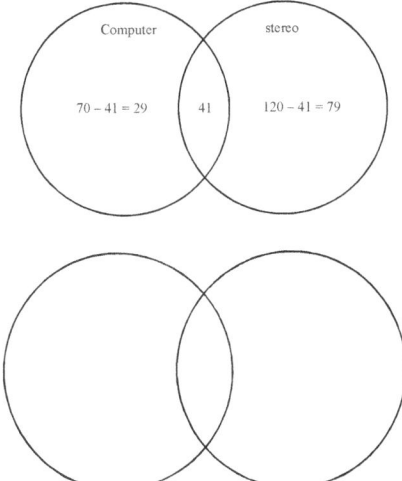

There are two overlapping circles. We pretend that the red circle contains all 70 students who have a personal computer. We pretend that the blue circle contains all 120 students who have a personal stereo. The overlapping part is in both circles and we pretend that the overlapping part contains only the 41 students who have both a computer and a stereo. So we write 41 in the overlapping part:

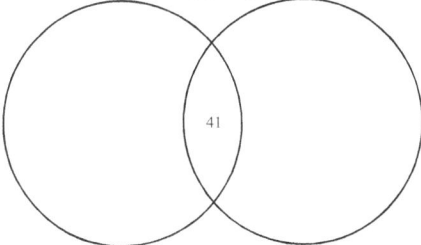

The red circle contains all 70 students who have a personal computer, and the 41 who have both are part of the 70, so that leaves 70-41 or 29 in the left part of the red circle, who only have a personal computer. So we write 29 in the left part of the red circle:

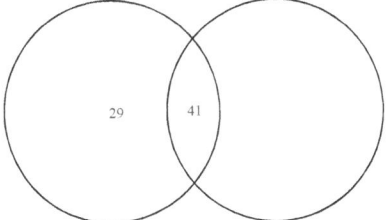

The blue circle contains all 120 students who have a personal stereo, and the 41 who have both are part of the 120, so that leaves 120-41 or 79 in the right part of the blue circle, who only have a personal stereo. So we write 79 in the right part of the blue circle:

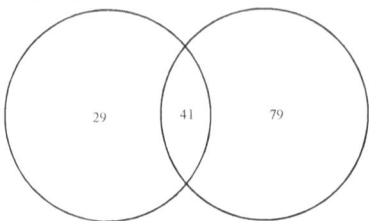

Notice that there are 29 in the red circle that are not in the blue circle.

So, 29 students have a computer but no stereo. Notice that there are 79 in the blue circle that are not in the red circle. So, 79 students have a stereo but no computer. And as we said earlier, the 41 in the middle that are in both circles are the 41 that have both a computer and a stereo.

So to determine how many students have one or the other (or both), that is, at least one, we add the three numbers together:

29 students have a computer but no stereo

41 students have both a computer and a stereo

+79 students have a stereo but no computer

----

149 students have at least one of the two devices

(c) $^{1000}C_{98} = {}^{999}C_{97} + {}^{x}C_{901}$. Find x.

Ans. By properties $^{n}C_{r} + {}^{n}C_{r-1} = {}^{n+1}C_{r}$

$^{999}C_{97} + {}^{x}C_{901} = {}^{1000}C_{98}$ ...(1)

$^{999}C_{97} + {}^{999}C_{98} = {}^{999+1}C_{98}$

$^{999}C_{97} + {}^{999}C_{98} = {}^{1000}C_{98}$

$^{999}C_{97} + {}^{999}C_{999-98} = {}^{1000}C_{98}$

$^{999}C_{97} + {}^{999}C_{901} = {}^{1000}C_{98}$ ...(2)

Comparing (1) & (2) we get

X = 999

Q3. (a) Draw logical circuit for the following logical expression:

$x_1 \wedge x_2'$

Ans.

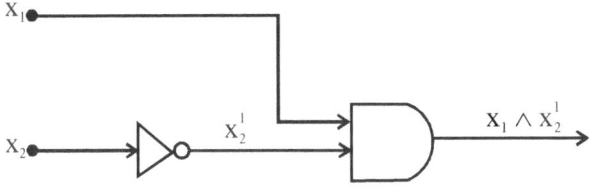

(b) Find the probability of getting the sum 9 or 11 in a single throw of two dice.

Ans. For a sum of 9, In two throws of a dice, n(S) = (6 x 6) = 36.

Let E = event of getting a sum = {(3, 6), (4, 5), (5, 4), (6, 3)}.

$$\therefore P(E) = \frac{n(E)}{n(S)} = \frac{4}{36} = \frac{1}{9}$$

For a sum of 11, there are 2 combinations: (5,6) and (6,5).

$$\Rightarrow P(\text{sum}=11) = 2\frac{1}{36} = \frac{2}{36} = \frac{1}{18}$$

(c) A drawer contains contains ten black and ten white socks. What is the least no. of socks one must pull out to be sure to get a matched pair?

Ans. Let the socks pulled out (pigeons) be denoted by $S = \{s_1, s_2, \ldots, s_n\}$ and consider the function f that maps each sock to its colour (pigeon holes) C. If n = 2, f could be one to one correspondence (if the two socks pulled out were of different colours). But if n > 2 then the number of elements in the domain S of f is larger than the number of elements in the co-domain of C. Thus, by pigeon hole principle, $f(s_i) = f(s_j)$ for some $s_i \neq s_j$. Thus, if at least three socks are pulled out, then at least two of them have the same colour.

Q4. (a) A problem of discrete mathematics is given to three students whose chances of solving it are $\frac{1}{2}, \frac{1}{3}$ and $\frac{1}{4}$. What is the probability that exactly one of them solves it?

Ans. We shall find the probability that the problem is not solved. Probability that A, B, C do not solve the problem are

$$1-\frac{1}{2}, 1-\frac{1}{3}, 1-\frac{1}{4} \text{ or } \frac{1}{2}, \frac{2}{3}, \frac{3}{4}$$

By the law of multiplication

Probability that the problem is not solved $= \frac{1}{2} \times \frac{2}{3} \times \frac{3}{4} = \frac{1}{4}$

Probability that the problem is solved $= 1 - \frac{1}{4} = \frac{3}{4}$.

(b) A house has 4 doors and 10 windows. In how many ways can a thief rob the house by entering through a window and exiting through a door?

Ans. The number of ways through which he can enter the room there are 4 doors and 10 windows so in total 14 ways (4 + 10) through which he can enter the room.

(c) A committee of 2 hawkers and 3 shopkeepers is to formed from 7 hawkers and 10 shopkeepers. Find the no. of ways in which this can be done if a particular shopkeeper is included and a particular hawker is excluded.

Ans. To find the number of ways in which a particular shopkeeper is included. Therefore, the number of ways in choosing 2 shopkeepers from remaining 9 shopkeepers is given by

$${}^9C_2 = \frac{9!}{7! \times 2!} = \frac{9 \times 8}{2} = 36$$

Again, to find the number of ways in which a particular hawker is excluded. Thus, the number of ways in choosing 2 hawkers from remaining 6 hawkers is given

$${}^6C_2 = \frac{6!}{4! \times 2!} = \frac{6 \times 5}{2} = 15$$

Therefore, from the fundamental principle of counting, the total number of ways to include a particular shopkeeper and to exclude a particular hawker is

36 × 15 = 540

Q5. (a) Show that 5 divides $n^5 - n$, where n is a non-negative integer.

Ans. Let P(n) be " 5 divides $n^5 - n$ ", where n = 0, 1, 2, ...

- Basis step: 5 divides $0^5 - 0 = 0 => P(0)$ is true.
- Inductive step: Assume P(n) is true, i.e. 5 divides $n^5 - n$.

Then $(n + 1)^5 - (n + 1)$

$= n^5 + 5n^4 + 10n^3 + 10n^2 + 5n + 1 - n - 1$

$= (n^5 - n) + 5n^4 + 10n^3 + 10n^2 + 5n$

MCS-013: DISCRETE MATHEMATICS
June, 2020

Note: Question number 1 is compulsory. Attempt any three questions from the rest.

Q1. (a) Check whether the following formula is tautology, contradiction or contingency:
$\sim\left((P \to Q) \to \left((R \vee P) \to (R \vee Q)\right)\right)$

(b) Two finite sets have x and y number of elements. The total number of subsets of the first set is four times the total number of subsets of second set. Find out the value of x − y.

(c) In a group of 400 people 250 can speak in English only and 70 can speak Hindi only.
(i) How many can speak English?
(ii) How many can speak Hindi?
(iii) How many can speak both English and Hindi?

(d) If f : A → B and g : B → C are injective function, then g o f : A → C is an injective function. Prove or disprove.

(e) Use the method of proof by contradiction to show that $x \in R$ if $x^3 + 4x = 0$, then x = 0.

(f) Three persons enter in a railway compartment. If there are 5 seats vacant, in how many ways they can take these seats?

Q2. (a) Given:
A = {1, 3, 5, 7}
B = {2, 3, 5, 8}
(i) List the elements of (A × B) × (B − A).
(ii) Is (A × B) × (B − A) a subset of A × B?

(b) Prove that:
$^nC_r + {^nC_{r-1}} = {^{n+1}C_r} \, (0 \le r \le n)$.

Q3. (a) Show that in any set of eleven integers there are two which are divisible by 10, by applying pigeonhole principle.

(b) How many solutions are there of:
x + y + z = 17
subject to the constraints:

$x \geq 1$
$y \geq 2$
$z \geq 3$.

(c) If:
$$P(A) = \frac{1}{4}$$
$$P(B) = \frac{2}{5}$$
and $P(A \cup B) = \frac{1}{2}$

Find:
(i) $P(A \cap B)$
(ii) $P(A \cap B)$

Q4. (a) Five balls are drawn from a bag containing 6 white and 4 black balls. What is the probability that 3 are white and 2 black?
(b) From the digit 1, 2, 3, 4, 5, 6, how many three digit odd numbers can be formed when
(i) repetition of digit is allowed?
(ii) repetition of digit is not allowed?
(c) How many numbers divisible by 2 lying between 50,000 and 70,000 can be formed from the digits 3, 4, 5, 6, 7, 8, 9, no digit being repeated in any number.

Q5. (a) Show that:
(b) Write the negation of the following statement:
If it is raining, then the game is cancelled.
(c) Draw the circuit represented by the following Boolean function:
$f : xy + \bar{x}y$

MCS-013: DISCRETE MATHEMATICS
February, 2021

Note: Question number 1 is compulsory. Attempt any three questions from the rest.

Q1. (a) Show using truth table whether $(p \wedge q \wedge r)$ and $(p \vee r) \wedge (q \vee r)$ are equivalent or not.

(b) Using Mathematical Induction, prove that:
$$1 + 2 + 3 + \ldots + n = \frac{n(n+1)}{2}.$$

(c) Prove that if A is a set with n elements, then $|P(A)| = 2^n$.

(d) If there are 7 men and 5 women, how many circular arrangements are possible in which women do not sit adjacent to each other?

(e) Find Boolean expression for the following logic circuit:

X_1
X_2
X_3
C

(f) If $f : R \to R$ be a function given by $f(x) = x^3 - 2$, find whether f^{-1} exists or not. If f^{-1} exists, find it.

Q2. (a) How many words can be formed using the letters of the word "DEPARTMENT", if each letter must be used at most once?

(b) Give geometric representation for $\{1, 3\} \times \{-2, 3\}$.

(c) Show that $(p \to q) \to q = p \vee q$.

(d) Find the number of ways to distribute 20 distinct objects into 10 distinct boxes with at least 4 boxes remaining empty.

Q3. (a) Draw Venn diagrams for the following expressions:

(i) $A \cup B \cup C$

(ii) $A \cap B \cap C$

(iii) $\overline{A \cap B \cap C}$

(b) Draw logic circuit for the following Boolean expression:

$$(X_1 \wedge X_2') \vee (X_1' \wedge X_2')$$

(c) Write the following statements in the symbolic form:

(i) Everything is correct.

(ii) All birds cannot fly.

(d) Explain Principle of Duality with the help of an example.

Q4. (a) Show that $\sqrt{11}$ is irrational.

(b) What is an indirect proof? Explain with the help of an example.

(c) Explain De Morgan's Laws with the help of Venn diagram.

Q5. (a) In a ten-question true-false exam, a student must achieve five correct answers to pass. If he selects his answers randomly, what is the probability that he will pass?

(b) In how many ways can an employer distribute 50 twenty-rupee notes among 5 employees so that each gets at least one note?

(c) Show that in any group of 30 people, you can always find 5 people who were born on the same day of the week.

(d) Draw truth table for:

$(p \rightarrow q) \rightarrow p$

MCS-013: DISCRETE MATHEMATICS
June, 2021

Note: Question number 1 is compulsory. Attempt any three questions from the rest.

Q1. (a) Write the truth value of the conjunction of:
"The earth is round" and "3 > 4".

(b) Use Mathematical Induction to prove that:
$$1 + \frac{1}{4} + \frac{1}{9} + \ldots \frac{1}{n^2} \leq 2 - \frac{1}{n} \ \forall \ n \in N.$$

(c) If $f : R \to R$ is a function such that $f(x) = 3x - 2$, prove that f is injective. Also find the inverse of f.

(d) Show that $p \vee (q \wedge r)$ and $(p \vee q) \wedge (p \vee r)$ are logically equivalent.

(e) A and B are two mutually exclusive events such that P(A) = 0.4 and P(B) = 0.2. What is the probability that:

(i) A does not occur?

(ii) A or B does not occur?

(iii) Either A or B does not occur?

(f) Find the number of ways of placing n people in n − 1 rooms, no room being empty.

Q2. (a) What is integer partition? Write down all the partitions of 8. Also find P_8^4 and P_8^7.

(b) Find Boolean Expression for the following logical circuit:

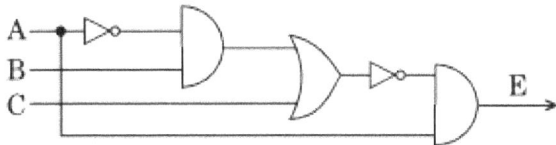

(c) Let two functions be such that $f(x) = x^2 + 2$ and $g(x) = 2x$. Define fog and gof.

Q3. (a) Reduce the following Boolean Expression to simpler form:
$$E(X_1, X_2, X_3) = (X_1 \wedge X_2 \wedge X_3) \vee (X_1 \wedge X_2) \vee (X_2 \wedge X_3)$$

(b) Show that $\sim(p \to q) \to p$ is a tautology.

(c) Prove that $\sqrt{2}$ is irrational.

Q4. (a) What is Relation? How is relation different from function? Explain any two properties of relations with an example.

(b) A company has the following professionals: Project Leaders – 5, Team Leaders – 6, System Architects – 3.

Find how many different committees can be formed of 10 professionals, each containing at least 2 Project Leaders, at least 3 Team Leaders and at least 1 System Architect.

(c) Find the dual of $A \cup B \cap C$.

Q5. (a) Explain the Identity Laws of Boolean Algebra.

(b) State and prove the Addition Theorem of Probability.

(c) Verify that $p \wedge q \wedge \sim p$ is a contradiction.

(d) What is Exclusive Disjunction? Write truth table for $p \oplus q$.

MCS-013: DISCRETE MATHEMATICS
December, 2021

Note: Question number 1 is compulsory. Attempt any three questions from the rest.

Q1. (a) Explain if the following sentences are proposition or not and why:
(i) Sun rises in the east.
(ii) Prepare for your exam.
(iii) Raju is 10-year old.
(iv) How far is Mumbai from here?

Ans. (i) Yes, Its True, it declarative sentence, "Sun rises in the east".

(ii) No, Because its Imperative sentence "Prepare for your exam".

(iii) Yes, Its True, it declarative sentence, "Raju is 10-year old".

(iv) No, Since a question is not a declarative sentence, if fails to be a proposition. "How far is Mumbai from here"?

(b) Prove that: $\frac{1}{1\times 2}+\frac{1}{2\times 3}+ \ldots\ldots\ldots = \frac{1}{n(n+1)} = \frac{n}{1\times 2}$ using mathematical induction.

Ans. Refer to June-2008, Q.No.-3(b)

(c) What is a proper subset? Explain with the help of a suitable example.

Ans. A set A is said to be a proper subset of a set B if A is a subset of B and A and B are not equal. We represent this by $A \subset B$.

For example, if A = {4, 5, 6} and B = {4, 5, 7, 8, 6}, then $A \subset B$.; and if A = {Java, C, C++, Cobol} and B = {Java, C++}, then $A \supset B$

(d) Find number of integers between 100 and 999 consisting of distinct even digits.

Ans. Let us assume the three digits number as xyz.

Hundred's placing - x

Ten's place - y

One's place - z

The digits can be formed from 0 to 9 numbers.

The first digit x can be 1, 2, 3, 4, 5, 6, 7, 8, 9

Therefore, the digits has 8 number of ways.

The second digit can be 0 to 9 and the numbers are not to be repeated.

Therefore, it has 8 number of ways.

The third digit can be 0, 2, 4, 6, 8

therefore, it has 5 number of ways.

The total number of ways = 8 × 8 ×5 = 320 ways.

Hence, there are 320 number ways can be formed between 100 to 999.

(e) If $f(x) = x^3$ and $g(x) = (x^2 + 1)$ $\forall x \in R$, where R is the set of real numbers. Find:

(i) (f o g)

(ii) (g o f)

(iii) (g o g)

Ans. (i) f o g (x) = f(g(x)) = f($x^2 + 1$) = $(x^2 + 1)^3$ = $x^6 + 1 + 3x^4 + 3x^2$

(ii) g o f (x) = g(f(x)) = g(x^3) = $(x^3)^2 + 1$ = $x^6 + 1$

(iii) g o g(x) = g(g(x)) = g($x^2 + 1$)

$\qquad = (x^2 + 1)^2 + 1$

$\qquad = x^4 + 2x^2 + 1 + 1$

$\qquad = x^4 + 2x^2 + 2$

(f) Find the number distinguishable words that can be framed from the letters of the word "UNIVERSITY".

Ans. $\dfrac{10!}{2!} = 10 \times 8 \times 7 \times 6 \times 5 \times 4 \times 3 = 2,01,600$

(g) Find dual of $(A \cup B) \cap C$ and $(A \cap B) \cap C$.

Ans. Dual of $(A \cup B) \cap C$ is $(A \cap B) \cup C$

Dual of $(A \cap B) \cap C$ is $(A \cup B) \cup C$

MCS-13 Discrete Mathematics   303

Q2. (a) Show that $\sqrt{17}$ is irrational

Ans. $\sqrt{17}$ is irrational essentially as a consequence of 17 being prime - that is having no positive factors apart from 1 and itself.

Here's a sketch of a proof.

Suppose $\sqrt{17} = \dfrac{p}{q}$ for some integers p, q, with q ≠ 0.

Without loss of generality, p, q > 0 and p and q have no common factor greater than 1.

[If they did have a common factor, then you could divide both by that common factor to get a smaller p_1 and q_1 with $\sqrt{17} = \dfrac{p_1}{q_1}$]

Then $p^2 = 17q^2$ and since p^2 is a multiple of 17 and 17 is prime, p must be a multiple of 17.

Let $k = \dfrac{p}{17}$

Then $17q^2 = p^2 = (17k)^2 = 17.17k^2$

Divide both ends by 17 to find:

$q^2 = 17k^2$ hence q is a multiple of 17.

So both p and q are divisible by 17, contradicting our assumption that p and q have no common factor greater than 1.

So there is no such pair of integers p and q.

(b) Find the Boolean expression for the following logic circuit:

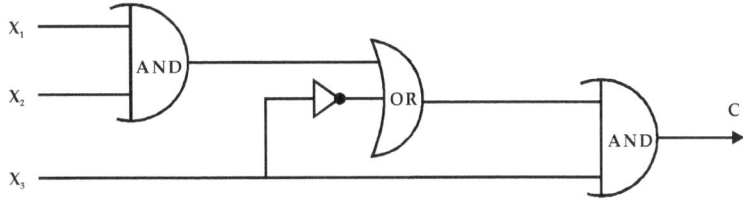

Ans. Same as Chapter-3, Q.No.-14

(c) Show that:

$\sim (p \vee q) =\sim p \wedge \sim q$

Ans. Refer to June-2005, Q.No.-3(a)

Q3. (a) Write the set expressions for the following Venn diagrams:

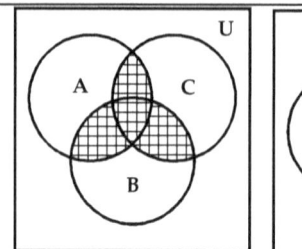 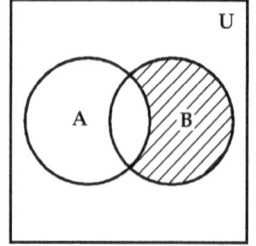 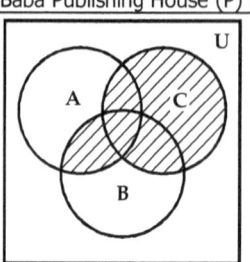

Ans. $(A \cap B) \cup (B \cap C) \cup (C \cap A)$

$(A' \cap B)$

$(A \cap C) \cup B$

(b) Prove that:

$$^{n+1}C_r = {}^n C_{r-1} + {}^n C_r$$

Ans. $^{n+1}C_r = {}^n C_{r-1} + {}^n C_r$

$$= \frac{n!}{(n-r)!r!} + \frac{n!}{(n-r+1)!(r-1)!}$$

$$= n!\left[\frac{1}{(n-r)!r!} + \frac{1}{(n-r+1)!(r-1)!}\right]$$

$$= n!\left[\frac{1}{(n-r)!r(r-1)!} + \frac{1}{(n-r+1)(r-1)!}\right]$$

$$= \frac{n!}{(r-1)!}\left[\frac{1}{(n-r)!r} + \frac{1}{(n-r+1)!}\right]$$

$$= \frac{n!}{(r-1)!}\left[\frac{1}{r(n-r)!} + \frac{1}{(n-r+1)(n-r)!}\right]$$

$$= \frac{n!}{(r-1)!(n-r)!}\left[\frac{1}{r} + \frac{1}{(n-r+1)}\right]$$

$$= \frac{n!}{(r-1)!(n-r)!}\left[\frac{n-r+1+r}{r(n-r+1)}\right]$$

$$= \frac{n!}{(r-1)!(n-r)!}\left[\frac{n+1}{r(n-r+1)}\right]$$

$$= \frac{(n+1)n!}{(n-r+1)(r-1)!r(n-r)!}$$

$$= \frac{(n+1)!}{(n-r+1)!\, r!} = {}^{n-1}C_r$$

(c) A die is rolled once. Find the probability of each of the following events:
(i) getting an odd number
(ii) getting at most 3
(iii) getting at least 3
(iv) getting at least 7

Ans. Same as Chapter-5, Q.No.-20

Q4. (a) Make truth table for the following:
$p \to (\sim q \vee \sim r) \wedge (p \vee \sim r)$

Ans.

p	q	r	$p \to (\sim q \vee \sim r) \wedge (p \vee \sim r)$
F	F	F	T
F	F	T	T
F	T	F	T
F	T	T	T
T	F	F	T
T	F	T	T
T	T	F	T
T	T	T	F

(b) Give geometric representation for the following:
R × {4};
where R is a natural number.

Ans.

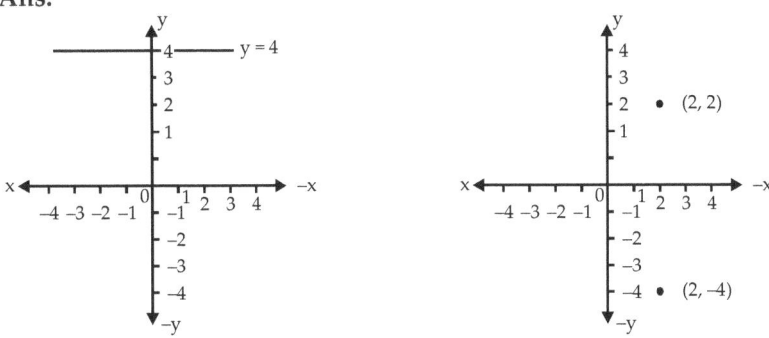

(c) What is Relation? Explain equivalence relation with the help of an example.

Ans. Refer to Chapter-4, Page no.-81

(d) State and explain Pigeonhole principle

Ans. Refer to Chapter-5, Page no.-111

Q5. (a) Draw logic circuit for the following Boolean expression:

(X' + Y + Z) + (X + Y + Z') + (X'. Y)

Ans. Same as Chapter-3, Q.No.-5

(b) In how many ways 10 students can be grouped into 3 groups?

Ans. Same as Chapter-6, Q.No.-13

(c) What is power set? Find power set of set A = {1, 2, 4, 6}.

Ans. Refer to Chapter-4, Page No.-78

The subsets of {1, 2, 4, 6} are:

{1}, {2}, {4}, {6}, {1,2}, {1,4}, {1,6}, {2,4}, {2,6}, {4, 6}, {1, 2, 4}, {1, 2, 6}, {2, 4, 6}, {1, 4, 6} and {1, 2, 4, 6}

P(A) = {φ, {1}, {2}, {4}, {6}, {1, 2}, {1, 4}, {1, 6}, {2, 4}, {2, 6}, {4, 6}, {1, 2, 4}, {1, 2, 6} {2, 4, 6}, {1, 4, 6}, {1, 2, 4, 6}}

www.ingramcontent.com/pod-product-compliance
Lightning Source LLC
Chambersburg PA
CBHW070800170426
43200CB00007B/847